About the Author

A M Gleason lll was born in the United States but migrated to Australia with his wife in the `70s. As a child, he was always fascinated with 'Down Under.' They meant to stay only two years but liked the place so much they decided to stay permanently. In the city of Melbourne, Augustine taught high school English and history in the public school system. In 2016 he retired after forty years. He has a BA and an MA, and graduate teaching credentials. He has been married for forty-five years, and he and his wife have three grown children and one grandchild.

Gustav's High School Diary

A M Gleason III

Gustav's High School Diary

Olympia Publishers
London

www.olympiapublishers.com
OLYMPIA PAPERBACK EDITION

A CIP catalogue record for this title is
available from the British Library.

ISBN: 978-1-80074-486-8

Although snippets of this story are based on personal experiences and
recollections, the names and characters are the author's imagination. Any
semblance to actual persons, living or dead, is purely coincidental.

First Published in 2022

Olympia Publishers
Tallis House
2 Tallis Street
London
EC4Y 0AB

Printed in Great Britain

Dedication

To my wife – K

Acknowledgements

Thank you to my wife and kids for encouraging me to write this book. Thanks to the Publisher and Staff. Thanks to Sunbury Radio - Melbourne Australia. Thanks to Eugenia Kozlevcar for her assistance. Thanks to all who read or listened to my stories and encouraged me to go on.

JANUARY 1,
1966
Saturday – New Year's Eve

Saw the New Year in at the local Teen Canteen dance club in Jakstown – a city in the northeast USA. I hoped to be with a girl when the midnight hour came, but the three or four I talked to during the night had better offers. At one point, the band played the 'Rolling Stones' song 'I can't get no satisfaction.' Appropriate under the circumstances.

One girl weighed damn near 200lbs. She seemed a bit receptive toward me early in the evening, but my best friend Danny Hepburn, aka 'Hep', told me I would be better off going to a pound. So, I left her well enough alone. Before the new year arrived, I saw a girl from my school named Barbara Geist. Hep told me to forget it as she was out of my league. I said hi to her and she returned the greeting, but that was the end of it.

Meanwhile, I got talking to a hairy dude obviously on the booze. He was going around telling everyone how much he loved them. I snuck away when it looked like he was going to barf on me. I struck up conversations with other girls, but in baseball speak I struck out. They must like the athletic types.

It's not that I'm ugly – at least I keep saying that to myself. If I say it often enough, I might start believing it. I'm 16 years old and neither fat nor thin. I might kind of look overweight because I have a prominent chest – what my dad calls the 'Gaughan' look. Dad often refers to me as husky which drives me nuts as I'm sure he means fat. I'm about 5'8 inches tall. I have brown hair and hazel eyes. Unfortunately, I have the family nose – not long, but with a bump in the middle. I have a prominent chin and a fair complexion. I wear dark-rimmed nerdy glasses.

I'm told I look more like my mom than my old man. That's good, cause he's balding. I have a driver's license as of last October and have access most of the time to my dad's Buick Wildcat. My mom says I'm a good catch, but then she would say that.

Anyway, one girl I talked to, Amy Sing - the daughter of the local laundry guy - showed some interest and offered me a discount if I brought my shirts to her dad's place. But she abandoned me for her friends. Later I saw her with the hairy guy – kissing on the stroke of twelve.

I was surprised when I saw Hep with the 'pound girl' at midnight. They were going at it hot and heavy while I had nothing to show for my night but that hairy dude on the bottle, possible cheap laundry and a mountain of ego-busting rejections. I wasn't about to kiss the dude, and my mom washes my clothes. As for the latter, I got a few pecks on the cheek from some girls, but I suppose that's what one does on NYE when the clock turns over and the dreadful 'Old Lang Syne' is sung.

So, the New Year started out pretty badly. I stayed another hour – still with no luck - then went with Hep and my other friend, Dordison French, to another friend's place to see Bob, aka 'The Egghead', or Eggy', Racovic. When we got there, we didn't see any lights on.

We honked outside his home for 10 minutes - causing quite a stir with the neighbours, but not his family. If they were even awake, they probably thought it was part of the new year festivities. The three of us then each had a beer, which I had taken from my old man's stash, to toast in the new year. It was late so I dropped the others off at their houses and drove home - not feeling all that crash-hot.

I hope this night is not an omen for the rest of the year.

Cop-u-later.

JANUARY 1,
1966
Saturday – New Year's Day

I know my friends and I only had a beer each last night, but I swear I had a hangover this morning. It was after two a.m. when I got home, and I crashed. Thank God no one was awake to see me and tell me off. My sister says giving a drink to one of our family is like giving whiskey to the Irish. You'd better believe it!

Still, I was up and downstairs by ten a.m. – bright-eyed, bushy-tailed and ready to face a new year. Well, not really. My head felt all of Xavier Cugat shaking the maracas, and you could throw in his wife Abbe Lane and her pet chihuahua as well. In addition, I felt my insides were inside out. I was barely able to wish everyone a Happy New Year, and certainly was not in a condition to put up with numerous first-day wet kisses and bone-crushing handshakes.

As everyone except my brother Will had eaten breakfast, we had the kitchen table to ourselves. Will said he was out late with his girlfriend – Cheryl. I didn't ask if he had any drinks but knowing him, he surely had. I was in no position to say anything to reprimand him. My head hurt too much. So, I ate my Wheaties ('Breakfast of Champions'), had some dry toast and felt right as rain by noon. That is, somewhere between a drizzle and a thunderstorm.

After an afternoon watching college football bowl games, I was called to the family dinner. My mom cooked a traditional roast pork for New Year's Day. My dad told us eating pork on the first day of the new year was an old German tradition and his mom was descended from an old German.

In my delicate condition, I was forced to eat it – my father insisted! I just hope it was cooked as I hear you can get a tapeworm from undercooked pork. I can't imagine having that long thing in my intestine. I'd be forced to drink beer continuously in order to drown that damn creature.

The worst thing about these formal dinners (we eat these in the formal dining room) is that the gang's all here; from sisters, brother, parents, boyfriends and my grandmother on my mother's side, Gran-King. Gran's a bit mad so I try to avoid her if I can. Otherwise, it's gummy wet kisses and her crapping on.

Gertrude King's husband died two years ago, which is sad, but she goes on and on about him. Sometimes she shows me a picture of his grave which she carries with her. As for her politics, she's kind of like Groucho Marx – 'she's against it!' Everything! Man, I hope her genes aren't dominant in me.

My sister, Bridget, twenty-two, and her husband to be – Duane Oss - were there. Bridget Marie is my oldest sister. She's a student at Steel City University in the big smoke. About 5'5, she isn't fat, though perhaps looks that way because of the loose clothes she often wears. She has a mature-looking face with the same prominent 'Gaughan' nose – as Dad calls it. Her ears stick out and she wears glasses – except when someone's taking a photo. She has a nice smile and a kindly-looking face.

Bridget, aka 'Biddy' to us, is often referred to as St. Bridget by us kids because she never has anything bad to say about anyone. If you need help with anything, go see Biddy. She's always ready and willing to lend a hand. She's a strict Catholic with high moral values and a regular church goer. Indeed, she briefly studied to be a nun. She's due to be married in April to Duane Oss, aka 'Dorky Duane' or 'DD', who's going for his doctorate in Chemistry at the same university as Biddy.

At dinner, Biddy naturally went on and on about the wedding which was a big yawn for me. Dad didn't seem all that interested. Paying the bills and giving his daughter away is enough for him. DD is nice enough in small doses, but he speaks with an air of superiority that reeks of 'Look at me. I'm almost a doctor.' Not a real one in my eyes.

Duane is slight and bespectacled, which kind of goes with the territory. My dad pulled him up at dinner when DD buttered his bread with the butter knife next to the butter. A lack of class in Dad's eyes. Dad believes the butter knife is used to transfer butter from the butter plate to your bread plate. Then you butter your bread with your own knife. Sounds like a lot of hooey to me. I find it hard to understand why one would be that concerned about spreading a piece of bread. Still, it was embarrassing for Duane and hence funny as all hell.

Later, my dad asked DD if he thought I was handsome. The embarrassment was now my hell. Just as well he said yes, although if he had said no, I'd have told him he's nothing to write home about either. Maybe he's a good kisser because I don't know what my sister sees in him.

DD knows nothing of sport and, when we later retired to the TV viewing room to watch more football, I asked him lots of meaningless questions about the game. He couldn't answer most of them. In this instance I was able to show my superiority. Not that he would have thought that way.

After dinner, Gran-King was taken home, and the family went to the living room to play Bridge. I barely know the Brooklyn Bridge from the Charles Goren one, so I excused myself. Besides, after a long day following a long night, I was tired. By now I was feeling better. So, I went to my room and left the group to their trumps and no trumps. I fell asleep within seconds.

Cop-u-later.

JANUARY 2,
1966 – Sunday

Got up early after a long sleep. My older sister Biddy was already awake and making breakfast. She went to the bother of making eggs, bacon and coffee, but I was more interested in my favorite – hot cocoa with toast. The toast had to be buttered, and then was dipped into the cocoa until the toast soaked up the hot chocolate. A mighty fine breakfast if I do say so myself.

Soon the other members of the family arrived: Pippa, twenty-one this week, my second oldest sister; Will, fourteen, my brother; Kitty, eleven, my youngest sister; Duane; and Dad and Mom. Anyway, after breakfast, Dad insisted we all go to Mass at the local Catholic Church - the Fear of the Lord parish. All went except Mom who said she wanted to start dinner.

After getting on our cold-weather jackets, hats and gloves, Will, Kitty, Dad and I jumped into his big Buick. DD, Biddy and Pippa decided to walk the 3-blocks to the church. Dad couldn't find a parking space near the church, so he parked 3 blocks on the other side. We had to walk in the wet snow without boots to get there.

When we got to the church, Biddy, DD and Pippa were already seated. As it was crowded, the rest of us had to stand in the back. This was OK with me as now I didn't have to listen to the blowhard priest and his hypocrisies. If a friend was around, I figured we could have a gab. In this case no one I knew was there, so Will and I BS'ed throughout.

Dad believes Mass is official if you get there before the bell is rung at the Offertory. We just made it in time for the end of the sermon. Thank God (no disrespect intended) I missed the fire and brimstone rant from old Father Ward, aka Pappy to us kids. We dutifully knelt for the Consecration of the Eucharist and took Communion. At this point, Dad told us we were leaving. We'd hardly been there 20 minutes, but, according to Dad, it was an official Mass and fulfilled our obligation.

Before we went home, we stopped off to see Dad's mom – Grandmother Gaughan. Almost 80, she's a very classy lady. She lives in a big house near the church. Her husband was a wheeler-dealer in this town and made lots of money. He died years ago so I never knew him. Her sons and daughters are all high achievers – professional types. Her oldest son – Andy, the patriarch of the family – is a lawyer and very influential in town.

Grammy – as we call her – lives with her three spinster sisters in this house. All elderly, it's a miracle the four are able to manage. She gave us caramel rolls and tea – with lots of sugar – while the older ones had coffee. We had a nice chat about this and that – hardly riveting stuff – before Dad said it was time to go home for dinner. Dad's side of the family loves to kiss, and it took a while to get through this leaving ritual.

As Dad pulled into the driveway, we spotted Columbus – the chauffer and handyman for our next-door neighbor Mrs. Pride – and waved to him. Dad is a dentist, and we live in an all-white suburban neighborhood called Westwood. Columbus is a Negro, a rare sight in these parts.

The City of Jakstown, commonly referred to as the 'City', is in a valley surrounded by 2 major hills. Westwood is located on top of one hill. The Negroes tend to live on the opposite hill of the valley called Prospector's Hill, or just 'The Hill' as it's known. Dad likes Columbus, but he doesn't have a lot of good to say about the black race or any non-white race. Perhaps he had a bad experience with Negroes when he was younger, or maybe he's a product of his times.

My school is an all-white Catholic High School. The Negro kids go to the public school – Jakstown City High School. So, I don't see any Negroes except when I go to the City. Even then, I don't have much contact, if any. Columbus and I talk occasionally, and he seems like a decent guy. I can't say I think a lot about the different races. I admire Martin Luther King, a Nobel Prize winner and preacher, but Dad says he's a Communist.

When we got home, we had our roast dinner. The rest of the day we just lounged around. We had a family 'Monopoly' game in the afternoon (I cleaned up by buying all the reds and putting hotels on).

In the evening we watched 'The Ed Sullivan Show' ('a really big shoe,' Ed, the host, says). It had Topo Gigio the mouse and Robert Goulet (ugh) the singer. Later we watched 'Bonanza.' Dad says I look a bit like Hoss which pisses me off no end. Finally, it was time for bed. School starts tomorrow and I can't wait to catch up with my friends.

Cop-u-later.

JANUARY 3,
1966 – Monday

School resumed this morning at Our Lady of Perpetual Succour Catholic High School - after the Christmas break. I'm a Junior (Year 11) about to start my second semester. I'm Gustav Martin Gaughan Jr.; the name is a mixture of German and Irish. Grammy comes from a German background, but her late husband – my grandfather - was Irish to the bootstraps. Gran-King's ancestors could have come over on the Mayflower for all I know of her background.

My friends nicknamed me 'Augoos' after the name my French teacher calls me. This is often shortened to 'Goose' which I tolerate but hate. I prefer to be called 'Gazman' or 'Gaz' - as most family and friends call me. Almost everyone – student and teacher, male and female – gets given a nickname. If I live to be 100, I'll never figure out the process for getting assigned this name. It just happens!

The first thing I did when I got to school was to look up my old friend Hep – though I had just seen him three days ago. Hep is slightly taller than me and a little bit overweight, but far from fat. He has a face only a mother could love. Kind of a 'Fred Flintstone' type. His hair is always messy, and he has big ears. He also wears glasses. We're good pals. When we first spotted each other, it was as if we were greeting each other after a long absence.

'How's your mother?' I said, 'I was with her last night.'

'Yah?' he replied, 'Yours was with a gang of sailors and she still had enough left over for my cousins'.

'No, it was the whole fleet'.

'How often did she do it?'

In our strange way we had to top the other one with insults – even at our own expense.

I spotted Barbara, aka 'Babs', Geist – also a Junior – who I had seen at the Canteen the other night. Babs was small, but well-proportioned with short, blonde hair (a peroxide blonde or a 'peroxy' as we joke) which flipped up on the sides. She had beautiful brown eyes, a great smile, a nice figure and the cutest face. I often said 'hi' to her but stopped short of having a conversation.

She returned my greetings, but that was the extent of our contact. Hep again said I didn't have a chance with her, but as she wasn't a cheerleader, I thought I had a maybe – or maybe a maybe - chance. I made a mental note to try to talk to her in the coming days.

Another NYE guy I ran into was Dordison French, a 200lb (at least he seems that big) man-mountain who tells everyone he's from France. Although his first name could be French, it doesn't sound French. I've met his parents and they don't have a French accent. Besides, I've seen him eat lots of food, but never snails or frogs, though he does like French fries. He may go wee-wee, but I've never heard him say oui, oui.

'Frenchie', a nickname which took about 10 seconds and little imagination to come up with, was big, with a round face. He had a dopey look about him but was actually quite bright though good at hiding it. His hair was always messy. He was a medium tall guy – a little taller than Hep or me - and had huge hands. Frenchie was a good kid who shared mine and Hep's sense of humour. He was a loyal friend and someone I could count on.

There were others I caught up with including Katie Petrane. Katie seems to pop up regularly where I am at school. I often think she actually follows me because I tend to run into her a lot. Although I don't dislike her, she's a bit intense. She often makes up reasons to be near me and to talk to me. Today, her mom's Pineapple Upside-Down cake was not a topic that interested me.

Bob Racovic, a thin, brainy and nerdy-looking guy we tried to see on NYE, said hello. Hep and I are often to be seen in his company. He's not so bad, just strange and about as uncool as a hot shower. Unfortunately for him, he often gets shit from us. Yet he likes hanging around. Go figure. The day went quickly as the time was spent catching up and talking about the holidays.

The Junior class play auditions were advertised and I decided to try out – much to the amusement of my so-called buddies who called me Shakespeare and implied even worse things. What's the big deal? I could be another Laurence Olivier, or better yet, Steve McQueen!

After school, I fronted at the school theatre and read a few lines. 'To be or not to be…' was the line I jokingly recited, but not the line wanted by the director. Instead, I read something from the play we were doing - 'Arsenic and Old Lace.' I was told to check the school bulletin board on Thursday for the casting.

Cop-u-later.

JANUARY 4,
1966 – Tuesday

It's only the second day of school, and already I'm in the shits. Got a ride to school with Dad, but I have to take the public bus or hitchhike home. There's talk of a school bus, but I'll be Rip Van Winkle before that comes to pass. I already have History and Chemistry work to do and tests coming up. Why don't the teachers give us a break?

It's only the second day for crying out loud! I'm not a genius, but my grades are good, not because I'm overly smart, but because I work hard at it. I started looking at the periodic table last night for Chemistry but dozed off.

When I got to school, I spotted the guys. Hep greeted me by telling me to suck his...I didn't have to hear the rest. I told him to show it right then and there if he wasn't bluffing. I added that I'd probably need a microscope to see it. We both laughed at the absurdity of it all.

We then broke into what's been an on-going argument over the relative merits of 'The Addams Family' vs. 'The Munsters' TV shows. I contend the 'Addams' is much cleverer than the latter. The jokes are better and the characters weirder.

All 'The Munsters' have going for it is Grandpa and some stereotypes. Hep insists 'Thing' is the only funny one on my show. This could have gone on longer, but we had to get ready for Home Room. This is where the roll is taken, and any announcements are made before the first class. HR is organised alphabetically, so I sit near Babs Geist.

All last semester, Babs and I went our separate ways, but today I decided to talk to her. I started by mentioning that I saw her at the Canteen on NYE. She said she remembered, though I doubted it. We laughed at one of the teachers – Sister Mary St. Albans, aka All Buns because of her wide girth. We talked about the holidays and then whatever came to mind. HR only lasts fifteen minutes so we didn't have much time, but – from my end – it was a start.

First period was Chem lab. As luck would have it, praise the Lord for alphabetical order because, again, I sit near Babs. The Chem class is usually beyond boring. The only interesting thing is the lab, though today even that was sleep-inducing.

We were lectured in the dos and don'ts (not for the first time I must say) of working in the lab by the Chem teacher, Sister Mary Bodecelli, aka 'Chubs'– another fat nun. During the class, I passed a note to Babs, but it never came back. It seemed to disappear into a black hole as I never saw it again. If it fell into my friends' hands, I'm toast. I'd never live it down.

Next it was History and the French Revolution. Mr. Ranan – our teacher – is a hard task master. He loves to give those damn pop quizzes. He's probably too lazy to do a normal lesson. He even makes us correct them and read out the grades to put in his mark book. I hope he chokes on those quizzes someday. The rest of the day was as always – footloose and unfortunately Babs free. But I had made 'alien' contact.

Anyhow, despite a Chem test and probably a pop quiz in History tomorrow, when I got home, I called Hep to go to the basketball game at the Memorial Arena in the City. We were playing our rivals, the 'Trojans' of Jakstown City Public High School - often referred to as City High. They are so damn big, and their players look like they need a shave. Yet we have a powerhouse team and won easily, fifty-six to forty-two. We are talking state championship this year. Go Cruisers!!

Hep and I arranged with Frenchie for him to open a side door to get us in without paying. The national anthem was being played so it was dark, and a piece of cake to sneak in. We managed to avoid the attendants. Frenchie wanted some money for his effort, but we fobbed him off.

Once we were seated, Hep threw a jam doughnut at Frenchie. He threw one back, but Hep ducked and it hit the unfortunate Egghead Racovic. One couldn't help but laugh. Hep wasted a bit more money on cheap doughnuts. He took a bite, then threw them at random, thereby pissing off the lot of us.

Undeterred, we returned the favor. Hep continued with this weird doughnut ritual until his supply was exhausted. By the end, he was covered in sticky jam doughnut crap. Would you call this behavior an obsession?

While there, I ran into the laundry girl, Amy Sing, and said 'hello'.

Amy is a Junior at City High. She actually remembered me from NYE much to the amusement of my pals. Amy is short, but thin with an interesting and not unpleasant face. She has dark eyes and long dark hair which she wears down. She has a bubbly personality which makes her quite attractive and somewhat exotic as there aren't many of Asian descent in this town.

I wonder how my father would react if I brought a Chinese-looking girl home for Sunday dinner? Gran-King, who hates anyone not Anglo-Saxon, would have a conniption fit!

Cop-u-later.

JANUARY 5,
1966 – Wednesday

Everyone at school was over the moon after our big win against City High last night. City H. has lorded over us too often throughout the years, so it was good to get one back on them. We sat near some of Hep's public-school pals last night, so I kept my gloating to a minimum. City H. guys tend to be aggressive bastards and not prone to losing. Let's just say we were quietly satisfied after the game was over and didn't feel the need to rub their faces into the dirt.

I'd hoped to renew my acquaintance with Babs today, but she wasn't at school. Instead, I lost myself in my work. There was Chem work to complete and a History quiz to take – the latter which I aced. In gym class, we were introduced to soccer. As far as I'm concerned, it's a sissy game played mainly by Europeans and Mexicans. It's boring to watch and even more boring to play. Who would go to a game to see a 0 – 0 tie?

At lunch, I saw Katie by herself so thought she'd like my company. She seemed very happy to see me – perhaps too happy. She sat very close to me and called out to her nerdy friends on more than one occasion to show them she was sitting with a real boy. Pinocchio, I'm not, though sometimes when I talk to her, I feel my nose would rival the puppet's.

After school, I had to rush home as it was my sister Pippa's 21st birthday. Dad had arranged a special surprise party for her. But he needed to get her out of the house so the guests could arrive without being seen and arrangements made for the celebration. He told me to go out with her for an hour or so to keep her away from the house.

Siobhan Philippa, aka 'Pippa' or sometimes 'Pip', is like a rattlesnake. She has a short temper and can be violent when she loses it. She once stabbed me in the ass with a fork over a disagreement. She can be nice, but you have to be careful around her. She can be wickedly sarcastic when riled. She's short – only 5'2. She has blue eyes, blonde hair and a beautiful face. Dad describes it as angelic. She is quite petite in stature. She should wear glasses but is vain, and only wears them if she has to.

Pippa's a favorite of Dad's because of her 'fairy-like' appearance. She plays him like a Stradivarius. He rarely turns down any request from her. She's engaged to a guy named Ennis Lysaght who often makes himself scarce at family gatherings. That's OK with me. Dad reveres him. I don't hate Ennis, but he can be a jerk at times.

In this state, you are legal to do most anything – including buying and drinking alcohol - when you turn 21. Today my sister Pippa becomes legal. To get her away, I suggested we go out to get her first legal drink at the local bar.

Once there, as I'm not even seventeen years, I figured I'd have to deepen my voice and show a few chest hairs to convince the barkeeper to serve me. As it's winter, I wasn't about to do the latter, and I don't do deep voices, so I had about as much chance as a snowflake in a desert of getting a drink.

But I tried. I entered the bar and sat in a corner booth as Pippa went to buy us drinks. As she's as small as a church mouse, the bartender didn't believe she was 21 – even after she showed him her driver's license. So, we settled on going to a liquor store where she secured a bottle of Seagram's, but only after experiencing the third degree from a prim and proper attendant.

'How old are you? You don't look 21', he said.

'But I have a license,' she answered.

'Where did you steal that from?' And on and on it went. I didn't contribute to the argument as it might have made things worse. But he gave her a form to fill out in which she swore she was of legal age. Then she bought a bottle of Seagram's whiskey. So, we were in.

Fortunately, Pippa wanted to take the booze home. Just as well, as it was time for me to get her to her party. When we got there, we were confronted by a large group of people who yelled, 'Surprise'. My diversionary tactics had been successful. Present were Pippa's friends, relations, our family, the largely irrelevant Gran-King and, of course, Ennis.

'En-ass', as I call him, though not when he's around, is a big, dumb, but good-looking athletic type who all the girls love and, if the rumors are true, he loves them back. But Pippa likes the guy even if he can be an asshole. Who am I to stand in the way of love?

Anyway, the party went on for hours with food, drinks, a cake, presents. I managed to grab some of the Seagram's. Now, was it no. 6 or 7? I wouldn't know the difference anyhow. By bedtime, I wasn't feeling too hot. Pity tomorrow's a school day.

Cop-u-later.

JANUARY 6,
1966 – Thursday

Every Thursday, I'm driven to school by Katie Petrane's father – Aldo – whose family lives down our street. Katie is a decent girl and very smart, but she likes to smother me. She makes sure I sit by her in the car, and she rubs up against me. Ugh! I wonder if Aldo notices.

It's not that Katie's ugly or anything, just ordinary. She's short with medium dark hair, usually worn in pigtails. Of Italian descent, she has a dark complexion. Her face could be nice if she worked on it. She has a pretty smile, but she wears glasses and has braces. How would I kiss her?

Anyway, I like to be footloose and fancy free, and she often shadows me at school – especially when I'm talking to another girl. Today I was waiting in the foyer of my house when Mom yelled from upstairs that Aldo had honked three times. I must have been daydreaming cause my mom came downstairs and started yelling at me.

I doubt Mom ever worked a day in her life. She is the atypical housewife of her generation. Aged 46, we think, she's short, and petite with thin legs, but a bulging body. She has brown eyes and brownish hair, slightly greying now. A lovely face, but not much of a smile. She's smart as a whip and very artistic. She's embroidered and created many paintings and wall hangings for the house.

Mom's quite introverted outside of the house, yet inside she runs the show. She isn't afraid to speak out if she has something on her mind. If she doesn't want to do something, wild horses couldn't get her to budge. She's not easy to talk to, but if you get her into a conversation, you can tell she knows the score.

Mom's a good judge of people and can be very helpful when someone's in need. She smokes constantly and likes her drink. Her first name is Elizabeth, but she's better known as Bette after her teenage idol Bette Davis.

'Why don't you stand outside so he doesn't have to honk?' she said, quite aggressively.

I ignored her and ran to the car. The trip to the school in the City was the usual. It took about fifteen minutes to get there. There were three other girls in the car, but, as always, the only seat available was next to Katie – by her design. My dad takes me to school the other days, but he goes to work late on Thursdays, so I need alternative transport on that day.

Katie started talking about the Sadie Hawkins dance coming up next month - a formal dance where the girl asks the boy. I'm worried she might ask me. I really need to stay away from her at school as much as possible until someone else invites me. I figured she'd be too shy to ask in front of her dad.

School was – for lack of a better word – school. I had lunch with the boys as I want to stay away from Katie for reasons already mentioned. We played lunchroom table-top football. You flick the milk carton and if it hangs over the edge of the table without falling off, you score a touchdown. Then you try to make an extra point by flicking the carton through your opponent's index fingers, connected with the thumbs up to make a goalpost.

As always, the game ended with an argument. Someone claimed a touchdown when the carton didn't quite go over the edge. The claimant insisted the carton edge was slightly over the tabletop. This is a situation where threatening words take place, and a show of male bravado is required. It rarely goes beyond the word stage. Most times we go back to playing – until the bell rings for class.

Babs was at school, but at lunchtime she was with her friends. I didn't see or talk to her all day except briefly at Home Room. She said she missed school yesterday due to a cold. It is wintry outside, so people are getting sick. I'll have to work harder if I'm to get her to notice me.

After school, I checked the music bulletin board to see if I was in the class play. It was not to be. Damn. I would have made a great Teddy Roosevelt. I can yell 'Charge' and run up the stairs with the best of them. I was told I could be part of the stage crew, so I signed up. My beautiful thespian career had ended before it had even begun.

When I got home in the afternoon, my mom again brought up the stupid honking. I got pissed off and I told her where to go. This wasn't too smart as I had a research project that needed typed. She often does this for me, but tonight, she refused. I had to do it myself.

When will I ever learn? Will I ever understand women?

Cop-u-later.

28

JANUARY 7,
1966 – Friday

Friday – at last. For a first week, it sure was damn long. Saw Babs at Home Room. I asked her about her cold as I couldn't think of anything else to say. This led to a brief chat, soon to be interrupted by the school counsellor asking each of us to make an appointment with her to discuss our future.

It's hard for me to think of a post-high school life when my future is about what I'll be doing this weekend. Still, I guess I should give it some thought. I mainly think about being rich. I just have to figure out how to get there.

Talked to Hep and asked if he was going to the Canteen tonight. He wasn't sure, as he said his family had planned something else and he didn't think he could get out of it. Pisser. I could ask Frenchie but having him around at a dance was detrimental to my chance of scoring. Then again, I'm detrimental to myself. In the end I decided against asking him.

I did have a nice lunch. Babs was with her girlfriends, so I wasn't about to interrupt her. Besides, anything that would interest that group would hardly be of interest to me. I played a bit of table-top football then sat for a short time with Katie until the bell rang for class. I was relieved she didn't ask me to the Sadie.

Friday night. I was keen to go – even if by myself - to the Teen Canteen to pick up girls (not probable, but my intentions were good). Perhaps I might have run into Babs or the mysterious Amy. I can't get either of them out of my head for some reason.

Anyhoo, my plans were curtailed when the Old Man decided to take me to see some friends and patients of his who were celebrating what he calls Russian Christmas. Something to do with the old Orthodox religion calendar.

Dad, Dr. Gustav Gaughan Senior, fifty-three, is a dentist who has an office in the City. He's a short and stocky guy. He has curly hair, which is grey on the sides and balding on the top. He wears a hearing aid due to deafness he got during the Korean War. That's his dubious story.

Others have different versions. Thus, you have to shout to get him to hear. He also wears thick 'Coke bottle' glasses.

Dad's outgoing and has a good sense of humor. Indeed, he often cracks jokes at other's expense. He makes decisions quickly and decisively. Unlike Mom, he's an easy mark for money and for the use of the car. He's particularly partial to anything to do with the Irish. He smokes regularly and drinks probably more than he should.

Well, he took me to an area of the City specifically populated by ethnics of the Eastern European persuasion. I'm not sure they were Russian, but they certainly knew how to have a good time. The food was to die for. There were halupkies (stuffed cabbage), perogies (a kind of dumpling filled with potato) and so many cakes that I felt like a kid in a candy store. My favorite was walnut roll, but there were a variety of poppy seed rolls as well. And moon-shaped cookies with powdered sugar on them.

So, Christmas in January, complete with trees, presents and - if I do say so myself - some good-looking daughters and their friends. I know I'm only sixteen but perhaps I could pass myself off as 18 years. Then again, these girls would eat me alive. As Maxwell Smart says, 'and I would love every minute of it.'

Now, the booze. Anything you wanted. We went to half-a-dozen homes and my father took liberal advantage of Canadian Club and a guy named Mr. Walker. For my part I had a couple of beers which more or less made sure I looked sloppy and acted the same. Thus, I couldn't have gotten lucky even if I tried.

At one house, I ran into Babs, actually of Polish descent, who was visiting a friend. Who would have thought? We talked a bit and she said she would see me at the school dance tomorrow. I can't believe my good fortune! Christmas has come early... or is it late? Doesn't matter!

The trip home was a bit hairy as my dad insisted on driving. Naturally in his condition after one (or ten?) too many, he was all over the road. I think I had my eyes closed and my hands in prayer most of the way. I should have had my ears closed as well as he insisted on singing Army songs. 'Over hill over dale...'

Cop-u-later.

JANUARY 8,
1966 – Saturday

Went to the school dance this evening. The school runs an informal dance most weekends for all students. Got there late because I wanted to watch the TV show the 'Honeymooners'. Funny as all hell. Like when Ralph goes, 'One of these days, Alice – to the moon.' Not that I'd ever hit a woman.

Well, I got there and saw Babs making out with a Senior boy. I know we're not going together, but damn, that hurt! Particularly as I was so encouraged after our talk last night. Anyway, I brooded with the other losers on the chairs at the side of the dance floor. The 'dogs' were on the opposite side. To pass the time, Frenchie, Hep and I amused ourselves by making fun of the Egghead Racovic, because he wore a tie!

Truthfully, we were too scared of rejection to ask any of the girls across the room. Some of them were not bad looking - particularly out of school uniform. But the thought of being tagged by your pals forever as a loser by asking one to dance and being snuffed prevented any movement across the 'no man's land' of the dance floor. Besides my heart had been ripped out by Babs. Out of jealousy, I called her every nasty name in the book to Hep and Frenchie.

Now Babs wanted to get in good with the guy she was with. She knew Hep from Home Group and cornered him during a break in the music. She asked him to say some good things about her to Carl Mirgat, the Senior (12th grade). From the way Mirgat and she were going at it, this ploy didn't seem necessary.

Hep knew I was hurting and hatched a diabolical plan to foil their romance. He would talk to Mirgat and make up things to say about the sub-hygienic condition of Babs. In addition, he would throw in some unkind references about her reputation. I'm not sure I cared for this underhanded scheme, but I was too hurt to worry. Not long after, I saw Babs crying. I don't know exactly what Hep told Mirgat, but he soon left the dance with his friends.

Now, Hep motioned for me to move in. I gave Babs my most sincere look. I asked her what was wrong and, when she confided in me, I showed the utmost sympathy. I even held her hand. Obviously upset, she indicated she wanted to leave the dance, so I offered to take her home! She readily accepted.

I parked by her place, and we talked for the longest time. I confessed to what Hep had said to Mirgat. She wasn't happy about this turn of events at all. She wondered why Hep would do such a thing and said she would never speak to him again. I played it cool and agreed with her. Though I didn't like what Hep did, I secretly was happy about the outcome. I told her what a rat he was. I hated to bad mouth Hep, my best friend, but this was Babs I was talking about.

Before she got out of the car, she kissed me on the cheek. Naturally, I was in seventh heaven as I drove home. The only downer was later when I noticed a forlorn Katie Petrane, who had been at the dance, as I drove past her house. She was sitting on her porch outside in the cold. It looked like she was crying. Broken hearts are as contagious as colds this time of year.

What a dilemma I'm in. I finally got what I wanted and kissed Babs. I got her away from Mirgat and on my side. But then I bad-mouthed my best friend, Hep, and the girl I like now despises him. I returned to the dance.

Afterwards I had Hep, Frenchie and a couple of others – J.D., his friend Con from City H.S. (who had snuck in thanks to Hep) and Zlatko Woznefski, aka the 'Boob' – over to my place to play pool. I have a table in my basement. The unfortunate Boob once gave a wrong answer to a question in class. The teacher called him a Boob and he's been branded with that name ever since.

JD, however, is the epitome of cool. He walks cool, he talks cool. It's hard to put my finger on it. He's just cool. He's average height and slight in appearance, but nothing rattles him. He's quiet but has a good sense of humor and he's very loyal.

As for Con, well I didn't care for him from first sight. He had that arrogant swagger. He was reasonably tall, and his face was full of zits. He spoke to us with a sarcastic bent. You couldn't tell if he was making fun of us or just being an asshole. Both no doubt. The public-school boys never liked us Catholic guys.

The others laughed when Hep said what happened tonight at the dance. I conveniently did not tell Hep everything. What a cad I am. We played 9 ball (five and nine in gets the money for the person who pockets them) doubles and Hep and I won $2. Hep and I are friends, but I can sense a storm brewing! Hep took the others home at 1am.

Cop-u-later.

JANUARY 9,
1966 – Sunday

Last night, I made arrangements with Hep to catch a bus to leave from school to go to a basketball game in Steel City. Steel City is a major metropolitan American city of over two million people about 70 miles from Jakstown. Our town is small by comparison.

It's been said there are 125,000 in our area, but the counters may have included dogs and cats as well as people in their census! Steel City is known for its large steel industry and is a hub for all major activities in its focus area. Jakstown is also known for its steel production, but on a much smaller scale.

Anyway, I met Hep at school in the morning. We used bogus cards secured by Hep to sneak onto the bus to go to the school basketball game. It was easy to get on, flash our fake cards and pull the wool over the teachers' eyes. Are they dumb or are we just too clever?

On the way there, I told Hep that Babs knew he gave Mirgat false information about her. She wasn't happy things got messed up with him and said she didn't want anything further to do with Hep. I told him I had to pretend he was a jerk as things ended up good for me.

Naturally, I didn't tell him I'm the one who told Babs about him. It wouldn't go over well even if we are best friends. I told him this was only temporary, and things would eventually get back to normal, but I couldn't help but think he would find out the truth and do something to get even.

Our b-ball team is super good, and many are confident we can win the state championship this year. Rudy Mingo is the only Junior starter, so he's revered by our class. Yet he's a decent guy without a big head so how can anyone be jealous of him? When we got to the basketball venue, we said hello to Rudy. He talked to us for about five minutes despite having to get ready for the match.

We won the game against Bishop McCrea 86-74. Rudy had 18 points. So, we were happy. On the way to the bus, I said hi to Karen King. Karen, a second cousin of mine on Gran-King's side of the family, also

34

happens to be a cheerleader.

I didn't know her that well, but she's about as close as I'll ever get to one of her lofty status. Yet she seemed very down-to-earth. A Sophomore, she spoke to Hep and I and introduced us to her friend Kathy Mason - also a Year 10 girl. Unlike the blonde Karen, Kathy's a tough looking brunette.

Hep seemed particularly interested in Mason and sat with her on the bus going back. I sat with Egghead Racovic who had paid full price to go to the game. He was wearing a hat and a scarf in team colors with the OLPS initials. On the way back, Racovic constantly cleared his throat and sneezed into a handkerchief which he put back in his pocket. Carrying that cloth of germs couldn't have been very sanitary.

Racovic spoke of a number of nerdy things. I think one topic was about astronomy, and another the perils of red meat. I ignored him. I was thinking mainly of Babs. I fell asleep and thought about her and me on a desert island. Unfortunately, I woke up as our bus arrived at school, just as she was going for a dip in the ocean in her bikini. Crap!

When we got to school, I said my goodbyes – not that Hep noticed with Mason around. I think he was getting a phone number. I had to call to get a ride home. Dad picked me up from school. When we got home, I noticed Columbus outside Mrs. Pride's house. This being January, it was quite cold. He was in his chauffer outfit but didn't seem to mind.

So, I went over to say hello while Dad pulled into the garage. Columbus and I exchanged pleasantries and then he asked how I was. I told him about Babs and how she liked another guy. He encouraged me to continue to woo (his speech and manner were very old fashioned) her. Things always turn out for the best he said.

I then said goodbye and went inside. When in the house, Dad asked me what I talked about with Columbus. I gave him a pretty vague answer. He told me he liked Columbus, but that I should be careful. I'm not sure what he meant by that and didn't ask. However, I thought that Columbus was one smart cookie. I liked his advice. I wouldn't give up the ship. I think some American naval officer said that during a war.

Cop-u-later.

JANUARY 10,
1966 – Monday

School again. All I could think of was Babs Geist. She's in some of my classes so I couldn't keep my eyes off her (although I tried to hide it). I flirted shamelessly with her by passing notes during our Problems of Democracy (POD) class. I was pleasantly surprised when she responded.

'How's your mother,' I wrote.

'OK, why do you ask?' she replied.

'How about a threesome?'

'She's a bit old'.

'But spry'.

Anyway, it went on like that until the teacher caught me and made me read aloud something about the House of Representatives from our text. Still, my connecting with Babs was fun, and well worth getting three demerits (if you get twenty-five of these marks against you, there is a suspension) from the teacher. After class, I briefly talked to Babs who's still mad at Hep. It will take a lot to smooth things over. Hep was hardly seen as he spent his spare time in the year 10 locker area with Mason.

Around noon, we had a school assembly. Here the Principal introduced a Spanish exchange student from Argentina. He might as well have held out a red cape to the bulls. She attracted boys like bees to honey. She was tall, dark, with long, black, luxurious hair, a beautiful body and figure, and the longest legs - in a short mini skirt.

She stood on stage and said a few words in broken English. She had the cutest Spanish/English accent. I managed to push through the throng and was about to introduce myself, but the jocks (sports guys) surrounded her which made it difficult for me. What a chick! I admit, I was smitten. I temporarily forgot about Babs, Hep and all my girl problems.

Anyway Lisbeth, the exchange student, had this wonderful smile. I wanted to introduce myself, but the jock factor was too much to overcome. My turn would come. I would make sure to talk to her later. Unfortunately, I took French, not Spanish, which would make conversation with her difficult, but not impossible, as she knew some English.

I was able to get close enough to her to quickly glance at her class schedule which she openly bandied about. She is in my Chemistry class, so I'll get my chance there. She'll be here for the term we were told.

Back to reality. Had lunch with Babs. I'm hoping she's forgotten all about Mirgat the Maggot (as I now refer to him). I like to think Babs and I are on to something, but it will take more than a lunch to straighten things out. Of course, I didn't mention the lovely Lisbeth, but why would I? How's the saying go, 'Love the one you're with.'

Home and some drama. Mom decided not to get up during the day. Dad screamed bloody murder when he saw she hadn't made dinner. He particularly didn't like that she hadn't made the beds. Then followed one accusation after another replete with yelling. Both sides gave as good as they got.

The argument was so heated that one might have expected fisticuffs, but Dad wasn't the type. Mom wouldn't budge, and that was that. Afterwards, Dad asked me where Mom hid the alcohol. I wasn't sure how serious he was when he said that. I didn't know anyway.

While this was taking place, I told Will and Kitty to come downstairs with me. I found some fish sticks in the freezer and put them in the oven. At some point, Dad joined us at the table to share what he called 'this crappy meal.' Beggars can't be choosey, I thought.

After dinner it was right up to my room - which I share with Will – to work on my homework. I really don't need this Dad/Mom confrontation in my life.

Cop-u-later.

JANUARY 11,
1966 – Tuesday

Dad drove me to school. Before he dropped me off, he apologised for last night. He said sometimes married couples have disagreements. It wasn't our fault. I said it was OK, though I feared otherwise. I felt sorrier for Will and especially Kitty as they are younger and more impressionable.

Kind of cold this morning with a bunch of snow flurries. It's heavy coat season, but not too heavy. The wrath of your peers awaits those who bundle up too much. It's not considered 'manly' to overdo things in winter. To hell with colds or flu - unless you're the Egghead Racovic. He had 3, maybe 4 layers on. Did I mention the wrath?

I was really keen to get to school as I wanted to see Babs, of course, but also, I wanted to possibly talk with Lisbeth. I got a break in Chem class. Babs was my lab partner, but the teacher wanted someone with experience, not that kind, to partner the new girl. Goodbye Babs, hello Lisbeth. I told Babs I didn't want to do this, but I lied. This was what dreams are made of.

The lab experiment centered on what occurs in a chemical reaction when two different coloured chemical elements are brought together. Something went wrong because Chubs - our porcine Chem teacher – turned on the ventilation. A strange greenish looking cloud was sucked into the vent apparently without causing any damage to object or person. Get back to me in thirty years to see if there's been any long-term effect!

Resuming ten minutes later after an evacuation, I needed the Bunson burner, and asked Lisbeth if she would pass it over. She's only 16, but more of a woman than any of the girls in the school. What eyes, lips, hair. Babs who? I thought. The teacher brought me back to earth when she asked me a question about our experiment.

I pretended I couldn't hear her, so she moved on to another victim. Hep didn't notice Lisbeth as he's in a love trance over that year 10 jail-bait Mason. I can only think of one reason he likes her. Maybe – as she's quite well-endowed - it's more than one.

There wasn't much interaction between me and Lisbeth. Let's just say it was a get to know you type thing. In my case, a get to know I exist. We didn't talk about anything personal but stayed on the Chem path right down the middle of the road. It was only a matter of time, I thought. Despite language differences, I was sure we could communicate when the time was right.

Anyway, saw Babs at lunch. My head must have been screwed on tight, as otherwise I might have blown my stack when I saw her talking to the Year 12 jerk Mirgat the Maggot from afar. I kept thinking they could be getting back together. Maybe Hep's undermining of her reputation to him was losing its bite. I felt relieved when the Maggot stormed away.

I just happened to be there to rush in to console a crying Geist. Her head rested on my shoulder. I wiped a tear away from her cheek and told her things would get better before she knew it. Who cares why she got close to me? The important thing is she did!! We had lunch together, but occasionally I snuck a peek at Lisbeth who was sitting nearby. It was hard to keep my eyes off her. What a dish!

After school, my intermural basketball team 'The Baileys of Balboa' (named after a TV show) played a piss-weak Year 10 side. We won 29-9 and I had eight points, so as Captain I was happy with the result, but that was only our second win out of 6 games. We struggle against the big jock teams.

Hep is hopeless as are most of his fellow players – Mike Kang, a goofy, wiry, eerie looking guy, and Frenchie and JD. But then I'm no Wilt the Stilt. So, two out of six may be not so bad! Fortunately, we have the Hesse twins who seem to know their way around a basketball court.

Tonight, when I got home, Mom was dressed, beds were made, and dinner was being cooked. Dad was pleased when he got home. His smile didn't last long as Mom left the table after serving dinner. There's still trouble in paradise.

Dinner over, I called Babs and talked for an hour about things I can't even remember. The talking wasn't the important part. Connecting with Babs was. Katie later phoned to remind me we had History and Chem tests tomorrow. I think she just wanted to hear my voice. Just as well she phoned to remind me. I spent the rest of the evening studying.

Cop-u-later.

JANUARY 12,
1966 – Wednesday

I guess I did OK on the History and Chemistry tests, but the French Revolution and periodic tables are not my forte! I was somewhat distracted in Chemistry class by Lisbeth who actually looked at me and, before the exam, greeted me with an 'hola' in that sexy accent. I assume that means 'hi' in Spanish.

Lisbeth often touches her long dark hair and pushes it back when she speaks. This only adds to her mystique and makes her even more appealing. Despite the distraction, I think I did all right on the Chem test and aced the History one. In the former, maybe I should have tried to copy Egghead Racovic, who always gets an A. But he guarded his paper like it was Fort Knox.

Had lunch with Babs again, but I can't help thinking she still likes that maggot Mirgat. She certainly stared at him when he walked into the cafeteria. Other than that, I felt we were getting on quite well. I even got a giggle from her when I asked her if she had a dog. She did – a cocker spaniel named Milly.

We both chuckled when she talked about her dog. Babs even touched me when she laughed. The big Sadie Hawkins formal is coming up soon. I have my fingers crossed that Babs will ask me. She hasn't yet – I'm holding my breath on that one. I'm not sure how long I can hold off Katie.

Today, after school, we had auditions for the musical 'Brigadoon'. The musical director Sister Mary Georgakopoulos – tall for a nun, and with a face that would scare a Werewolf - had us sing a song and then read a passage. We all had to sing 'Secret love' – the old Doris Day song from the movie 'Calamity Jane.' UGH! As a secondary audition song, I went with 'It's almost like being in love' from the musical.

Next, we had to read a passage with a Scottish accent. I sounded like Scotty in the new TV show 'Star Trek'. ('I canna hold it no longer, Cap'n. It's gonna blew'). I sounded unconvincing, so I figured I better go for one of the American roles – preferably not Tommy, but Jeff.

There's a bit of humour in the Jeff character and he doesn't have to sing much. Not that I hate singing, I just like that role. There was some real talent trying out for the leads, but I was called back for a second audition tomorrow. Babs also tried out but didn't make the cut. This gave me another chance to console her.

It was a pretty quiet evening. I studied for Algebra and French tests. I don't have a clue what's happening in the latter, but I'll try to fake it. Before the studying, I watched the first episode of the TV series 'Batman'. I thought it would be an adventure show, but it was more of a weird comedy with a fat Batman who danced. There were signs like 'kapow' and 'crunch' when he hit a bad guy. The humour is a bit dumb, but I'll stick with it for a while.

Mom, again, made dinner for us – spaghetti with meat sauce. Once again, she didn't eat with us. I hope this isn't the beginning of a worsening relationship with Dad. Time will tell. At bedtime, I thought I'd dream of Babs, but my thoughts turned to Lisbeth and then gulp, Katie. My mind is certainly playing tricks on me.

Cop-u-later.

JANUARY 13,
1966 – Thursday

Thursday, and my ride to school with Katie's dad. I was the last one picked up, so I was funneled to a place by Katie who had saved me a seat next to her. She snuggled up to me on the trip. I'm surprised her dad didn't notice. Anyway, when we got to school, I made an excuse about needing to study for tests, so ran away to avoid her in case she was planning to ask me to the formal. Will Babs ever invite me to the Sadie?

When I opened my locker, it exploded. I guessed that Hep had somehow found out that I did the dirty and spilled my guts to Babs about his bogus words to the Maggot at the dance. He somehow got into my locker and rigged my books tightly against the door.

The release of pressure on opening the locker threw books and other unmentionables everywhere. I could see Hep chuckling at a distance. I laughed as well but vowed to get back at him somehow. I'll come up with something dirty about his year 10 girlfriend, Mason, to spread around the school.

Babs was away sick today, so I decided to have another crack at talking to Lisbeth – the tough Argentinian gaucho. I went up to her at lunch and asked if she needed help negotiating the cafeteria line. She said she didn't, but that didn't stop me. I helped her choose a kind of runny tapioca pudding they serve. I was going to sit with her, but she thanked me and went to the table with the jocks. As they are not my type of people, I decided to find Hep.

Hep was in kind of a dream world thinking about Mason, so I sat by Frenchie. Frenchie weighed a ton on any scale and was eating everything not nailed down. I could not stomach his eating habits. He snarfed down two of those awful puddings and wore a good part of them on his face and clothes. He spoke as he ate, so I couldn't understand him anyway.

I decided to take a chance she wouldn't remember the Sadie and sat near Katie. She was alone reading a book 'A Tale of Two Cities' – I think by Charles Dickens. 'This is the worst of times and the best of times,' she quoted. She might have been talking about my life.

She went on to talk about the book, but I'm a bit thick and couldn't make out what she was saying. On second thought, I didn't really want an explanation, as I probably wouldn't have understood her as it was. I was grateful she didn't pop the Sadie question as I'm not sure how I would have reacted.

After lunch, I secretly spent a whole Chemistry period staring at Lisbeth. Sometimes life can be great. Part-way through the lesson, I leaned over to her and asked what some of the periodic table symbols meant - even though I knew the ones I asked her about. I just wanted to talk to her. This caused a few problems with Chubs, but I think I covered my tracks.

After school, I had my second 'Bridgadoon' audition. I read for the Jeff part and made a damn good fist of it, if I do say so myself. I should find out if I get one of the leads in the next four days. As I was leaving school, I noticed Hep's locker was open. Hep tried out for a musical part but didn't get a role so he left early with Mason. He forgot to secure his locker.

This was an opportunity I couldn't let pass and rigged his locker to explode with books tomorrow morning. Now I can abandon my plan to spread the rumour that Mason has crabs. As I said before, sometimes life can be cruel, but sometimes great. The worst of times and the best of times.

Cop-u-later.

JANUARY 14,
1966 – Friday

I hadn't arrived at school when it happened, but I heard Hep's books sprayed far and wide down the corridor when he opened his 'booby trapped' locker. A job well done, but I'd best be on the lookout in case he retaliates.

We spent the first two periods decorating our home room for the big game on Sunday. We play our archrival Bishop McGuillicutty, and if we win, we'll be closer to winning the state championship. What a team! I ran into Rudy Mingo between classes and wished him luck.

The theme for our room was the German Beer Hall. We decorated the room in an alpine setting with fake beer mugs and German clothing. There were fake mountains in the background covered with fake snow and tables with checked tablecloths just like a real beer hall (except no beer). Of course, there were crepe paper buntings with our school colors.

It looked quite impressive. Georgina Hansel, aka 'Gretel' for obvious reasons, was in charge of the decorating. A big, burly girl, Gretel is so sweet she'd make sugar melt, but a wonderful organizer. I've got to give her credit.

Mike Kang, though, almost ruined it by dressing up like Hitler. He combed his hair back and wore a fake black moustache above his lip. He even gave the 'Heil salute.' It was funny in a way, but we got him out of there before the judges came as we wanted to win the big prize.

After lunch (as yesterday, I again tempted fate by spending lunch with Katie as Babs was sick), a panel of judges came to the rooms to deliberate on the winner of the grand home room decorating prize. We won, though it would have been a tough choice.

Second place was the ice room – a re-creation of an igloo decked out in school colors with toy penguins along the sides; and third was space rangers – a planetary view of the world with our school in our colors in the center.

All the work we put into it was worth it as we won $25 to spend on something for our room. Mr. Ranan - called Doc because he's the sports teams' trainer - was our homeroom teacher. He was particularly overjoyed we won and had a grin as big as Broadway. Well, maybe Fifth Avenue.

The only drawback was that we had to clean up afterwards. It was dark when we finished, so I suggested to some of the guys (even E-H Racovic who was still at school) that we get some pizza and then go to my house and shoot pool. Frenchie and JD were goers, but not Hep who was pissed off about his locker and went home.

It appeared Mom and Dad had worked things out, as she cooked and ate with the family yesterday. Today - Friday as always – is fish day for our family. Don't know where the Friday fish custom started for Catholics, but we follow it – dare I say – religiously.

There is a rumor that the ban on Catholics eating meat on Fridays will be ended by the Pope. Dad says it doesn't matter, as we'll always be Friday fish people. He buys this crappy haddock every week that only needs to be warmed up.

Thankfully, I was with my friends and didn't have to stomach it. I was happy with pizza, but I dare not tell Dad, as it had pepperoni on it.

Anyway, I'm praying he forgets all this nonsense about sticking with fish. Maybe if it's fish fingers that would be different. I'm not sure what part of the fish they're made from, but these fingers can't be beat – as long as there's tartar sauce available.

We had an enjoyable evening talking about girls and cars except for the Egghead Racovic. He likes Ronald Reagan – the washed-up actor – who is running for Governor of California. He wanted to talk about his conservative policies. That discussion ended when JD threw some pepperoni at him. Still, it was an enjoyable evening and we stayed till midnight. I think I won $2 playing 9-ball. It was late, but Dad let me take the boys home.

Around ten p.m., I had left the group to make a phone call to Babs, but she wasn't home. Funny, as she wasn't at school today. As it was late, I was a bit puzzled. My first thought was that the 12th grader maggot might be up to his old tricks. My second thought I'd rather keep to myself.

Cop-u-later.

JANUARY 15,
1966 – Saturday

Had to stay home for part of the night as it was Mom's birthday. No one really knows how old she is, as she changes her birth year depending on who she's talking to. I assume she's about forty-six or forty-seven, but then anyone in their forties looks old to me.

Anyway, we had a meal of crab cakes - a local delicacy that can only be described as crab meat mixed with breadcrumbs, spices and whatever's available, then patted flat and baked. It's not bad, but kind of an acquired taste – meaning you have to have been born and lived a minimum of two decades here to like it. I'm about four years off.

We sang Happy Birthday to Mom. My dad always yells WOW at the top of his voice when the candles are blown out on the cake. Then presents – perfume, scarf, and an ashtray to cater for her nicotine habit. Then cake and ice cream.

After I ate a piece of the sponge with that sickly-sweet icing that you can only get on birthday cake, I gave her a kiss, wished her a happy birthday and left for the school dance. I picked up Frenchie, but Hep is still pissed off I rigged his locker. He blames me for spreading a story linking Mason with a sickening sexual disfunction. I took the fifth on both counts. I drove to his house anyway and with a lot of pleading and coaxing, I finally persuaded him to come along.

As I got to the dance late, I didn't see Babs anywhere. My friend JD (I don't know what the initials stand for) told me he saw her there earlier, but she left. I didn't see the Maggot either. So, I ended up sitting with the other losers.

Unless you have a girlfriend, these dances are all the same. It's like being in the World War I trenches. The boys hold their position at one end of the dance floor and the girls on the other. The middle may as well have barbed wire.

The girls dance the fast dances with each other. Woe to any two guys who try that. Occasionally a boy will ask a girl to dance. I decided to be bold and ask Gretel from Home Room to fast dance. She's what's known as a 'nice' girl if you know what I mean. She's friendly but safe – no boyfriend, few expectations. I took a lot of shit from the others for my effort. In their minds, I danced like a wounded rhino.

After the dance, I spotted Lisbeth. My heart started pounding and my palms sweating. Unfortunately, she was with the jocks, and it didn't pay to talk to those prima donnas.

I moved on. I spied Babs' younger sister, Elaine – a sophomore. We danced and mildly flirted for a while until I saw Babs, who had arrived late. She was without the Maggot, and thus I went over to her. I told her I had tried to call her yesterday. She explained that she had missed the last two days of school due to a cold and didn't answer my call as she didn't feel all that well.

She explained that she needed air and went outside occasionally to catch a bit of the fresh stuff. As it was cold outside and she couldn't have been out for long in that weather, I had the distinct impression she was making excuses. I thought it best not to mention that she wasn't home at ten p.m. when I phoned the previous night.

After the dance I took Hep, Frenchie, Babs, JD and his girl Arua Marhilles to my house to play pool. We didn't stay long as it got late. I took everyone home - saving Babs for last. We kissed once - softly on the lips - before she left the car. The feeling was wonderful, but why can't I stop thinking that the Maggot is still out there?

Cop-u-later.

JANUARY 16,
1966 – Sunday

Sunday, and the big basketball game with our rivals from Altona – a nearby city – Bishop McGuillicutty. We needed to win this to qualify for the state championship. I went with Hep and Frenchie. Racovic tagged along. A friend of Hep's – a fellow Junior – was to join us. Charles Podbottle or the Chief as he is known. The Chief, so-called for his boastful manner and big girth, didn't have any money according to Hep. He said we had to sneak him into the arena.

The National Anthem was being played in darkness at the Memorial Arena. When the attendants weren't looking, Hep opened the side door and the Chief ran in – unsighted. When we asked him for a couple of bucks for letting him in for free, he laughed and went on his merry way.

After he left us, I said something sarcastic about the Chief being a cheapskate and a tight asshole, but Hep convinced me to calm down and play it cool! The Chief was a big SOB who weighed damn near 200lbs. Well, he looked that big. I wouldn't doubt he weighed that much. He wasn't all that tall, but he had a big gut and powerful arms. His hands were surprisingly small and girly.

He had short, dark hair, a prominent nose and spotty red skin. He had more chins than a Chinese phone book to use an overused and probably derogatory reference. Hep said I should keep my opinions about the Chief to myself as he was known to have Negro friends. Their reputation is such that you don't want to mess with them.

Anyway, Hep spied Mason and sat with her. I had asked Babs if she wanted to go to the game with me when I saw her last night, but she turned me down. She's still getting over her sickness – so she said. I didn't see the Maggot either.

I'm getting suspicious, worried – all of the above. I asked her about the Maggot the other day and Babs said, 'There is nothing going on.' Would she tell me the truth if there was? Was she really sick on Friday night at ten p.m.? Why hasn't she asked me to the Sadie Hawkins dance?

Soon the game started, and it was really over before you could say woo, woo, woo like Curly of the Three Stooges. Our year 11 main man Rudy Mingo scored twenty points and the boys breezed to an 84-54 victory. We're now two games away from qualifying for the state championship game. We then sang our school song – or mouthed it as no one has a clue what the words are or mean. To wit:

By the banks of the mighty Stringybank,
We dedicate our lives to you,
Dear old lady of success,
Today may be passing, tomorrow we'll be through,
But we will never forget (we always say 'lick') you,
Our Lady, we love you.

What dribble. Frenchie gave a raspberry while we were fake singing which was quite embarrassing when everyone looked our way. With that, temporarily, I forgot about Babs and thought only of basketball. Temporarily being the key word.

Cop-u-later.

JANUARY 17,
1966 – Monday

Saw Babs this morning at Home Room. She looked great and seemed happy to see me. I asked about her health, and she said she was over her illness. We agreed to have lunch together.

After Chem class, Lisbeth was having trouble opening her locker. I decided to be gallant and give her a hand. Maybe she'd remember me. Besides, how could I resist helping her? Those eyes, that body, that beautiful hair, those legs. Her voice – particularly the accent - takes my breath away.

It took a while, but I opened the locker, and it didn't explode. I'm a bit gun-shy these days. Anyway, she thanked me and then touched my hand. With that gesture, all I could think of was marrying her. I soon snapped out of it when I remembered Babs and lunch. So, I said good-bye and hightailed it late to the cafeteria.

When I got there, I could hardly believe my eyes. Babs was sitting with that maggot Mirgat, and they certainly didn't look unfriendly towards each other. His arm was around her waist, and they were laughing in a way only two people with a thing for each other would. And they were cuddled so close to each other that one would have needed a crowbar to separate them.

Well, I went a bit crazy and went over to her table. I tried to be calm, but that lasted about ten seconds. I asked what was going on? The Maggot stood up and said nothing and started laughing at me. I pushed him. He pushed me back. I then emptied a nearby opened carton of milk on him. He jumped on me, and we started wrestling – while Babs was yelling. Things looked grim when I saw five of his Senior friends coming to his rescue.

I was a goner until I noticed the figure of Charles Podbottle – the Chief – above me. His imposing near 200lb frame scared off most of the gang. The Maggot let his grip loose when one of his friends told him a teacher was coming.

I too jumped up when I saw Mr. Rosen – a math teacher. Rosen being there was a break as he was a reasonably good guy who I expect wouldn't send us to the principal. Anyway, I told him it was a mishap over some spilled milk. He made us shake hands which the Maggot reluctantly did, though I'm sure only for show.

Rosen, aka The Rock - who was also my math teacher - didn't call the principal but gave us both after school detention and five demerits. I was lucky. With the Sadie coming up and the State Basketball Championship games, I could have been banned from both events.

Now I really am stuffed. Babs is pissed off at me. In fact, she stormed out of the cafeteria after the incident and didn't speak to me the rest of that day. I felt like a real 'ning-nong.' After school, I went to the detention where I saw the Chief. A regular at these things, he kept count of his detentions and bragged about the number he had attained. Kind of a badge of honor. It was amazing that he never accumulated enough demerits to get a suspension.

'Thanks, Chief, for sticking up for me. But why?' I asked him.

'You let me in the game yesterday and I never forget a favor,' he replied. I felt somewhat weird considering I said some nasty things about him being a miser and an asshole at the game because he wouldn't give us money for getting him in for free. I was going to tell him we were even, but Rosen told me in no uncertain words to 'shut up'. That was that.

Cop-u-later.

JANUARY 18,
1966 – Tuesday

I'm still getting over the big fight with the Maggot yesterday. What a fool I was. Now, Babs isn't talking to me, and she probably won't ask me to the Sadie. I kept an eye out for the Senior boys all day as I feared there could be reprisals. But the Chief made it clear they better not touch me, and – as Hep mentioned - he hangs around with the Negro guys from the public school. The Seniors are scared of those guys. I think I'm safe. Just the same I tread carefully.

The day went slowly. I ate lunch with Katie as Babs settled with her friends and without me or the Maggot. With Babs out of the picture, I'm almost resigned to Katie asking me to the Sadie, but I'm not sure I want to go anyway. Katie's a good kid, but not much to look at. She'll probably ask me on Thursday when her old man picks me up. I better be on my guard!

So, I kept a low profile. After school, my Intermural Team – Baileys of Balboa – played a game. We got kicked badly 56-18 by the Red Corpuscles – a team of jocks so dumb that they odds-on live in caves and communicate with grunts. But they know how to play basketball. I only scored four points and we stunk. Our record is now 2-5 with little chance to make the play offs.

After the game, I checked the bulletin board in music to see if I got a part in the musical 'Brigadoon'. I did, but not what I wanted. I wanted Van Johnson's role (in the film) of Jeff, the funny American side kick, but was given the part of Frank the Bartender instead.

I have a few lines toward the end of the show but nothing to write home about. I also get to play one of the townspeople and wear a kilt. No girl, no major role. Seniors after me. 'You reap what you sow' says the Bible.

When I got home, the Old Man was walking around in his underwear as is his habit and gave me some crap about picking up my youngest sister – Kitty - and her friend from the movies. Kitty is a student at the local Catholic elementary school. She's taller than my other sisters – about 5'7, but she's a bit overweight.

Actually, that's putting it mildly. She's certifiably obese. She probably takes up two seats at the movies. She loves to eat. Dad buys her these diet supplements to suppress her appetite, but she eats them like candy – and then overeats anyway.

Kitty's opinionated and, as the youngest, tends to get her own way. She doesn't care what others think. She has a nice face. I think she'd look good if she lost weight – a lot of weight. She has the best sense of humor in the family and, although sometimes the butt of jokes, she has a snappy comeback for anything you throw at her. She gives as good as she gets. She's easy to talk to and makes friends easily.

Her best friend is Missy Procco. Although only twelve years old, Missy shows real potential to be a beauty. Great skin, a nice light tan complexion and the most beautiful dark, wide eyes you'd ever want to see. Almost doe-like. Very hypnotic and sensual. She's also a sister of my public-school friend – Tom Procco. I doubt if he'd want me hanging around her. I wasn't about to do anything with her at this time, but a guy's got to think of his future.

So, I picked the two up and struck up a decent conversation - mainly with Missy. When I got home, Dad asked me to pick up my grandmother, Gran-King, for dinner. I was so pissed off I yelled at him. Dad rarely gets angry, but this was the exception.

He said I couldn't drive the car to go to the basketball game tonight. It wasn't a qualifying game for the state championships, so I was thinking of skipping it regardless. I still had to pick up the old bat, but I wasn't allowed the car for the game.

Our team won the non-conference game easily anyway. Instead of cheering our boys on, I had to put up with that old fart, Gran-King, who could only talk about the mess the Jews and Negros had made of this country. I took her home at midnight. She was quite tipsy. There's certainly bats in her belfry. Then again – she is my grandmother. Now I'm worried!

Cop-u-later.

JANUARY 19,
1966 – Wednesday

I'm almost resigned to not going to the Sadie Hawkins dance unless I accept an expected invitation from Katie. She's not a bad person – I could do worse. What do I do if I'm asked? Two girls fighting over me. Only in my dreams!

Babs still isn't talking to me after my fight with the Maggot Mirgat. I assume now she'll ask him. I really blew it. Racovic said I had a "brain explosion". His advice was that I ignore her and eventually she'll ask me. Is that the same as playing hard to get? What girl was Egghead ever with?

Anyway, today I got measured for a kilt for the musical. I got the expected catcalls and whistles from the boys when I tried on a model, but my legs weren't nearly as hairy as Hep's. I figure this production could be a lot of fun and, if anything, take my mind off Babs. My mom was thrilled that I got a part, even if I only speak a few lines at the end. Rehearsals are soon.

Hep is still having his thing with Mason. I kid him about jail-bait and how he could be arrested. Not that he listens to anything I say. He told me to say, 'mother may I' and then spell c-u-p. Good one, I thought. I countered that by telling him to hold his tongue and say, 'my father works in a shipyard and cleans up all the ashes.' We both got a kick out of these and laughed self-indulgently.

During music class I sat near Lisbeth. She gets better looking every time I see her. She's a real cutie-pie, but what would my Old Man say if I brought her home to have dinner? What would he think about a dark Argentinian girl? He has a poor view of non-white races as many people of his generation tend to have, but would a Latino girl be preferable to him over a Negro girl?

Sam Signoria, our weird music teacher, likes it quiet in class. When I talked to Lisbeth, he yelled at me. Short guy, Napoleon syndrome, I thought. I had to stay back after class and listen to his 'bull dung'. But I played it cool, nodded, apologised and pretended to agree with everything he said. He let me go without detention and demerits. The dumb S.O.B.

When I was leaving school to catch the bus, I ran into Babs. I asked her if she was still angry about yesterday's fracas. She said she was, but then asked me about a POD report due tomorrow. I made something up as I wasn't sure what she was on about, but I got a sneaky feeling it wasn't the assignment on her mind. The ice was broken and all of a sudden, I had thoughts of getting back together. We departed on good terms. There is a God, I thought, and She is looking after me.

Cop-u-later.

JANUARY 20,
1966 – Thursday

Thursday morning, and I dread this day. I got a ride with Katie's dad and, as always, Katie arranged it, so I sat right beside her. Her leg touched mine and there was nothing I could do. I kept wondering what I would do if she asked me to the Sadie in front of her dad and other passengers. If I said no, she'd start crying and I'd look like a real cad.

I almost made it to school without her asking the expected question. Right before we got there, she asked if she could talk to me. I quickly changed the subject. When we reached school, I made an excuse about whatever and took off. Now I know I have to keep out of her way. It's a big ask, as the Sadie is still three weeks away.

As luck would have it, I spotted Babs as soon as I got in the school building. She looked pretty good, yet she seemed preoccupied. Will she ask me or the Maggot? Or not go? I told her I'd see her at lunchtime, but she only grunted. So, Babs is indifferent and Katie needy. Which way will the scales tilt?

During the day, we had an assembly where our Congressman, John P. Singer, spoke. A Republican, Singer's been representing our area for about seventeen years. He's like a comfortable old shoe that no one wants to toss out. From what I gather, he doesn't do much for this town.

He sprouted the usual crap only a politician could get away with. He told us (in our case erroneously) what fine young people we were, a credit to our school, and all that suck up shit. I might have fallen asleep if I hadn't been focused on my Sadie dilemma.

My dad likes Singer, but I can't wait to be twenty-one years and vote against him. The best thing about the speech was that I got to sit near Lisbeth. A second reason for not paying attention to the speaker. My mind was firmly on the here-after – if only she knew what I was here after.

I stammered blindly through an inane conversation with her – she with those sensuous lips and beautifully accented Spanish/English words. While speaking to her, I daydreamed about that beautiful body... then abruptly I snapped out of it. As Singer finished, there was clapping, the cue to leave. I came this close to asking Lisbeth on a date, but I chickened out. I may never get this chance again. At least I talked to her. Second time in two days.

The rest of the day was an anti-climax. I had lunch with Babs, and I think I got on her good side. I managed to avoid Katie and so delay the inevitable tears on her part, and I faked my way through the first singers' rehearsal for 'Brigadoon' after school. But it all paled into insignificance when compared to my encounter with Lisbeth. I'm in dream heaven, so please don't wake me.

Cop-u-later.

JANUARY 21,
1966 – Friday

Friday, end of the week. I managed to avoid Katie for the most part. However, I still have Lisbeth on my mind. I'd ask her out, but the jocks always have her covered. I figure I'd better wait until after the Sadie in three weeks. I had lunch with Babs, then asked her if I could come over tonight. She liked it. I know it's a crap date, but it's the best I can do under pressure. However, things are picking up!

Anyway, my brother Will asked me to take him to see his girlfriend, Cheryl. She lives out in 'the country', but I had time to take him before I went to Babs'. Not that I had a choice. Dad insisted this task be completed for me to get the car.

Will, real name Amos Wilhelm, is fourteen and a Freshman at Westwood Suburban Public High School. He hates the name Amos (Grammy's deceased father's name) and goes by a shortened version of his middle one. He's a bit taller than me. He has blonde hair and blue eyes, an athlete's physique and, though I hate to admit it, is quite good looking. Dad often refers to him as 'the Gaughan' because he looks like Dad's deceased father.

Unlike me, Will's a natural at sports. He's very outgoing and popular with the girls, but not the smartest link on the chain. Like most brothers, we have our little spats, but he is my brother and I try to look out for him when I can.

Well, we went down this road, called Old Ridge Road. It was snowing and visibility was poor. To make a long story even longer, the car ploughed into a snowbank. I tried like hell to back it out, but it wouldn't budge. Will and I took turns pushing it – nothing. We both pushed it – again, nothing. It was stuck like Elmer's glue.

I was pissed off and cursed Will to hell and back. I guess it wasn't his fault, but I had to blame someone. We had to walk a mile to Cheryl's place where I phoned Ted Shark aka Sharky – our local gas station serviceman – to free the car out. Sharky owns the Esso service station in

Westwood.

With all that was occurring, I forgot to call Babs and tell her I'd be late. Damn, if I was pissed off before, my anger now multiplied to the nth degree. Sharky took an eternity to get there as I waited at the car - freezing my tush off. Will stayed at Cheryl's in her warm house! Around half past nine, Sharky finally arrived and towed the car out of the snow drift. I thanked him and told him to put the fee on my dad's account. Then I rushed to Babs' place.

It was ten p.m. when I got there. When I rang the bell, Babs' mom answered and told me Babs had gone out. My heart sank right there. I was already on her bad side and here she had gone out without me – to who knows where? I'm sure now I can kiss the Sadie goodbye.

I went home and cursed my brother again. Around 11.30pm I tried to call Babs, but her father answered and told me it was too late to talk. I was sure she had gone out with the Maggot and that's that. Ironically, around midnight, my old man saw I was up and asked me to pick up Will at Cheryl's.

'Ladies and gentlemen of the jury, it was insanity that caused me to kill my brother', I thought. This time I wouldn't get caught in a snowbank. Maybe!

Cop-u-later.

JANUARY 22,
1966 – Saturday

After last night, I'm doomed to miss the Sadie Hawkins dance. I tried to call Babs this morning, but she wouldn't take my call. Or should I say calls, as I tried multiple times. I needed to get my mind off everything currently going on in my life. So, I went to Herb's Barber Shoppe for a haircut. Herb, the local barber, surely learned his trade at the turn of the century. Herb, aka the Butcher as we call him, knows only one cut – short back and sides.

Herb has an old war injury – anyhow that's my understanding - and he walks with a limp. He breathes heavily when cutting, and his breath smells like he slept with a sock in his mouth. It's disgusting. But he only charges $1.25 a cut. More importantly, he has the best old comic collection in the world. I get there early for my cut so I can read the comics.

After this very mediocre haircut (I know it was bad because later my Dad and Mom said they liked it), I played basketball with Hep - and a few guys - at some local gymnasium near my home called The Groove. Hep couldn't resist and gave me shit about my cut. I ignored his taunts.

Hep told me he's already been asked to the Sadie by Mason and encouraged me not to give up on Babs. I think he wants to double with me 'cause I can drive my old man's Buick. The car certainly makes a good impression with the ladies. Hep and I then made plans to meet at the Teen Canteen dance in the evening.

I went to the school dance first to see if Babs was there. No luck! I got out of there quickly when I saw the Maggot and some other seniors who might remember my run-in with them earlier in the week. So, I left and made a beeline to the Canteen. Here I met Hep and his friend Calvin Pigeon.

What surprised me about Pij, as Hep called him, was that he was a Negro. I didn't think there was a problem, but it surprised me, nonetheless. I never considered that Hep might have Negro friends. I thought about what my dad said about Negroes and looked at Pij warily. Pij was taller and thinner than both Hep and me. He had black curly hair, dark eyes and smooth medium brown skin. He spoke rapidly when he talked. Hep said he had street smarts – whatever that meant.

Outside of our neighbour's chauffer – Columbus – I don't think I ever really talked to a Negro. We had an awkward chat as I didn't know what to say to him. Pij realised that because in the midst of the conversation, he actually called me 'bro.' Coming from a black person, I suppose this was a compliment.

Pij had a chip on his shoulder a mile wide for who knows what reason. He railed against everything. The music was too 'white bread.' The guys had no dress sense. The people were drab and boring. There was no understanding of the situation. I wasn't sure what he meant by that last statement.

Pij had been wronged by people and he wasn't about to let it slide. He was quite good-looking – a bit like Cassius Clay - and super charming with the ladies. But he had this aggressiveness toward most guys he met – not necessarily just white guys. Pij appeared to be looking for a fight. It didn't matter the color.

When relaxed, Pij had a good sense of humor, a wide smile and an engaging, if intense, personality. Hep later said Pij took a liking to me, but maybe he liked me because I lent him $10 when he asked. Hep said I'd get it back - though none too convincingly.

While at the Canteen I talked to Amy Sing for a long time. We danced, joked and flirted. What a great gal, I thought. Cute, too. I don't see her much as she doesn't go to OLPS. I promised to visit her dad's laundry and catch her at the Canteen in a week.

Hep and I were ready to leave with Pij to get something to eat, but we got the hell out of there when Pij challenged a couple of large white guys to a fight. Hep asked, but Pij said he didn't need our help. Just as well. I'm a lover, not a fighter. We were out of there.

Cop-u-later.

JANUARY 23,
1966 – Sunday

I finally got through to Babs on the phone this morning. We talked for an hour. Surprisingly, she didn't seem as angry as I thought she'd be. I explained what had happened with my brother. She said she understood my reason for standing her up (my words) on Friday, despite the story, though true, being so unbelievable that even I would have been skeptical.

She talked to me for a long while before ending the conversation. She'd see me at school on Monday. I never did get around to finding out her whereabouts last night. Best I didn't know anyhow. So, why am I even more suspicious? She seemed to forgive me too readily.

Ironically, I hung up and turned on the radio and 'Barbra Ann' by the Beach Boys was playing. ('Went to a dance, looking for romance, saw Barbra Ann so I thought I'd take a chance'). I love that line. I planned to drive up to Babs' place to see her in person, but it started to snow like hell. The streets were covered with the white stuff and slippery to boot. The old man told me it was too dangerous, and I couldn't have the car.

So, I called Hep and said I'd meet him at the basketball game in the afternoon against the school 'Flower of the Carmelites' (we call them the 'Carmel Apples'). This game didn't have any bearing on the state championship, but we expected a big win as we're getting close to playing for all the marbles.

Anyway, my dad told me I had to attend Church. With no car, I had to walk. On the way, I met Tom Procco, aka Cooey after his little brother's unpronounceable gibberish of his name, and another mate Tom Bailey, aka Beetle after a comic strip character of the same name. Both go to the public high school – the same one as brother Will. We decided to skip Church and walk to the local fountain store – Clarke's Confectionery.

When we got there, we spotted Father Bellodhiro, the assistant priest at the local parish. It was a bit awkward, and he asked us if we'd been to Church. We all lied and answered affirmatively. To a priest! I guess they should reserve a place in hell for us.

Well, afterward, I went home, got $5 from the old geezer and left for the city. I took the Inclined Plane – a cable car that goes down the side of the hill at a very steep angle. It was snowing like mad, and I could hardly see 2 feet in front of me. When I reached the City, I realised I was going to be late as I had to fight the elements to get to the game.

After a hard slog walking to the Memorial Arena, I found the basketball had been cancelled. Crap! Here, I was cold, wet, tired and I had to get home. I didn't fancy the long, cold walk to the Inclined Plane, so I called Will from a pay phone, but he said Dad wasn't home. Damn Will. After all the trouble he caused on Friday, I figured he could have made more of an effort to find Dad to pick me up. I told Will to tell Dad, when he saw him, to meet me at Gran-King's place.

Gran-King lived near the arena, so I bit the bullet and went to her place to shelter from the cold. The problem was I had to talk to her. She obviously had been drinking. The thermostat was turned up to extra hot.

She only wanted to talk about her late husband, who died two years previously! She again showed me a picture of his grave and told me she couldn't wait to join him. It was so hot in her place that meeting him in hell seemed appropriate. I was in my own hell now.

I shuddered at her morbid thought and needed to find a way out of there pronto. I called Will and offered him $5 if he could find dad within twenty minutes to pick me up. He agreed. It didn't take long for Dad to get there which begged the question - why couldn't Will find him earlier? Money talks!

When Dad arrived, the snow was a foot deep. I thought if it got any worse, school might be called off tomorrow. Dad, not to waste a trip, stopped for some hot dogs before we slowly and carefully made it home.

Cop-u-later.

JANUARY 24,
1966 – Monday

The way my luck has been going, I should have known there would be school. Despite a foot or two of snow (well it seemed like that much), and a number of schools cancelled on top of our basketball game yesterday, we had to go. Crap! Not only that, but we have tests coming up on Wednesday in English and French. Sacre Bleu!

Because of the snow, I got to school late and had to walk into the classroom in front of all my so-called friends. Hep and a few others gave me raspberries, but were told off by our math teacher, The Rock.

I found out the game against the Carmel Apples has been re-scheduled for tomorrow. But the big one's in March. We're going all the way. Said hello to Rudy Mingo who was with his girlfriend - cheerleader Sally Rationello. She's so far out of my league that I won't even talk to her without an appointment. I put her on a pedestal with Raquel Welch and Ursula Andress (or 'Undress' as we call her).

I'm a bit down in the dumps about the Sadie. Babs doesn't seem interested in asking me, although I don't think she's asked the Maggot or anyone else. I'm sure I would have heard about it. I talked to her today, but she seemed a bit distant. The Sadie's only a couple of weeks off so I wish she'd get her ass in gear and make a decision – hopefully the right one. Ask me!

I know I could go with Katie, but I'm just not interested. If she asks me, I'd feel terrible if I turned her down. I guess I could do worse. Woof, woof! Had lunch with Hep who wants Babs to ask me because he wants us to double with him and Mason. He really wants to impress his girlfriend by riding in my dad's Buick. I sometimes think that if he could score the car without me that he would, but I come with the auto. Eventually, the drama will work itself out I suppose.

I stayed late and played intermural basketball. My team, the Baileys of Balboa, lost to the jocks 35-14. I did get six points, but the team was a shambles. We're not doing well, so I suggested someone else should be

Captain. No one else wanted it. Lucky for me, the season is almost over!

I didn't get home until after five p.m. and it was dark. When I got there, I could hardly believe my eyes. An ambulance was in my driveway and my mom was on a stretcher. What the hell? I rushed into the house and asked Kitty what was afoot? Apparently, my mother complained of pains and collapsed.

Kitty called my dad, who rushed home and called an ambulance. Mom was taken to the hospital. After a long wait, my Dad called and said she was resting well. He didn't tell us what was wrong.

Cop-u-later.

JANUARY 25,
1966 – Tuesday

I had trouble sleeping last night. All I could think of was Mom. Dad spent most of the night at the hospital. When I woke up, I asked him if everything was all right. He assured me that Mom was fine, and that she'd be home in couple of days after undergoing a number of tests. She was conscious and eating (and probably smoking, knowing her).

The word about Mom's jaunt to the hospital had gotten out because this morning Columbus knocked on the door to pass on Mrs. Pride's and his sympathies. He gave us a cake. This touched me a lot as I always had a lot of time for him. Being the only Negro I knew (I guess Pij is now the second), I felt that perhaps if people of his race were like him then they couldn't be all bad. Could Dad and Gran-King be wrong about Negroes? Was Columbus the exception?

My father was less than kind about the non-white races – especially the Negro. Although he had good words for Columbus ("A good boy,"), he said others of the Negro race were lazy and worthless. He said I should treat the Negroes respectfully, 'but they weren't our people. You have to watch them closely,' he said.

Mind you, a lot of the sports he watches have Negro competitors. Baseball, football, boxing. He loves to cheer for the Americans at the Olympics. Many of these competitors are black. I trust Dad. He's always been up front with me. I didn't think he would steer me wrong.

We have lived at our current address on Ticonderoga St. for ten years. I can't remember a time when Columbus wasn't next door working for Mrs. Pride. A rather tall, thin and distinguished-looking man, Columbus (I never asked him if this was his first or last name) had very fine features. He had a light brown complexion, a smooth face with some brown spots on it, short dark curly hair with just a touch of grey and green eyes. He had a thin moustache above his upper lip.

Columbus, I guess around fifty, although I couldn't really tell his age, was a muscular man of medium height who looked as if in his younger days he once worked as a laborer or did some strenuous work. He was polite and soft-spoken to a fault. He usually wore a form fitted grey chauffer outfit with a grey cap. He kept Mrs. Pride's car shiny, clean and spotless at all times. He was well-spoken, and quite loyal to his employer.

Anyway, Columbus said Mrs. Pride offered her car to be used to take me to school. He said he was happy to drive me in his (Mrs. Pride's) 1948 Packard – a beautiful car that looked as if it had just come off the showroom. He asked me about Babs. I told him I was hoping to get together with her but had experienced problems. He told me to have faith. He dropped me off at school and I thanked him.

In Home Room, before school, I had a brief chat with Babs. She asked if I wanted to sit with her at lunchtime. Does a wild bear shit in the woods? I eagerly accepted. After he took roll, Mr. Ranan asked what the class wanted to do with the $25 we won for decorating our room.

Ideas ranged from a big party to buying a record player to play our records in the room during free times. He said those ideas weren't practical, and suggested we give it to the Catholic charity that baptizes overseas pagan babies into the Faith. I suppose it's a worthwhile cause, but I liked the music or party ideas. As expected, Doc's idea carried the day.

The day dragged. All I could think of was the Sadie Hawkins Dance. I looked forward to seeing Babs at lunchtime. It finally arrived. Indeed, Babs and I had a great time at lunch – laughing and flirting. I wondered if she had asked anyone to the Sadie, but I wasn't game to inquire in case it was in the affirmative.

She was quite sympathetic when I told her about my mom. I thought I was still in with a chance until I spotted her talking with that 12th grade maggot later in the day.

After school, I had musical practise. We learned 'Brigadoon' songs and a dance for the song 'Come home to Bonnie Jean'. I suffer from three left feet so Gene Kelly I'm not. Hep, was just as bad. We learned the steps (kind of), but eventually we'll have partners, so it was important we knew what we were doing. I wonder who I'll get!

I got home late, and Dad told me Mom would have to stay in the hospital for ten days to get her gall bladder removed. Dad said he'd cook, and he made pancakes. I hope we don't have breakfast every evening. I was going to stay in and study for English and French tests tomorrow, but Hep called and asked if I wanted to go to the basketball game. I hated to leave Dad, but Will and Kitty were there to console him. We won by twenty points against 'The Caramel Apples.' I'm screwed because I didn't study for the tests.

Cop-u-later.

JANUARY 26,
1966 – Wednesday

Got to school knowing I was up shit creek without a paddle, as I hadn't studied for the French or English tests. I managed to feign illness and got out of French – not that it mattered as I suck at the subject and would have failed regardless. The nun told me I could take it on Friday.

English was a different proposition, as Sister Mary All Buns was a difficult person, and not one to fall for any shit excuse. I was resigned to failing the test. When I had told Hep earlier about my dilemma, he commiserated with me. He, too, hadn't studied. During lunch, as I was talking to Babs, Hep came up to me and asked to speak privately.

He gave me a folder that he got from his friend Ronald Homulkyo. The sheet inside had all the answers for the test. I don't know where Homulkyo got them, but I wasn't about to throw away this pot of gold at the end of the rainbow.

I didn't have much of a moral dilemma about using the sheet as I was desperate and didn't know anything that might have been on the test. Just the same, I didn't tell Babs as I figured she wouldn't understand. Besides, we were getting along well – laughing and flirting. And not a maggot in sight!

For once, I didn't think about the Sadie. I was having too good a time with Babs. If she didn't ask me, well, it couldn't be helped. I walked her to her English class and said goodbye as she has a different teacher. I said I'd see her tomorrow.

True to his word, Hep's (or Homulkyo's) answers were spot on. Hep was pretty quiet when I asked him where Homulkyo had got the test answers from, but I didn't really want to know. He did say I owed $5 for the test. It was worth it, so I paid the blood money. A good day after all. I aced the test and would soon be back with Babs.

The world was looking pretty good. Last period, in History, we saw the movie 'The Ugly American' with Marlon Brando. I didn't understand much of it except the Americans were the bad guys. I always thought it was the Russians.

When I arrived home, I was told that Mom was still in the hospital. Her operation was scheduled for the weekend. So, we went to have dinner with my Dad's mom, Grammy Gaughan. She was about eighty years old, but very classy – albeit semi-deaf like my dad. I wondered if I'll be deaf too when I get older.

Everything went well, even if I had to yell to get my point across. Grammy lived with her three sisters – all around her age, so it wasn't pleasant to spend too much time there. All that 'dinosaur' talk and sloppy kisses. She offered me a beer, but I decided at sixteen years old I wasn't ready to drink alcohol in front of Grammy and the matrons. So, I refrained.

We ate what we always did when we went there for dinner – hash. Grammy must have roasts coming out of her wazoo for all the hash she serves when we dine there. We stayed late so I didn't have much time to study for Friday's English test – part 2. But I'm confident Homulkyo will come through.

Cop-u-later.

JANUARY 27,
1966 – Thursday

Thursday, and I went to school with Katie and her father. For once, Katie didn't cuddle up to me. She seemed nervous and hardly said anything. When we arrived at school, she asked if we could talk. She seemed very serious. I lied and told her I'd see her at lunchtime as I had to see a teacher. I was a bit anxious as I figured she was going to ask me to the Sadie. What would I do? I wanted to go, but with Babs! But I hadn't been asked. Perhaps, I could hide somewhere or go home.

In the morning, all I thought about was the impending lunchtime meeting with Katie. I was certain she was going to ask me to the Sadie. What did FDR, a former US President, say about only fearing fear itself? In the end, I decided I would let fate decide. What happens, happens! I'd play my response by ear.

One thing took my mind off things. Lisbeth sat by me in Chem class. If you asked me, I couldn't tell you what the class was about, because I was in a trance the whole time. I kept daydreaming that she'd ask me to the Sadie, but I'm sure she would prefer to ask some jock.

She spoke broken English, but, somehow, we managed to communicate. I was having a ball flirting during class and forgot all about my impending dilemma. That is until the bell rang for lunch. It went way too soon for my mind.

I walked slowly to the lunchroom for my date with destiny. Katie would be there, and I'd have to say something. Even I didn't know what I was going to do. On the way, I made excuses to stop and talk to people. I spent snail-like time at my locker. Finally, I made it to the lunchroom to face my destiny.

When I got to the entrance to the cafeteria, Babs was waiting. She stopped me. She smiled, greeted me warmly, looked me in the eyes and asked me to the Sadie Hawkins Dance. I couldn't believe it. It had finally come off. And I thought she was going with the Maggot.

Naturally, I accepted. We both smiled. I bottled up a cheer. I was relieved the whole thing was over. As we walked into the cafeteria, I spotted Katie sitting by herself at a table. I told Babs I had to do something and walked over to her.

Katie smiled nervously and asked me to sit down. She didn't beat around the bush. 'Would you go to the Sadie with me?' she asked.

Any sense of euphoria abandoned me. I actually felt sorry for her and almost wished I hadn't run into Babs. Almost! 'Sorry, I've already been asked,' I said.

'Oh,' she said quietly. Her eyes filled with tears although she didn't cry. I admit to some moist eyes as well. We sat quietly for a few minutes (it seemed like hours) and then she ran out of the lunchroom. I felt bad, but I had gotten the outcome I wanted. Even if it was at someone's expense.

I returned to Babs and mentioned something about Katie and homework. I'm sure she didn't believe me. We talked about the Sadie and what we would do, who we would go with and what she would wear. Actually, I don't remember much of the conversation as all I could think of was Katie.

Cop-u-later.

JANUARY 28,
1966 – Friday

I'm still not feeling good about Katie. Although a bit behind in the looks department, she's a good kid. Could I have let her down more easily? But I'm going to the Sadie with Babs, and that's what I had always wanted.

At lunchtime I talked to Babs. She sat close to me. We said stupid lovey things to each other amidst eating our food. Mercifully, none of the guys were around to hear me. Naturally, the Sadie was high on our agenda. I asked Babs if she wanted to go out this evening, but she said she had something to do. I hate to be suspicious, but I can't help thinking about Maggot.

I looked around for Katie but didn't spot her. I thought of the 'Loving Spoonful' song, 'Did you ever have to make up your mind?' I guess I still feel guilty about letting her down.

I barely studied yesterday for today's English test. I just hope I'm not getting addicted to this easy path. Once again, Homulkyo came through with the answers - at a price. He gave us the golden cheat sheet right before we entered the room, so I had to hide it under the exam. After it was over, I put the answers in my pocket.

I was spotted by our Junior Class President Regis Hoss who called me a cheat. I ignored him, but I felt like everyone in the class was staring at me and shaming me. Although he wasn't about to tell anyone, I decided then and there not to do this again.

I got home and was surprised to see Mom. Apparently, her blood pressure was too high for the operation, so the doctor asked her to spend a few days at home to rest. She was to return to the hospital for the gall bladder removal next week.

I talked to her, and she was in good spirits. It was strange - though it shouldn't have been - to see her smoking. Mom couldn't avoid a smoke if you paid her, as she was a two-pack a day advertisement for Raleigh's. It couldn't have been good for her blood pressure as a prelude to a serious operation.

After dinner, I asked Dad for the car. He said 'OK,' but I had to take Will to his girlfriend's place again. On the way, Will asked me to pick up some of his friends. Although only fourteen years old, they all were smashed on booze of some sort and talked about a party. I assume it was at Will's girlfriend's house and, to be expected, unsupervised.

I made sure the chains were on the tires as it was snowing. I wasn't about to get stuck like last week. Things went well, although Will's asshole friends tried to get me to go faster. I put up with a lot of abuse from the little shits. I was glad to drop them off and I hoped I wouldn't have to pick them up.

I drove to Frenchie's house where we played pool with his friend, Dick Howell. Dick, a Senior, often bragged about his conquests with girls and how happy he made them. So, we nicknamed him 'Little Dick Howell' or 'LDH' for short (I don't feel the need to explain the reference). As usual, he was full of bluster. It made me wonder if he was such a charmer with girls, why he was with two guys on a Friday night?

I easily took $2 off Frenchie and LDH. We then each had a can of beer, compliments of Frenchie, which made us a bit tipsy. Soon after, I called it a night as I wanted to go out tomorrow. To make certain I make Dad happy and get the car, I went home early. As expected, I had to pick up Will in spite of my condition - which I admit wasn't bad considering.

When I collected him and his pals, they were much worse than me – pretty much out of it. I had to drive each one home. It could have been worse, as they could have thrown up in the car. Instead, they stuck their heads out the window to spill their guts out on the outside of the car. I knew what my morning task would be tomorrow!

Cop-u-later.

JANUARY 29,
1966 – Saturday

I am still basking in my triumph of being asked to the Sadie by Babs but, at the same time, also a bit down about Katie. Two weeks to go and counting. This afternoon, I took some dirty clothes to Ye Sing Laundry in the City with the hope of seeing Amy Sing.

Not knowing where the place was, I accidently walked into an auto parts store. When the attendants saw me with laundry, they put on fake Chinese accents. 'No tickee, no laundry,' they repeated. Everyone's a comedian.

They then pointed me to the right place. I didn't really have any dirty clothes that needed cleaning, but I needed an excuse to see Amy. So, I grabbed a few items from home. I guess I've grown accustomed to her face (shades of Rex Harrison). Mom can't wash things in her condition, but a housekeeper, Merle Groggin, performed that duty. I had my druthers.

I took the laundry into the shop and immediately spotted Amy. It looked as if she was behind the counter collecting clothes, returning the clean ones, and receiving and organizing the money from the customers. Though small, she's very well-proportioned and has a beautiful smile. I kept thinking my dad would kill me if he knew I was seeing a non-white girl. If only he knew Amy. We talked a bit before I told her I'd see her at the Teen Canteen dance tonight.

When I got home, I decided to call Babs and see what she was up to. Again, she told me she had something to do. That's two days in a row. So, I said I'd see her on Monday. I called Hep and organised to meet him at the school dance. After dinner, Dad gave me the car to drive and I stopped off at the dance, but it was a drag. Mainly Freshmen and Sophomores. Saw EH Ravovic there and once I found Hep (Mason-less) we decided to go to the Canteen.

It was cold and snowing, and we got wet walking the short distance from where I had parked the car. When I got to the Canteen, I spotted

Amy and, despite getting razzed by my so-called pals, I danced with her. We clicked immediately. I flirted with her between dances, and we held hands. Was I being a rat to Babs?

After a while, I asked Amy if she wanted to go for a walk. Although it was freezing, she agreed. When we got outside, I couldn't resist and kissed her. I figured I needed some practice before I went at it with Babs. Amy was OK with us making out. This led to some heavy-necking on a frozen bench near the canteen entrance.

I couldn't have cared less if anyone saw me – except Babs of course. We were only at if for ten minutes 'cause of the cold, but man could Amy kiss! She showed me a thing or two that I could use with Babs or – for that matter – Lisbeth, or any other girl. When we returned to the dance, I saw Hep and Racovic standing like deer; in the headlights. I said good-bye to Amy and said I'd call her but somehow forgot to get her number.

After this, I didn't think anything I did would top my time with Amy. I was on cloud nine and decided to go home. When I got home, I saw my two sisters, Saint Bridget the do-gooder and Pippa, the devil in the blue dress. They had come to see Mom as it was decided she would go back to hospital on Monday for her operation.

Biddy asked if I was going to Church tomorrow, and Pippa offered me a drink. I said 'yes' to the former and took the offered Seagram Seven from the latter. It was the best of both worlds, I figured.

Cop-u-later.

JANUARY 30,
1966 – Sunday

It was snowing like hell when I got home from Church this morning. Surprisingly, Mom came to the Mass. I guess she's discovered religion with her impending operation. I went with Biddy and her husband, Dorky Duane. DD, like Biddy a charismatic Catholic, asked me if I spoke in tongues. I said I did and made some smart-assed nonsensical sounds.

I saw them later when we had a fancy dinner in the dining room. Pippa was there with En-ass – her boyfriend – who had come late. Mom later told me she was sure he had been out with another woman. I laughed, but he has that sleazy reputation, so I didn't discount it.

The food consisted of a big roast, spuds and some green vegetables. Apple pie afterwards. Dad eats in huge bites which scares the crap – literally – out of the diners at the table. On the other hand, watching him eat defies description. It really is a site to behold how he fits those huge bites into his mouth. One prays he doesn't get the food wedged in his throat and can't breathe. Who would know what to do in this instance?

Our conversation is even more bizarre. Dad dominates the topics and takes a rather earthy view of things. This will lead to a mild rebuke from Mom followed by an 'Oh, dear' and a hand placed on her upper chest. Today, the main topic was Biddy and Duane's wedding in April. Hardly riveting. A small mercy, Gran-King wasn't there to dampen the mood. It was snowing too heavily for someone to pick her up.

Mom didn't eat much as she goes to hospital tomorrow, but she had a smoke afterwards. Strange, but that's Mom. High blood pressure and all. I noticed the ashtrays were full. Not strange, as everyone smokes here save one. Afterwards, we played bridge in the living room. I don't know much about the game, but I was allowed to drink while playing so I joined in. Really, no one in the family knows how to play properly.

Except Dorky Duane, who fancies himself a Charles Goren-Class player. Unfortunately, he always loses when he plays with us, as he can't adapt to our unorthodox, amateurish play. It pisses him off, but then that's the charm of our game. We're happy with it. This time Mom won, which made us even more happy as she'll be away for a while. The fact that she couldn't drink gave her an advantage.

After our game, I called Babs. She sounded in good spirits, and we talked about our big Sadie date on February twelfth. The call lasted over an hour. We laughed and flirted like old lovers. It almost made me forget that I had made out with Amy Sing, the previous night. I told Babs I'd catch up with her tomorrow.

Hep called soon after. By now the snow was falling quite heavily. He had his fingers (and toes and whatever else he could) crossed that school would be called off tomorrow. I hung up and looked out the window. It looked bleak outside. And yet, En-ass was able to go out after the bridge game. His absence gave me a chance to talk to Pippa about nothing and everything and enjoy another seven and seven.

Cop-u-later.

JANUARY 31,
1966 – Monday

Listened intently to the radio this morning and prayed that school would be cancelled due to snow. After my 7 and 7s last night, I wasn't up to going as it was. There was a long list of schools named. Will, Kitty and I yelled please, please before each named cancelled school.

Kitty blessed herself. I cursed every time my school wasn't mentioned. Will and Kitty had theirs named, but it wasn't until toward the end of the broadcast that I heard OLOPS was cancelled. I was relieved and let out a huge scream.

Snow was still falling so perhaps a two-day cancellation was on the cards. But for now, we were basking in today's success. Now what to do for a day? Regardless of the bad roads, Dad had to take Mom to the hospital for her gall bladder operation. She was in good spirits, and we all hugged and kissed her. She then put out her cigarette and left.

I'm not sure of the date she goes under the knife – sometime this week. Biddy and Pippa also said goodbye to her and farewell to us as – despite the snow - they left for their respective homes. Biddy and DD to Steel City; Pippa to University Town. No sign of En-ass though.

Called Babs when I heard the cancellation news. We talked briefly, but I told her I wouldn't be able to get to her place because of the snow and slippery roads. Instead, I decided to go to the local shops. I had to rug up with a heavy coat, boots, hat and all the snow-wear paraphernalia.

The streets were beautiful with all the snow, but it was heavy walking on the sidewalk. On the way, I stopped over at Cooey's place - more to see his sister than him. Not that I said that to Tom. Missy's going to be gorgeous in a few years. I spoke with her for a while and reminded myself to bide my time.

Coming home I saw Mrs. Pride's house with her chauffer Columbus shoveling some snow off the walkway. Will, Kitty and I joke about his relationship with Mrs. Pride. There are added benefits (wink, wink) to his role. Today there was no sign of Mrs. Pride.

Mrs. Pride has to be about one hundred years old. She certainly looks that age. She has one of those craggy-lined faces that reminds me of a piece of paper after it had been folded numerous times and then unfolded. She's short-statured and stooped over. It's hard to get a handle on what she's like because as kids we don't have much to do with her. We always looked on her as a bit dotty.

To be honest, the youngsters were scared shitless of her because she reminded us of a witch. We would run away at the sight of her. She was quite wealthy as indicated by her large California-style house and her chauffer. My dad said her late husband had been a big shot with the steel company. She often could be seen in her kitchen from our place during the day. Just not today. I didn't think much about not seeing her and went on my merry way.

I actually did schoolwork today before I phoned Hep. We confirmed the double to the Sadie a week from Saturday. Of course, I would be driving in my dad's Buick. I hope Babs and Hep's date get along as Mason's only a sophomore. I also hope Babs has forgotten Hep ruined things between her and Mirgat.

I called Babs again and discussed a few more details about the dance. After, I watched 'Gidget' on TV. That Sally Fields is cute. I went to bed humming the theme song, 'If You're in Doubt About Angels Being Real'. I had no doubt about my angel being real. Babs was real all right and hopefully mine. It was still snowing, so I had high hopes we'd get off school tomorrow as well.

Cop-u-later.

FEBRUARY 1,
1966 – Tuesday

Once again, school was cancelled because of the snow. It had snowed most of the night so this time it wasn't a surprise when it was called off. We heard the news bulletin on the radio early in the piece. Although I was happy in a way, I was disappointed as well.

It was too cold to go out, it was snowing, and the roads were near impassable - icy and dangerous. I was homebound. Worst of all, I wouldn't get to see Babs. The Sadie is only ten days away. I called her and we had a nice chat, but it's not the same.

Dad had to negotiate the roads as he went to the hospital to see Mom. He called around ten and said Mom was to have her operation today. That was quick! I hope she didn't smoke beforehand. He told me to take out the garbage. I braved the ice and the snow to take the wretched rubbish to the bins outside the garage.

While out there I looked across to our neighbor's house and once again saw no sign of Mrs. Pride. Usually she's noticeable in her kitchen – cooking or pottering around. Sometimes, she goes for an afternoon ride with Columbus – though hardly today under these conditions. Columbus was around, but no sign of the old lady. It was odd, but I wasn't all that concerned as I had other eggs to fry.

Around noon, Will's friends came over. I guess when the cat's away and all that crap. They basically played pool in the basement, but later I heard Will raiding Dad's booze cabinet. With all the booze available and passed out freely, things got rowdy. This inevitably led to shouting and arguing over some inane matter. Inevitably, food was flying all over the basement. Pretzels, chips, popcorn.

I went downstairs and said something about the carnage, but the dolts continued their anarchy without regard to what I had to say. I mentioned to Will – in front of his buddies - to clean up this mess before Dad got home - only to be greeted by a symphony of raspberries.

I knew where I wasn't wanted, so went to my room to do some

homework – as I was bored – and listen to the radio. 'Georgy Girl' by The Seekers came on and I laughed when I thought of a parody of that song I had recently heard. It went 'Hey there Gorchki Boy, why do party members pass you by, could it be you hit the Commissar in the eye – and loved it? Hey there Gorchki Boy, I'll see you at your trial.'

The boys left around 4 – drunk as skunks. With the jerks gone, I came downstairs and had some Seagram's. Will and his pals had partially decimated Dad's vodka. I suggested he top off the remains of the bottle with water. Dad wouldn't notice – if he did at all - until next time he drank some. By then Will could plead ignorance. He thanked me for this crooked advice and proceeded to do exactly that.

Will and I then cleaned up the basement and put the remaining booze bottles back. It was tough sledding, but we got the place in order just before Dad got home. He was with Kitty, who had gone with him to the hospital. Dad told me that Mom had her operation, recovered OK and was feeling fine. I could picture her with a fag in her mouth lying in her hospital bed.

Anyway, Dad didn't feel like cooking, so he came home with 'Original Coney Island Hot Dogs'. You could barely see the dog for all the pickles, onions, meat sauce and whatever on it. It pays not to ask about the whatever. It was terrible looking, yet irresistibly delicious. After I was finished it felt like an alien had slept in my mouth. An alien who had recently completed a human probe.

The snow stopped and roads were clear, so it looked like we'd have school tomorrow. At last, I'd get to see Babs.

Cop-u-later.

FEBRUARY 2,
1966 – Wednesday

Back to school after two days off for snow. Had surprise History and Chem quizzes, but I faked my way through both of them. The whole quiz thing was pointless after two days away. But so be it! Except briefly at Home Room, I saw Babs at lunch for the first time since last Friday.

She seemed happy to see me and we talked about the Sadie. Hep and Mason came by, and the two girls discussed what they were wearing to the Sadie. Gag, gag! I can only think Hep assumes I'm driving though I haven't asked Dad for the car yet. Only ten more days!

At the bell, I left the lunchroom for my next class and ducked into the lavatory. When I came out, I saw Lisbeth, the Argentinian hottie. She knows me as her lab partner in Chem, but she seemed much more friendly when she saw me this time.

She actually called me by name and smiled at me with that beautiful smile that would melt an Eskimo Pie in winter. Her dark hair shimmered in the light and her figure was outlined by the sun shining through the window in the background. I liked what I saw.

Lisbeth came over and grabbed me by the hand and took me to a quiet corner of the school. She then kissed me on the lips. I returned the kiss and wondered if this was too good to be true. She pushed herself against me and I could feel her breasts against my body. She asked me if I'd go to the Sadie Hawkins dance with her. How could I say no as she was the most gorgeous girl I'd ever seen? We kissed passionately again.

Then I saw Hep leaning over me and asking if I was OK. I felt dazed and asked him where Lisbeth had gone. He laughed and told me I had hit my head on one of the toilet stalls and knocked myself out. I had only been out for minutes, but everything I experienced with Lisbeth was so real. This made me wonder if I really was that committed to Babs as I accepted a date from another girl – if only in my dreams.

Anyway, I told Hep I was hunky dory although I had a nasty bump on my head as I left the lavatory for the next class. On the way, I saw

Lisbeth who acknowledged me with an obligatory hi. I guess things were back to normal. We had an intermural game, but I didn't go as I used my bruised head as an excuse to miss something I'd lost interest in long ago. Instead, I went home.

At night I went to the basketball game - that had been cancelled on Sunday - with a local lad Damien Schuster. Damien was razor thin with curly hair and a face that seemed lopsided when you looked at him. He always wore a baseball hat – even in winter - that was two sizes too big for his head. His nickname was Mud - so called because his personality was 'meh' - if you know what I mean. Brown shoes in a black suit. But a decent fellow, nonetheless. Mud, who lived near me in Westwood, was a Sophomore at OLPS.

While there, I ran into Hep who asked me what I had dreamed about when knocked out. I told him I dreamed of Lisbeth but left out that I had dreamed of paradise!

Cop-u-later.

FEBRUARY 3,
1966 – Thursday

Got home late from the basketball game. We won 76-62 and have lost only one game all year. It looks good for the state championship in March. Went into a deep sleep last night and dreamed of Lisbeth. Something about a desert island and skimpy clothes, I think.

My sleep was so deep that I slept until half past eight in the morning. Even honking from Aldo didn't stir me. Eventually he gave up because he left without me. Normally Mom would have gotten me up, but she's still in the hospital. It's my dad's day off and he doesn't sleep with his hearing aid on. He wouldn't have heard the honking and woken me. As for Will and Kitty, they couldn't have cared less about waking anyone up. Not even themselves.

Anyway, I had to get myself to school by taking the City bus. Naturally, I got in late and had to sign the late book before I went to class. Everyone stared at me as I entered the classroom. Why is coming late to class such a big deal? Did they think I was with the principal? Or the police?

At lunchtime, I tried to explain my absence this morning to Katie. Not that she gave a flying fig, as she's still upset about being turned down by me for the Sadie. So, I sat with Babs. All Babs wanted to do was talk about the formal. I'm getting a bit bored with her clothing talk and there's still another week until the big day.

Got to see our report cards today and I did very well. I made the honor roll, which was not very easy for me because I stink in French. This time I guess I was less stinky (a different type of fromage?). For French, I usually get Mom to translate for me and otherwise fake my way through. Dad will be pleased with my grades. I should be able to get the car more often. Not to mention for the Sadie.

After school, we had dance practice for the musical 'Brigadoon.' I do Scottish dances with a girl in some of the scenes. I was looking forward to it and I thought my partner would be Kathy Wasp – a decent looking girl who I rarely see as she takes commercial subjects. Instead, I was assigned to dance with my cousin Vicki King – sister of Karen King, the cheerleader. Just my luck.

Vicki – a Senior – is cool and picked up the steps from the word go. It would take me longer to be as adept as her. Like her sister, she was quite striking in appearance with light brown hair, a slim figure and a beautiful face. She had a pleasant personality and joked with me about our relationship right off the bat. I'm sure my brother Will would have tried to pick her up in these circumstances, but I have my moral standards.

Truth be told, I'd really rather not have exercised these standards. The Pilgrims had the right idea. They considered dancing sinful. They forced their morals on their congregation. In this case I'd have to control myself. Sister Georgakopoulos wasn't happy with the rehearsal and yelled at us – especially when I talked to Hep. The bitch!

It was dark when we finished. I called Dad, and he picked me up and drove me home. He said Mom was OK after her gall bladder operation but was staying in the hospital a few more days. On the way, we stopped off and got a couple of large Clarke submarine sandwiches with everything on – especially the jalapenos. What a treat! We don't get these very often.

When I got home, there was a mysterious letter from a sailor from the US ship 'the Kitty Hawk.' The sailor explained he had gotten my address from a list given to him. I had given my name at school last year for some pen pal program with overseas servicemen, but I have to admit I'd forgotten all about it and never expected to hear from anyone anyway.

The sailor – Mark – was on maneuvers with the navy off the coast of Vietnam. As some of this information is classified, he told me what he could about what was happening over there. He asked a lot of questions about the home front. I'll write him back when I get the time.

The war in Vietnam has been proceeding for a few years against the Commies. I'm convinced we'll win the war eventually. It was only a matter of time. Only a few kooks were against our involvement. With our superior military and firepower, I figure the war will be over soon.

Cop-u-later.

FEBRUARY 4,
1966 – Friday

Slept in again, as Mom is still in the hospital and Dad's not good at getting us up. As for Will and Kitty, well the less said, the better! So, I got a ride to school from Dad. Getting there late for the second straight day was not cool. As soon as I arrived, I was told by the secretary - who checked me in – to report to the principal.

Father Georgia was a squirrely little guy who sucked his lips a lot and spoke in staccato words - a bit like the guy who narrates the TV show 'The Untouchables.' 'Mr. Gaughan …what…is...going…on?' We often referred to him as Georgie Porgie – 'Porgie' for short – behind his back.

I silently smirked at his voice and mannerisms and – as a result – didn't listen to a word he said. My inattention didn't go over well. He gave me five demerits and I was ordered to attend a detention on Monday after school.

I'm really not the rebellious type, so I felt a bit hard done by. But I apologised – for what I don't know, as all I did was come in a bit late. I have to suck it up because the Sadie is next week and there's also the basketball finals and the musical to consider. I wouldn't want to miss these events. And I wouldn't want to lose my honor roll pass which gives me the chance to go where others fear to tread. In other words, I don't have to stay in the lunchroom during lunch.

By the time I finished with Georgie Porgie, period one was over. The word had already gotten out about my meeting with the principal which I soaked for all I could by being deliberately vague. Girls like a rebel and guys are impressed with that bad boy shit.

Babs was particularly happy when I saw her at lunchtime. She cuddled up to me and gave me her dessert. If that isn't love, what is? I arranged to meet Babs at the school dance at night. Of course, the big enchilada is next Saturday night. As a result of my lateness, I missed an algebra test which I'll have to make up next week. But overall, I had positive vibes about the day.

After dinner, I picked up Mud Schuster and we went to the dance. When we got there, I couldn't believe my eyes. Babs was talking to the maggot Mirgat. My heart was in tatters as I had thought it was over between the two. Worse, he was with his Senior friends, so I was reluctant to confront him.

I figured I'd sit this one out and do my best James Dean brood. I managed a dance with Gretel from my Home Room, but the whole time we danced all I could do was stare at Babs and hope the Maggot would leave.

I couldn't help observing that the Seniors were somewhat hyped up for lack of a better word. It was as if they had too much to drink, but without the sloppiness that goes with it. There was an odd smell I couldn't identify around them as well. By their attitude one could tell they were looking for trouble.

The trouble soon came in the form of Jake St. Pierre – a Junior and our starting football quarterback. Jake was in good with the jocks I thought, but he was a cocky SOB and a bit of a blow - hard. He started mouthing off to the Seniors. The condition the Year 12s were in, it didn't take long for them to take offence. The group pulled him outside and smacked him around.

This left Babs alone, and I went over to her. Babs looked fantastic without her school uniform and seemed pleased to see me. She apologised for ignoring me. I saw no reason to ask her about the Maggot. We danced and enjoyed each other's company for the rest of the evening.

As for Jake, he wasn't looking so hot with a bloodied lip and a black eye. And the Seniors? They were kicked out of the dance by the supervising teacher so that took care of my problem. Though it was cold outside, Babs and I went out and kissed. I used some of the tricks Amy had taught me to great effect. What started out badly at the dance, took a turn for the better.

Cop-u-later.

FEBRUARY 5,
1966 – Saturday

Well, a week till the Sadie and if I may paraphrase a Christmas classic, there are 'visions of Babs dancing through my head.' Things are going so well that I can't believe my luck. Today I played basketball at the Groove with Cooey Procco and Mud. I'm not very good as one can tell by our intermural record, but I have my moments. It was snowy outside, but the weather was not as bad as last weekend. Still, there was a fair bit of the white stuff on the ground.

When I got home, I looked at Mrs. Pride's house and again saw neither hide nor hair of the old fart. I'm starting to wonder where she is as I usually catch a glimpse of her after school. I realise I shouldn't have done it, but I peeked in the window.

All the furniture in the living room was covered. She's rich enough, so maybe she went south for the winter. Many older people go to Florida this time of year. But no sign of Columbus. Where was he? Mrs. Pride's car was there. Not my problem, I thought.

At night, I went to an ice hockey game with Cooey and met Hep there. The local team – the Jets – aren't that good, but tonight Dick Roberge and Reg Taschuk, the stars, lit up the cage five times. The Jets – a semi-pro team – won 5-3 so we went away happy.

Cooey and I got a ride home with Dave Jones – Tom's neighbor. Dave takes up a good portion of the seat as he's quite porky. We sat in the back, which was just as well, as we saw a box of Clark bars opened on the seat. We each took a half dozen.

When Jones went to drop us off and found out about the missing candy, he started screaming blue murder. Tom and I laughed our asses off as we tore away from his vehicle.

When I got home, Will was playing pool with his girlfriend Cheryl and three other babettes. They were gorgeous year 9 girls – never mind the jailbait. I wonder how Will does it! Playing sport has its advantages. Also home were my sisters Biddy and Pippa. They are the yin and yang of sisters. Biddy – good; Pippa – bad. One old-fashioned and set in her ways; the other spontaneous and unpredictable. Neither had their partners with them.

I went down to the basement and started to chat up one of Will's friends – Mandy. Just when things were starting to crank up, St. Bridget came down and chased them away. She may have suspected some hanky-panky. On this occasion, I struck out. Or in baseball terms, one could say the game was called off on account of rain.

After Biddy went to bed, Pippa gave me a tall Seagram's 7 with 7up – a 7 and 7. Then she repeated the dose with a second. Both went down well for a sixteen-year-old. I went to bed with visions of more than just Babs dancing through my head.

Cop-u-later.

FEBRUARY 6,
1966 – Sunday

Didn't get up until past nine-thirty. Staying in bed is getting to be a habit! I guess I overdid the seven and sevens. The day started off quietly – which in my condition was a blessing. I couldn't even eat breakfast for fear of spilling my guts. Report cards are sent to the local church for collection, so I had to pick mine up. Still, I made it through the morning without emptying anything.

Around eleven a.m., Pippa asked me to drive her to her friend's house. I wasn't feeling the best, but I owed her for giving me the booze last night. I wonder if that was her plan. I suppose I shouldn't have been driving as the roads were still slippery and I only got my probationary driver's license last year. If Pippa was OK with it, then who was I to argue?

When I got home, Biddy asked me to take her to see Gran-King. I wasn't crazy about this trip as I had to be not only the driver, but a visitor as well. Now, I love my grandmother, but her battiness gets on my nerves. I had a pre-ordained signal with the Bidster that when I coughed twice, it would be time to go. It worked like a charm after an hour.

When I got home, Will asked for a ride to his girl's house. I was going to say no, but he offered to give me this 'dirty' book he was reading called 'Candy.' It was the adventures of a loose woman, he told me, and held little back. How could I resist? So, I took him to Cheryl's place.

On the way home, I stopped off at a local pizza shop for a couple of pepperoni pizza squares. By now the boozy feeling was wearing off though I still had a headache. Here I saw a classmate, Jerome (don't call me Jerry) Cavendish, who goes by Jack at school. He gave me $5 to take him to the City. How could I refuse? Four people to four different places.

Now that I was in the City, I decided to look up Babs. She wasn't home so I talked with her sister Elaine. She's not as good looking as Babs but has a good personality. We hit it off right away – laughing and joking. Perhaps flirting, though I'd hesitate to call it that. When Babs got home, she wouldn't have been excited about this behavior

Anyway, Babs and I talked about the Sadie on Saturday. The arrangements were finalized. I will drive and pick up Babs, then Hep and finally Mason. We'll go to the dance and grab something to eat later. As Babs' family was in the house, I didn't get a chance to kiss her before I left. Damn!

When I got home, I was told by Dad that I had to pick up Pip and Will. I was chauffer for a day. And I did all this with a headache so bad it was like Ringo Starr was drumming in my head. Once home, I ate dinner prepared by Biddy (some foreign thing - I couldn't tell you what it was). Afterwards I went to my room to read the book 'Candy.' I made sure Dad didn't see the book although it was Mom who would have made a fuss.

Candy Christian was an innocent girl who came to the big city and got in all kinds of adventures – if you catch my drift. Yet she always seemed to come out on top (again if you catch my drift). If I felt Babs danced through my head last night, reading 'Candy' gave the phrase a whole new meaning. They say the book was banned in Boston. That's good enough for me.

Cop-u-later.

FEBRUARY 7,
1966 – Monday

Back to school. Still a shithouse full of snow outside, but unfortunately not enough for school to be called off. Got my honor pass, which allows me to walk around the school at any time (except during classes) without permission. Now what to do with it.

Saw Babs at lunch. Considering the Sadie Hawkins dance is Saturday, she seemed a bit cool toward me. Perhaps my 'flirting' with her sister got on her nerves. Talked to Hep, and we finalized the Sadie travel arrangements. Hep seemed happy I was driving although I still have to talk to Dad to organize the car.

Had Chem Lab a day earlier than usual because of some work being done there tomorrow. After the mysterious green cloud of a few weeks ago, a new fumigation system being installed was long overdue. I had been trying to avoid my lab partner Lisbeth – the Argentinian goddess – ever since my fantasy dream about her. Too much temptation. Today she surprised me by referring to me by my first name. I thought she knew me only as 'you.'

Anyway, she asked me a question about the lab exercise we were doing. After I answered her, she then touched me on the shoulder. One cannot underestimate the power of a girl's shoulder touch. Any thoughts of avoiding her left my mind immediately. I smiled, said something funny, and went back to work. I could swear she laughed at my comment and glanced at me on a number of occasions. I hope Babs – who's in the same lab - didn't notice.

After school, we had a musical rehearsal. We practiced our Scottish fling. Vicki King, my dance partner, looked as tough as one could imagine. I wouldn't mind having a fling with her (boom, boom). I can really relate to her (again, boom, boom). I know - look, don't touch.

The director of the 'Brigadoon' production, Sister Georgakopoulos, or the 'Fuhrer' as we refer to her behind her back, talked about the choir performing at a music festival next month in in Jakstown and then

Altona, the rival city to Jakstown. We'll have to learn some new songs, but it sounds interesting. I'm all for it.

Got home from school, and Biddy and Pippa were both gone. Kitty heated Swanston TV dinners for the remaining members of the family. Rubbery chicken, lumpy mashed potatoes, cold peas and a peach cobbler. The latter is the best part of the meal.

Dad had had a few vodkas (when the mother's away, the father will play) after work so he didn't look too good. He continued at home. If he noticed the watered-down version from last week, he didn't say. I was wondering when Mom would get released from the hospital.

Dad crashed early, so I took a bit of Seagram's from his stash, added some Coke, and took it to my room. I went back to reading my book. 'Candy' was getting quite spicy. In my mind, I thought of Lisbeth, uh I mean Babs. Five days to the Sadie.

Cop-u-later.

FEBRUARY 8,
1966 – Tuesday

I used my honor pass for the first time. I wanted to leave the cafeteria early just to prove to myself I could and perhaps to show off. So, I left before the bell. Sister Mary Donatus, aka Donuts, stopped me and was ready to throw the proverbial book at me, but I just smirked and showed her my pass. I love it when you get one of those rare wins over a teacher.

Before I left, I had lunch with Babs – still uncool for some reason. It didn't matter as my mind was fully on Lisbeth. For the first time, I thought about asking Lisbeth out. What a coup that would be. She's such a living doll. Where to go to best get noticed? Bowling, pizza, the Canteen? This would take some thought and I obviously couldn't do it until after the Sadie. But it was on my to-do list.

Ah, the Sadie. Four days to go. I have to remember to ask Dad for the car or all our plans are kaput. Another reason I left the cafeteria early was because all Babs could talk about was the Sadie. Her dress, her hair (styled by her mom who is a hairdresser), her flowers and all that crap that I could care less about. I'm good at nodding my head and filtering out the unimportant.

After school, I played one of our last intermural games. Thank goodness as we were terrible. We lost to the jocks 45-14. I had four points and fouled out. After one of the fouls, one of the big jocks wanted to start a fight. I was intimidated, not by one jock, but by his friends who were ready to gang up on me. My guys didn't want to get involved and a black eye wouldn't be a good look on Saturday. So, I was out of there quick smart.

When I got home, I again noticed the emptiness of Mrs. Pride's house next door. I saw Columbus, but no sign of the old lady. The house looked deserted. I made a mental note to check it out after the Sadie. The whole thing was beginning to look awfully suspicious.

Once again, we had TV dinners. As much as I like them, a homecooked meal every so often would be a nice change! The meal was the same as yesterday. This time I had the apple cobbler for dessert. Except for the dessert, the food is ordinary, but passable. However, what fun is eating a TV dinner if you can't watch TV while eating?

Dad wanted us to eat as a family at the table. We gobbled down this tasteless meal so quickly that we hardly said boo to each other. He did say Mom would be back tomorrow after the successful removal of her gall bladder, but she'd have to stay in bed for a while. Mom likes her sleep, so this is right up her alley.

So, to bed. I stayed up late to finish 'Candy.' Very enlightening. This girl gets around – and around and around and around - in many different ways. There were mucho things going through my head: Babs, the Sadie, Lisbeth, Mrs. Pride, Vicki King, Columbus, Mom, 'Candy.' Sleep did not come easy.

Cop-u-later.

FEBRUARY 9,
1966 – Wednesday

You would think that only three days until the Sadie Hawkins dance Babs and I would be thick as thieves. You'd think that, but things seem worse than ever. Babs has been frosty ever since I gave her younger sister some attention. Then again, she may have seen me talking to Lisbeth in the Chem lab. Now, as I was carrying Babs' books (very old school) before lunchtime, I dropped a couple. Not on purpose. I swear! She said I was an oaf and an unthoughtful one at that. Ouch!

So, I ended up having lunch with Hep and Frenchie. It gave me time to finalise Sadie arrangements with Hep. I was going to ask Frenchie if he was going to the dance, but then I thought what girl would ask a guy who would cause an earthquake when dancing to a dance? I let it ride. Frenchie did mention later that he had a family commitment on Saturday, but Hep and I figured he was lying through his teeth, gums and tonsils. We didn't challenge his version as we didn't want to make him feel bad.

I went over to Katie toward the end of lunch period to say hi. She seemed a bit better toward me, but I didn't stay long enough to be certain. I expect there's still a lot of hurt there. I didn't have the balls to ask if she was going to the Sadie.

With all the hassles with Babs, the dance and assorted stuff ups, my mind wasn't on my work. I blew an easy Algebra quiz. I've got to get my head together. I still have yet to tell Dad about the Sadie – partly because of Mom's operation, but also because I wonder how he would respond.

I never tried to bring girls home in the past for fear he would embarrass the girl and me by walking around in his underwear. This doesn't bother Will, but my fragile ego couldn't stand it. Though one had to admire Dad's devil-not-care attitude.

I signed up earlier to be a backstage person for the school play but decided to skip an after-school meeting. Instead, I hightailed it home. I wanted to be home when Mom got back from the hospital after being picked up by Dad. When she arrived, she seemed a bit sore and tired. I suppose that's part of getting your gall bladder cut out.

Mom said she was glad to be home as she couldn't have taken another day of hospital food. I figured she missed smoking as well because she lit up soon after she came through the door. Dad joined her and – to my surprise – so did Will. As he's only fourteen, I wouldn't have expected my parents to allow this. Yet it was all go.

With all the smokers in our family, we have dozens of ashtrays around. Most of these were made by us kids at school as gifts for Christmas and Mother's Day. I doubt if ashtrays will ever go out of fashion. Myself, I had no compulsion to light up, as the fags don't do much for me.

Decided not to call Babs tonight as I hoped things would be better between us at school. I'll talk to her tomorrow. I went upstairs and watched TV (the show 'I Spy'), studied a bit, read some, then went to bed. 'Candy' was still floating around in my head when I nodded off.

Cop-u-later.

FEBRUARY 10,
1966 – Thursday

Only two days till the big Sadie Hawkins Dance. If it seems like I'm counting down the days, it's because I am. I can't wait to take Babs out. Katie was still sore as she sat up front with her dad on the way to school. I sat in the back with two Freshmen girls. Have mercy!

The two young chickadees went on and on about Prell shampoo and its merits. I couldn't care less if it left their hair soft and bouncy. With their zits, those girls will need all the help they can get. Between Katie and the follicle girls, I was happy when we got to school.

When I reached the school door, I found Babs waiting for me despite the cold. She was in a particularly good mood. She actually gave me a kiss on the cheek. I usually hate these public displays of affection, but in this case, I was as happy as a mosquito in a nudist colony to find out our boyfriend/girlfriend thing might be on again.

Babs' birthday is on the eighteenth, and she invited me to her party. Does it get any better than that? Today I spent most of my time with Babs – lunchtime, study halls, some classes, in the corridor. I finally felt we were a couple. When no one was around, she kissed me on the cheek. Then again before we went home. This time it was a real kiss! On the lips. I enjoyed it immensely. Valentino would have been proud.

After school, I found out I had been kicked off the stage crew for missing yesterday's meeting. Boo, hoo! One less thing to put on my college application. It saved me from a lot of work for something I didn't care much about anyway.

Instead, Hep and I rushed to town to rent a suit for the Sadie from 'Rent-All-Anything.' I have a suit at home, but I wanted something classy. It cost Hep and me $20 each, but it was worth it. We were measured head to toe and fitted with snug-fitting blue suits with a white shirt and one of those thin black ties.

Hep ordered a tartan vest with his suit, but I went au natural – vestless. They even threw in flowers for our lapels. We were told to pick up our suits on Saturday morning. Afterwards, we stopped off at a local flower shop and ordered corsages for our dates. We were going all out on this one.

It was set for the big night. All that was left was to tell Dad and secure the red Buick Wildcat for the night. Why have I waited so long to tell him? What if the car wasn't available? What if Dad meets the girls in his boxer shorts? Stay tuned for the next exciting instalment – same Bat time, same Bat channel.

Cop-u-later.

FEBRUARY 11,
1966 – Friday

The big night's tomorrow. There hasn't been this much excitement since Hoary Laurie dropped her drawers at a football game last year. Saw Babs briefly today. She told me it would take her quite a while on Saturday to get 'dolled up' (my words). But what had to be done? She looked OK to me. Women!

Talked to Hep and confirmed Saturday's arrangements. I'm sure he's getting sick of me going through the whole routine. I would get my dad's Buick, I would pick up Babs' first, then I would go to his place, and finally Moran's. Then it was to the dance. Afterwards, the six of us would have dinner at a restaurant.

Hep did request one change to our itinerary. He asked if we could go back to his place for photos after we pick up Mason. Why not? Tomorrow morning, we would get our suits and the flowers – and then we were in like Flynn! What could go wrong?

During lunch, JD came up to me and told me his old man's car was on the blink. He was taking Arua Marhilles to the Sadie and now he needed a ride. The idea of six in a car hardly appealed to me, but JD was a buddy so I couldn't let him down.

I talked to Hep and he said he'd ask Moran. Babs hung around with Arua – unlike the 10th grade Mason who she didn't really know – so I anticipated no opposition, but it could get a bit squishy in the back. I liked it `cause I'd have the whole front seat for Babs and me to make out in. Ha-Ha!

Hep got back to me later and said Moran wasn't too keen about the whole sharing thing, but he had persuaded her. Tonight, I phoned Babs and told her of the new arrangements. As expected, she was OK with it. My only concern was whether if Babs and I would be able to get some alone time.

The boys came over later to play pool – Hep, Frenchie, Boob, Eggy, who was going to the Sadie with the equally brainy Stephanie

Bronkowski (If they ever have kids, the world will not be safe), and JD. Frenchie brought his friend Al Fido – a fitting name and nickname as his face resembled a bulldog.

Both Frenchie and Fido said they would have gone to the Sadie, but they had something on tomorrow – a family thing. With Frenchie's weight and Fido's looks, a girl would have to be blind to ask them to a formal dance. I wouldn't have expected them to go.

Then there was the Boob, kind of a hanger-on, who said he wasn't going because he had bigger fish to fry. I wasn't sure if he was talking about dinner or a date but didn't care either way. We played pool until midnight before the boys went home with Hep.

Dad was still up so I thought it would be a good time to ask for the car. I went to the living room where he liked to read Zane Grey or Perry Mason novels. Before I could ask him, he said the car needed to be serviced and he would be taking it to the garage tomorrow.

I got all red and didn't know what to say. Dad asked me if I'd go along and take the VW Bug, our second car, and pick him up after he dropped the Buick off. This was highly unusual as Dad doesn't like us to drive the small Bug in the winter. He's worried the small car might slip on the icy roads and hit a truck.

I meekly agreed. What choice did I have? I didn't get around to telling him about the Sadie. 'The best laid plans of mice and men often go astray,' according to one of Aesop's Fables.

Cop-u-later.

FEBRUARY 12,
1966 – Saturday

Sadie Hawkins Day. The name comes from Al Capp's cartoon strip 'L'il Abner.' Once a year – on SH Day - the girls in the fictional town of Dogpatch are allowed to ask the boys to marry them. I don't read that particular comic so I wouldn't bet my life on that explanation. Maybe my sister Kitty told me about it. But that's neither here nor there. The Sadie Hawkins idea has been taken and applied to our formal where the girl asks the boy to the dance.

Got up in the morning and, after breakfast, drove to the City in our VW to pick up Hep, get our rented suits, and the flowers. When I tried on my jacket, it seemed awfully big. But the guy fitting me said it would ride up with wear. I bet he says that to all the boys!

Earlier I had to see Dad to ask for the Buick before he took it in for servicing. When I told him, he wasn't happy as he wanted to leave the car at the garage overnight. He suggested I take a taxi. When I told him about the four other people, he finally agreed to drop it off, have it serviced and then have it delivered to our home in time for me to drive to the dance. I was relieved, but also concerned it might not be serviced in time. I said OK, but what was my alternative?

While in the City, I saw Lisbeth sitting on one of the park benches. I mentioned this to Hep, who didn't really give a damn, but I thought I'd check things out. When I approached her, I noticed she was shaking and crying. I reluctantly asked her why. She said in her cute broken English that her Sadie date was sick and couldn't make it to the dance.

Lisbeth then asked me if I'd take her. I couldn't believe my ears. This was my dream come true. I had to decline of course as I was taking Babs, but what an opportunity. What a dish! I confess to briefly considering my options.

Pretend to be ill and dump Babs, but she'd surely find out the truth. Besides, she's already made heaps of arrangements. Take both of them. No way Jose. Two girls, one guy. A recipe for disaster. Suggest she go with Frenchie, but I'd never subject any girl to that embarrassment. I told her things would work out for the best or some other crappy platitude designed to make her feel better. It probably didn't.

I went home. I was so nervous I got ready three hours early. When the car still hadn't been returned at five p.m., my anxiety levels hit the roof. I had reason to be nervous. Dad again suggested a cab, but I declined as people were counting on me. The car was finally delivered at six p.m. – much to the relief of my chewed fingernails.

Around seven p.m., I went to Babs' house where there were smiles and photos and gawking parents, sisters, brothers, grandparents and assorted hangers-on. You'd think she never went out before. I gave her the flower and she pinned it on her wrist. Babs looked fantastic in a bluish, flowery dress. It almost made me forget Lisbeth. Almost. While there I saw Elaine, Babs' sister, who was going to the Sadie with some Sophomore loser. She too looked great. It was all I could do to keep my eyes off Babs though maybe a little bit on her sister.

Next, I picked up Hep. Then, to Mason's where the formula was once more repeated. Mason lived in a tough neighborhood, and I was glad to get out of there. Her dress was also blue and flowery. I thought Babs and she had discussed these things. Now it was back to Hep's for more photos, more smiles and more gawkers. Finally I picked up JD and Arua – more p,s and g. Arua also wore a blue, flowery dress. Very odd indeed!

Now the couples were together. Babs and I were up front. And four were crammed in the back. I was hoping to take the group to my place, but before I left for the dance, Dad passed on it. He said he was worried about Mom after her operation. Knowing Dad likes to 'prance around the ring like some boxer' in his shorts, that was one less worry for me.

At last, we made it to the school where the dance was held. Everyone looked great. My red Buick '65 Wildcat was a huge winner. The Sadie beckoned!

FEBRUARY 12, 1966
The Sadie Hawkins Dance – Saturday

The Sadie Hawkins Dance was all I thought it would be – for the first two hours. Almost as soon as we got there, Babs and I started dancing. She knows all the latest moves while I suffer by comparison. Still, I gave it my best shot and, anyway, she didn't seem to mind.

Music was by the Melodic Boys – basically our school music supremo and his friends moonlighting with all the top hits of the thirties, forties and fifties, but it didn't matter as I was with Babs.

After dancing, we sat down and got some drinks (lemonade I think). It was just Babs and me at the table. I told her I liked her a lot and asked if she'd like to be girlfriend/boyfriend (only my sisters' generation would have said go steady). She agreed and we clinked glasses on it. Kissing would come later.

I checked in with Hep and JD. That they said they were doing well with their ladies may have been fool's gold. I didn't notice much dancing or flirting.

I also danced with Elaine. I asked Babs if it was OK to dance with her sister and she didn't have any problem with it. I'd find out later if it really was all right. While dancing, I couldn't help but think Elaine was getting rather close to me, but I can't say I put up much resistance. Talk about fool's gold!

About two hours into the evening, Babs left to go to the bathroom. I spotted Lisbeth. She looked lost, disoriented and seemed the worse for wear. What was she thinking coming here? Without an escort. How did she get in? Many were laughing at her as she was slurring her words and falling down. I felt sorry for her. As it was cold, I took off my coat and put it over her.

I then led her outside and asked if she had a way to get home. When she said no, I told her I'd take her. Now she turned toward me, and she tried to kiss me. I admit I was tempted, but I decided not to take advantage of the situation. Even as much as it had been my fantasy.

I did notice her breath and unsteadiness. At first, I believed she had been drinking some alcoholic beverage - probably beer. On reflection she didn't smell as if she had been drinking, though all the signs of disorientation were there.

It was a similar smell to that I had experienced at the school dance last week, but I wasn't familiar with the odor. I went back inside and called Hep over to ask him to tell Babs I'd be back in a half-hour, and I drove Lisbeth to her home in Jakstown.

Lisbeth told me her address. She didn't live that far away. She also seemed to be sick. I motioned for her to stick her head out the window which she did and immediately puked over the side of the car. When we approached the house of the family she was staying with, she said she liked me.

Again, she tried to kiss me. A recently vomited-mouth kiss was not a turn-on – no matter how much I wanted a kiss from her. I brushed her off. Why couldn't this have happened yesterday, I thought?

When I got to her place, her host family was happy to see her. I helped her stagger into the house. Her family seemed grateful I'd brought her 'home.' She was taken upstairs to her bedroom. The older man then asked if I'd like a coffee, but I declined as I wanted to return to the dance.

I got back to the Sadie and saw the two couples I'd brought, but no Babs. Hep gave me the bad news. Babs had gone home – with the maggot Mirgat and his date. What a blow! What a threesome, I thought. We stayed a little bit longer. I had a dance with Elaine to try to explain my side of things. All she wanted to do was cuddle. That wouldn't go over well in the short run, I thought.

Now it was time to go. I had already booked a restaurant, so we went there, but it was pin-drop quiet throughout the meal. I can't remember much about it. Needless to say, it was a somber return trip to the homes where I dropped the others off. Hep was somewhat annoyed as he had hoped to make out with Mason after the meal. Save it for next time I told him.

Tonight, I had fun for a couple of hours, then did what I thought was right and helped someone. Did I have other motives? At first, I thought no, but on second thought, I couldn't help thinking of the helpless Lisbeth. Babs, Lisbeth. Babs, Lisbeth. Maybe I should have taken that cab like Dad suggested.

Cop-u-later.

FEBRUARY 13,
1966 – Sunday

I'm still reeling from last night. Got home well after midnight, but Dad was alright with it and asked if I had a good time. I didn't exactly tell him the truth, and with some exaggeration, I told him what I thought he wanted to hear. I told him – as vaguely as possible – that I got something. He winked at me thinking I did something special. 'T'would that I could!' I thought.

I tried to call Babs but got no response. Was she with the Maggot? I couldn't bear thinking about it. I tried to phone her a number of times, but each time I was told she was out. Were they covering for her? Were her pants on fire? I really think I screwed up big time.

On the other hand, I couldn't help but think of Lisbeth and how she wanted to kiss me. Did she mean it or was it because of her condition? What was her condition anyway? She didn't smell as if she had been drinking, yet she was out of control. I came to the conclusion that she probably didn't mean it when she said she liked me and wanted to kiss me. I would find out at school.

I needed to get my mind off last night's events. Mud Schuster called and asked if I wanted to go to a local dance at the Fear of the Lord Parish Church Hall in the evening. I agreed as I needed to get my mind off everything that had occurred last night.

As I was leaving to walk to the dance, I spotted Columbus tending to his car outside of the garage. I didn't let on that I suspected Mrs. Pride was gone. I'm sure he would have given me some sort of meaningless explanation anyway. When I asked if everything was OK, he said in that deep Lou Rawls voice of his that all was well.

I wasn't satisfied that things were well but didn't question it. I would pursue this later. He then asked me about my girlfriend. I told him about last night.

'You in deep shit brother,' he said. He suggested flowers and a card, but this was the 1960s, I thought, not the 1940s. I nodded, then said goodbye as I had to meet Mud at the hall.

The dance was mostly for younger kids – twelve-fourteen, but Mud knew someone, so we were allowed inside. I was only sixteen and Mud fifteen, so we weren't far off the mark. A bit of jailbait never hurt anyone as long as one looked but didn't touch.

I did notice my friend Tom Cooey Procco's sister – Missy. Although only twelve, she had real potential. She – like her brother – was a light brown color. She had beautiful dewy cow eyes, tiny freckles and the slightest lisp when she spoke that I found very attractive.

I went up to her and chatted a bit. I felt nervous and my heartbeat accelerated. I thought I'd better get away quickly before I said something I'd later regret. Around 1970, she would be old enough to ask out. I moved on.

While there, I noticed Katie. I went over to her to say hello. To my surprise, she seemed happy to see me. She said she was chaperoning the dance. Oddly enough, she looked very nice. Not great, but passable. Actually, better than passable. She was dressed in a simple, but attractive dress and her hair was worn down to her shoulders.

I didn't ask her about the Sadie as I knew she hadn't attended, but she volunteered that she didn't go. I felt bad about this as I'd turned down her invitation. Thankfully, she didn't ask me about last night. For once, I was grateful for small mercies. Anyway, we twisted once on the dance floor to a Chubby Checker song, but I soon got out of there as I didn't want her to think I liked her.

So, Mud and I went to my place to play pool – later to be joined by Cooey. I mentioned I talked to his sister, but he laughed it off and jokingly called me a 'dirty prick.' I easily beat Mud and Coo in pool. My dad was asleep, so I managed to get us some Seagram's.

The evening ended somewhere between eleven p.m. and midnight. It was good being with these guys, but for the moment I had other things on my mind. Tomorrow was another day. And unlike Rhett Butler in 'Gone with the wind,' I gave a damn!

Cop-u-later.

FEBRUARY 14,
1966 – Monday

The Monday following the Sadie Hawkins Dance was one of the more awkward days of my sixteen years. I thought of avoiding Babs entirely. Instead, I tried, on a number of occasions, to talk to her. She didn't seem interested by any stretch of the imagination and shunned me when I approached her. Indeed, at lunch she was with the Maggot. I guess I deserved this treatment.

One who didn't deserve to be treated badly was Katie, who handed me a Valentine Card on this special day. I felt like a real cad as I hadn't reciprocated. I read the semi-mushy 'roses are red, violets are blue' message, then gave her a kiss on the cheek when I saw no one was around. I figured that would satisfy her for the day.

At lunchtime, I ended up talking to Hep who told me what a fantastic night he had on Saturday. Hep told about getting it on with Mason, but I took that to mean he got a couple of kisses, maybe some tongue, but little else. I didn't see when he would have had time to do even that much. Frenchie also said he went out with a girl on Saturday, but as I didn't hear news of any beached whales, I discounted his story.

I passed Lisbeth and said hi. She was the main topic at school and I'm sure I was part of that conversation. The rumor was that she was on some drug, but I found the old South American/drug connection a cliché and discounted the story. Lisbeth returned my greeting and added she didn't remember much of anything from Saturday. If she did, she didn't let on.

As Babs' party was on Friday, I asked Hep, JD and Frenchie if they were going. Hep said yes, but JD and Frenchie first wanted to go to the big basketball game that night. We play Altona City Public High School – usually a top team and one that beat us regularly in the past. We have a good chance of beating them this year. It wasn't a state qualifying game, but it would give us an indication how good we are. This year it's all the way - though not with LBJ.

At night it took me a while to get up the nerve, but I rang Babs. I wished her a Happy Valentine's Day and told her I had a card to give her. She had ignored me most of the day and I didn't give the valentine to her at lunch as she was talking to Mirgat.

She mentioned that she and the Maggot (my word) were just good friends and that he was good enough to give her a ride home on Saturday when she thought I had left her.

I tried to explain about the situation that night, but she stopped me mid-sentence and said it was all water under the bridge. I hope so. I could have told her I asked Hep to tell her I'd be back, but then thought why. Would it make any difference?

I asked her if she still wanted to go together, but she said she couldn't give me a definite answer. I felt some resentment there but was hopeful that time would be the great healer. She said she still wanted me to come to her party, so things were cool in that regard.

At this, Elaine asked to speak to me. Babs said it was OK with her and handed me the phone. I didn't really want to talk to her, but it would have been rude if I hadn't. I joked with Elaine for a couple of minutes. She wasn't a bad sort, but I loved Babs.

When Babs got back on the phone, she made an unusual request. She asked to speak to my brother Will. I called him and then gave him the phone. It was a short conversation between the two before the phone came back for me to say goodbye.

When I hung up, I left with the idea that things were not great but there was room for reconciliation between Babs and me. That lasted about thirty seconds. I turned to Will and asked what Babs wanted with him. He said nothing much except that she invited him to her party.

It was then that I realised I had a lot of work to do to get back on Babs' good side.

Cop-u-later.

FEBRUARY 15,
1966 – Tuesday

I was more than pissed off this morning about my brother being invited to Babs' party this Friday. I couldn't help thinking this was revenge for me leaving her on Saturday night. Maybe even for dancing with Elaine after Babs left (I'm sure Elaine told her). I was going to tell Will in no uncertain terms not to go, but Dad was in a hurry to leave so I had to rush out.

During Home Group I greeted Babs and gave her the Valentine Card, but she barely said anything other than a muted thanks. I saw her later with the Maggot and was devastated as I thought Babs and I had made peace last night over the phone.

I was upset, sure, but I had confronted him once before over Babs and I didn't want to do it again. For one, it was undignified. That never stopped me from doing anything before. More to the point, his buddies might seriously harm me this time.

Had lab and saw Lisbeth. Man was she beautiful – even in a sexless school uniform covered by a white lab jacket. I tried to ignore her as much as possible but, as she was my lab partner, it was a tough ask. I stuck to the business at hand for the most part. Part way through one of the experiments, while mixing some chemical compounds, she turned to me and asked me to meet her after school. I was mystified, but we agreed on a place, and I said I would.

For the rest of the day my mind played tricks on me as I anticipated the meeting with Lisbeth. All I could think about was her. I kept wondering what our children would look like. During lunch, I was very quiet sitting with Hep and the boys. Babs was with Maggot, but even that didn't bother me.

After school I went to meet Lisbeth. As suggested by her, we met in an empty Language Lab. When I saw her from a distance, my heart started beating madly. This was no ordinary girl – or woman the more I thought about it. She came up to me and grabbed my hand. I looked into her eyes and had non-Catholic thoughts galore.

After a brief period where nothing was said, she thanked me for helping her on Saturday. She explained in cute broken English that her Sadie Hawkins date had gotten ill and couldn't take her to the dance. She was very upset, she said, and to calm herself had taken something she had gotten from a student.

I was intrigued and was dying for some details but decided not to continue this line of conversation. All I know is that she wasn't thinking straight when she was at the dance.

To me, these things didn't matter. All I wanted to know was if she liked me. Actually, more than just liked me. I never got around to asking her, as I don't remember saying anything except that's OK or some trite comment to make her feel better. She then handed me an envelope and told me to open it later. She looked at me and kissed me on the forehead. She was gone! I pledged never to wash that part of my face again.

I daydreamed that the envelope contained a letter expressing her love for me. She was just too shy to say the words in front of me. I wondered how I would respond. I opened it up and came across a note on coloured paper. But the writing came from someone older.

It was from the woman in whose house she was staying. The letter thanked me for helping Lisbeth and expressed gratitude for what I did on Saturday. Suddenly a crisp $20 note fell from the letter. It was for helping their charge get home safely.

To say this was like a kick in the groin would have been an understatement. It was deflating. Then again, perhaps I had deluded myself into making more of the situation then there was. It was all quiet after that, but if you listened carefully, you might have heard my heart bursting at the seams.

Cop-u-later.

FEBRUARY 16,
1966 – Wednesday

Another day of school, another day watching Babs with the Maggot. What does she see in him? I guess he's smart and good-looking. But aren't I? My mom would say so. Dad and even DD (granted under duress) said so. At least Babs hasn't uninvited me from her party on Friday. I decided to ignore the Maggot thing for now as I'm obviously not her flavor of the month.

Sat Chem and Religion tests. During the former, it was all I could do to keep my eyes off Lisbeth. After reading yesterday's letter from her guardians, I know I should be happy. Why wasn't I? I guess I scored $20. Should I expect more from her?

Soon she'll be heading back to Argentina, and I'll just be a footnote in her life, but there's no harm in fantasizing. For what it's worth, I can't help myself. I look on her as the Juliet to my Romeo. Perhaps not the best analogy. We all know what happened to them!

I am a bit concerned about what she said yesterday – about getting something to calm her down from a fellow student. People here believe she's on drugs. If that's true, what student is supplying her? Are there others taking these so-called substances? What type of drug? How is it taken? I'm pretty ignorant about these things, but it disturbs me to think someone - perhaps from this school - is peddling these dangerous things.

Back to reality, I think I did well on the Chem test. As for religion, I hope I made the right moral choices. My conscience is not functioning the way it should be these days.

After school, the Glee Club saw the film 'Brigadoon' in preparation for our school musical. I liked Gene Kelly's dancing with Cyd Charisse. But for me, Van Johnson stole the show. I liked his sarcasm and sense of humor. I noticed the dances I have to do with my cousin, Vicki. I also studied Frank the bartender's small, but significant role. The significant part were the Fuhrer's very words.

Afterwards, I looked for Babs as I wanted to talk to her about the mysteries of life and our puny role. Well, not really. Something much more important. Getting together again! Somehow, I missed her. I'd make sure to call her when I got home. My plan was laid bare when Dad insisted, we go to Grammy's for dinner.

We left as soon after I got home. I cringe when I think of being subjected to Grammy and her senile sisters – all of them other than Grammy smoke like fiends and have the breath to prove it. Not to mention their sloppy kisses. When I'm older I'm going to forgo any kiss that doesn't lead to something.

All of us - Dad, Will, Kitty and me – but without Mom who is still recovering from her recent operation – went to Grammy's. Her house is a rather large two-storey stucco building with a huge porch and thick pillars. As usual, we had hash to eat. I swear she stores this stuff in a freezer and saves it to serve to our family when we eat here. I didn't even get a drink – a real drink – as in this instance I wasn't asked.

When I got home, it was late, as Dad sat at Grammy's BS-ing for the longest time. I decided it was too late to confront Will about the party and too late to call Babs. Had I broken a mirror or walked under a ladder recently? My luck could not be any worse.

Cop-u-later.

FEBRUARY 17,
1966 – Thursday

Tomorrow is Babs' birthday and I'm still not sure where I stand with her. Maybe I'll find out at her party. I just wonder if the Maggot will be there. I do have fears my brother will show up. As is customary on Thursday, I got a ride with Katie's dad. Surprisingly, Katie left room for me to sit by her and rubbed her leg against mine. After her disappointment of not going to the Sadie, I guess it's forgive and forget. She seemed awfully perky.

Had lunch with Hep, Frenchie and Eggy. This wasn't Babs, but it was cool, nonetheless. Our conversations are without peer. Hep was still talking about the Sadie and how he scored with Mason. I disagreed, but I stayed quiet and let the dog have his day.

Frenchie then said he didn't believe 'Tony the Tiger' was a real tiger because real tigers wouldn't eat the cereal 'Sugar Frosted Flakes.' I don't know why I got involved as Tony is just an advertising cartoon character, but I couldn't help myself.

I argued that tigers liked sugar and would eagerly devour a large bowl of that cereal. I added that I wasn't sure about the milk. The innocuous debate continued with a life of its own. The Eggster mentioned that cats liked milk so why not tigers? JD said tigers liked meat, not corn. As always nothing was resolved.

As this debate raged on, I snuck a peak over at Babs and noticed she was with the Maggot. I also spied Lisbeth who was eating with the jocks. What a waste! Were the dummy jocks her suppliers? I happened to see Rudy Mingo – one of the good jocks.

When he was away from the others, I went to him and inquired if any of his group were involved in supplying any illegal substances to students. He said some jocks took steroids (he denied he did) but wouldn't sell them. It was more for personal use. He said he heard rumors of one person involved in this trade, but he wasn't a squealer and wouldn't reveal the name.

He was insistent that the supplier was not a jock. He told me to look to my own house for answers. I had no clue what he was on about, but I thanked him just the same.

After lunch, I had an English test. I can't say I studied for it, but luckily Homulkyo came to the party with the answers. It only cost me two bucks. I know I said I wouldn't use his services anymore, but I was desperate. I hadn't studied. Though I knew it was wrong, it was just too tempting to resist.

I had the answers under my test paper. The fat teacher, Sister All Buns, was somehow suspicious of me. Maybe I looked guilty. Indeed, I was. So, I had to be careful. Throughout the test, I swear she was staring at me. I couldn't chance looking at the answers. I only was able to read some of them. I didn't finish and cursed her as I was leaving the class.

I had a musical rehearsal after school. On the way to the rehearsal room, I passed Babs and she was kissing the Maggot – on the lips! I held my temper, but frankly I was livid. Tomorrow, I thought, I would get to the bottom of this.

Today I had dance practice with my cousin Vicki. I'm getting the hang of these steps after seeing the film yesterday. She helps me a lot with my dancing. Vicki's cool and quite funny. I don't think of her as my cousin when we're going around. I could really go for her if we weren't related. We could never have a serious relationship. We wouldn't want to bring two-headed children into this world, would we?

We learned a few songs during rehearsal. 'Come Ye to the Fair' and 'Come home to Bonnie Jean' amongst others. With the latter I kept picturing Hep as Gene Kelly and me as Van Johnson. The dance on the film looked like a lot of fun.

When I got home – late – I saw Will. I asked, pleaded, warned and threatened him not to go to Babs' party tomorrow. But I knew that nothing I said or did would have any effect on him. I only hoped and prayed he'd listen and not go. I didn't want the party to be more miserable than I already expected it to be.

Cop-u-later.

FEBRUARY 18,
1966 – Friday

Babs' party was tonight. I was in two minds whether to go especially as Babs has been flirting with the Maggot. I decided to go as I had nothing to lose but my dignity. The little I still had. Our final intermural basketball game of the season was after school and not before time. As usual, we lost – this time 25-23, but the other side used an ineligible player, so I guess we won a hollow victory. Good riddance to the season.

After the game, I went with Hep to get a birthday gift for Babs. I got her a stuffed dog – a big one – and a mushy card. It wasn't flowers as suggested by Columbus, but it was something to stir the emotions. I can't see either of these things changing her mind about going with me. I just hope she likes them.

Anyway, I rushed home after school to get ready for the party. Got the car about 7, picked up Hep and drove to the 'Friends of Poland' Hall where Babs' party was held. Thankfully, there was no sign of my brother.

When we got there, the place was crawling with Babs' girlfriends and only a handful of guys. Most of the boys went to the school basketball game and would arrive later. Seeing this many girls was unnerving away from school. Many I hardly knew, and even fewer had I ever talked to. A few resembled the stuffed animal I brought for Babs' present. Still, some washed up well and had a pleasant look out of their drab school uniforms.

The gift went over well. Babs seemed happy to get the dog and the card. She gave me a kiss on the cheek. The cheek? A bad sign! There was no sighting of the Maggot. Hep and I danced with a couple of girls we knew, but not Babs, as she was running around greeting her guests and organizing things for her party.

So, I got talking to Elaine. I'm playing with fire, I know. I danced with her a number of times (fast dances like the 'swim'). She was wearing this big turtle-necked sweater so Hep dubbed her the 'Turtle'.

Things were going well even without Babs' constant presence.

Around half past nine, the boys arrived as the basketball game had finished. JD, Frenchie, the Chief and – yes – the Maggot with some other seniors. JD mentioned our school had won the game tonight, so all were in a good mood. Perhaps too much of a good mood. Some of the seniors had that peculiar look and smell. Rudy said to look to my house as a clue to the seller of that shit. Could he have meant the Maggot?

At last, the food was brought out. Then the cake. We sang 'Happy Birthday' to Babs, and she blew out sixteen candles. Hep sang 'Happy birthday to you, you belong in a zoo, you look like a monkey, and you smell like one too.'

'Very mature,' I said sarcastically. We were given a slice of the white sponge.

Then, the Maggot gave Babs a long kiss on the lips. Maybe to make Babs jealous, I turned to Elaine to talk to and to dance with. Despite the antics of Babs and the Maggot, I was surprisingly having a good time talking and mingling with the Turtle and the other guests.

Just after 10.15, things turned sour. Brother Will and his freshmen morons arrived – unannounced and drunk as skunks. He sure acted drunk. He was waving a can of beer, slurring his words and talking to the girls like he was God's gift to women. I noticed some of his friends were smoking cigarettes. How humiliating for me.

Babs didn't look very happy. She came over to me and asked me to get him out of there. I thought about the irony of her inviting him and then asking me to get him to leave the party, but I refrained from rubbing it in.

So, I dutifully went over to my brother to escort him away, but Will didn't want to go. He took a swing at me which I easily dodged. Then he got a bit weird and told me he loved me. Eventually I persuaded him and his friends to leave. Some of his pals had transportation, so I suggested they take Will home. I escorted him to a car and laid him down on the back seat. Then he puked! At least it wasn't in Dad's car!

I stayed another hour or so. It was obvious that Babs had another agenda this evening. I wasn't part of it. We left and at the urging of the guys, we stopped at Coney Island for a hot dog. I wish I hadn't because ironically the Chief threw up in the car after eating four of the franks. JD thought he was on something. I figured he was on something – too much

118

food.

It was now late, so I took the boys straight home despite their yearnings to go to the local cathouse – Rachael's. You're dreaming, I thought. Do they even know where it is?

I was upset that I never had the chance to tell Babs how much I cared for her. All I could think of was Babs and that Maggot together. With perhaps thoughts of Lisbeth thrown in. When I got home, I found Will had made his way home safely. I was PO'd at him. During the night he got his comeuppance when he vomited a few more times.

Cop-u-later.

FEBRUARY 19,
1966 – Saturday

My luck has been so bad lately that I figure I'm due for a break. Even an exorcist would struggle to expel my bad vibes. For not only have I lost my girlfriend to that Maggot, but twice in the past week I've had to interrupt being with Babs to take care of other people. I'm sure Babs was concerned, and I may have pushed her toward the Maggot. I dare say I may never get back with her again.

I thought I'd impress Dad this morning by taking the car to the car wash to get it cleaned. After all, one of Will's half-wit friends had puked on the outside a few days ago and the Chief spilled his guts on the inside last night. Do I detect a pattern here?

I spent the morning cleaning the vomit on the outside and cleaning and vacuuming inside of the car. A gallon of industrial cleaner and a couple spray cans of deodorant couldn't eliminate the smell entirely but made a huge dent into it.

Oh yes, Dad was not happy about the mess. 'You had the car, and it was your responsibility to make sure nothing happened,' he said angrily. I copped it, but I put this all onto Will for a variety of reasons. He was still sleeping when I finished my nasty cleaning task. Thus, I couldn't confront him. Not that he would have remembered anything. He was still asleep at noon when I had to go out. I assume he was alive as I heard snoring.

I tried to call Babs but got her sister instead. I flirted a bit with the Turtle who eventually confessed that Babs didn't want to speak to me. I had to cut our conversation short as I was to meet Hep in the City. After last night's debacle, the car was off limits by order of Dad. So, I had to take the Inclined Plane downtown. I was lucky I wasn't grounded. He told me to stay home, but I had a musical rehearsal at school. I'm not sure he believed me when I told him, but he eventually let me go sans car.

The cast of the musical met in the City at St. John's Church Hall near where Hep lived. It wasn't a rehearsal per se, but another showing of the film 'Brigadoon.' I met Hep there and kind of hoped to see Babs. If she was there, I didn't notice her. The film started and I saw the early part, but then fell asleep. I dreamed I was Gene Kelly and Babs was Cyd Charisse.

We danced while we collected heather on the hill, went to Bonnie Jean's wedding and saw Harry Beaton and tried to keep him from leaving the village and stop the miracle (the Scottish village of Brigadoon only appears once every one hundred years and if someone leaves, it disappears entirely). Harry was stopped when he was accidently killed by Van Johnson.

At the end, I sang the sad farewell song to her. 'You and the world we know will glow till my life is through, for you're part of me from this day on. And someday if I should love, it's you I'll be dreaming of, for you are all I'll see from this day on.'

At this point, Sister Mary Fuhrer poked me which woke me up. She told me to watch the scene where the bartender does his spiel. It's a pretty minor role, but one takes what one can get. So, I dutifully watched. Though short in duration, it's not so bad.

It's the scene where Tommy at a bar in New York City sees visions of life in Brigadoon. He decides to go back to Scotland to find the lovely Fiona – the girl he loves. Being the bartender is certainly not the Jeff (Van Johnson) role that I wanted.

Afterwards, the lights went on and I saw Babs there. I tried to get her to go outside so I could talk to her and explain about last night, but she ignored me. A car drove up to the curb and picked her up. It was the Maggot. You could have ripped out my insides and fed my carcass to the dogs for all I felt. Hep consoled me, but I now realised that Babs and I as a couple was history.

The words from 'Brigadoon' came back to me as I sadly left. '...if I should love, it's you I'll be dreaming of, for you are all I'll see from this day on.'

Cop-u-later.

FEBRUARY 20,
1966 – Sunday

Sunday morning and I got a call from Father Bellodhiro from the local Fear of the Lord parish to serve Mass. I was no longer on the regular altar boy schedule, but I was available if the priests needed me. I hadn't served for a while, but I thought this would be one way to get my mind off Babs.

The thought of her with that maggot Mirgat made me think of un-Christian things to do to him. In the same vein, I've heard there are many fish in the sea, and Christ is the Fisherman. Or it was St. Peter if I remember my Bible.

The regular commentator for Mass wasn't available so Bellodhiro asked me to fill in. Well, I didn't know what the f (pardon my French) I was doing and made a meal of the whole thing. I think Father B. was aware of my incompetence as when it came time for me to commentate a second time, he stopped Mass and did it himself.

Got home in time for Sunday dinner. Gran-King was there, so there was plenty of talk about the failings of heebs, blacks and dagos. I guess I should have said something positive as we live near plenty of Jews, our neighbour's chauffer is a Negro and one of my best friends is Italian. But I let it go as, despite her idiocy, GK can't be stopped when she gets on a roll! These days I find myself morally bankrupt anyway.

I finally caught up with my brother Will before dinner. He couldn't remember much about Babs' party. He gave me the same blanket apology I often give the next day after a bender when I feel I did something stupid. Sincere, but equally insincere. Not having the foggiest what you're apologizing for. Dad grounded him for being drunk, but, knowing Will, he'll sneak out.

I tried to call Babs after dinner to no avail. If that makes me desperate, then color me guilty. I talked again to Turtle, but there's no way I could ask her out as to do that would add weird to weird. It certainly wouldn't endear me to Babs. I figured I'd bide my time and hopefully give the Maggot enough rope to hang himself.

In the evening, I went with Frenchie to the school auditorium to see the Junior play – the one I tried out for earlier in the year. The play was 'Arsenic and Old Lace.' It was surprisingly good. The student playing Teddy Roosevelt was particularly entertaining. I saw Babs and the Maggot together. During intermission, I went over to where she was sitting and, despite the Maggot being there, briefly talked to Babs.

I then took a piss break. As I was leaving the lavatory, I was struck in the back of my head by someone I didn't see. I was knocked down and it hurt like hell. When I got up and went back into the auditorium, I saw a group of Senior boys laughing their asses off.

Well, I was pissed off no end and ready to walk over to them and say some smart-ass comment to their group. That surely would have resulted in a pounding, but I wasn't about to let these goons get away with hitting me. Before that happened, Frenchie pulled me aside and told me to forget it for now.

He said there was a half-dozen of them, and I had no backup other than him. Their cowardly hit was obviously a warning from the Maggot and his buddies to stay away from Babs. I took Frenchie's advice and let it go, but – like an elephant – I wasn't about to forget. This event made me even more determined to get Babs back.

Cop-u-later.

FEBRUARY 21,
1966 – Monday

It's the first day of school since Babs' party and I expect things to be a tad awkward. First, there was Babs with the Maggot – holding hands and pecking at each other. That should be me doing the chicken thing with her. Then there was the ever-present senior gang literally running interference for the Maggot – thus keeping me from talking to Babs.

I wasn't too worried about another cowardly smack from behind as I had friends here. The Chief - and his always in the seniors' minds Negro friends - would be a deterrent against a repeat of the whack I got last night.

Nonetheless, it was a typical lunchtime with Hep, Frenchie, Eggy and JD. We passed the time rating every girl who walked into the cafeteria. We gave them a number from one to ten (ten being the top) based on looks, reputation and 'bedability.'

Not that any of us had ever experienced the latter. Hep carried rubbers in his wallet (he once showed them to me), but I suspect it was all for show. From what I saw it didn't look as if any of them had ever been out of the packet of three.

I'm not sure this exercise was all that appropriate, but it got my mind off Babs (whom I rated a nine – just below cheerleader status; the others, knowing my feelings for her, gave her the same score). Eggy suggested we add personality and brains to the equation, but he was shouted down in no uncertain terms and had food thrown at him.

Surprisingly, Frenchie gave Katie a six where I only gave her a two or three. Go figure? The cheerleaders all got tens as expected, but there were some surprises. Janet Voohaus, a non-cheerleader, got 9.5s and tens from the group. Hep – the self-proclaimed expert – claimed that he could tell if a girl 'did it' by the way she walked. Voohaus rated highly by this standard.

Laurie Zoller, aka 'Hoary Laurie' – not the best-looking girl – got high marks mainly because of her trashy reputation. Too bad she scares the hell out of us. Soon we tired of this sordid academic exercise. If the shoe was reversed, I'm sure all of us would pale in comparison to the other lads at our school.

I finally got to talk to Babs at musical practice after school. We're learning songs for 'Brigadoon,' but also songs for the upcoming Music Festival in March in Altona – about thirty-five miles from here – and in Jakstown. Other schools will also be there to highlight their musical abilities. I just hope the festivals don't interfere with the basketball playoffs scheduled around that time.

We play one of our last regular basketball games on Friday before our first knock-out qualifying finals game on the following Wednesday. I expect we'll win that one. Then on to the state championship. It's ours to win. I don't want to miss it. Besides, following the team is a good way for me to get my mind off Babs, if that's possible. For now, it's 'Come Home to Bonnie Jean,' 'Harry Beaton' and 'Welcome to the Fair.' I have some lines to learn as the bartender as well.

After school, there was a big party for the cast and the crew of the junior school play. I tried to crash it as I was briefly a crew member, but some fat nun kicked me out. Pity. Speaking of the devil, scary Laurie was one of the party goers.

Cop-u-later.

FEBRUARY 22,
1966 – Tuesday

Now that I'm Babs free, I'm ready to ride the horse again. Not literally. I'm regularly eyeing the chicks. Fat ones, skinny ones, ugly ones, tough ones – all except smart ones. My ego couldn't take going out with a girl smarter than me. For that matter, add cheerleaders to the avoid list. They are so far out of my league that I can't even fantasize about them. Usually they go out with jocks, the socials, seniors, college guys and even male teachers (if you believe the rumors).

I did say hello to the cheerleader Sally Rationello once. She is so gorgeous that when I talk to her, I mumble, stumble and choke. So, I settled for a 'hi' and left it at that. She returned my greeting. That's progress!

But I digress. Hep told me about this dance for teenagers of all high schools at the Masonic Lodge tonight. It's Mardi Gras Tuesday with Lent starting tomorrow. All I could think of was Lisbeth even though she's not Brazilian where the MG originates. Anyway, I said I'd meet him there.

After school we had another rehearsal for the Music Festival. The festival rehearsal is a week from Friday, the concert the Sunday following. A guest director was a Mr. Bowles who was a conductor of some piss-ass choir whose name escapes me. Of course, that opened up the musical possibility of a 'Bowel movement' which we had a lot of fun with.

Well, we practiced until five p.m. which didn't leave me much time to get home, get ready and meet Hep at the dance. As I was leaving the practice, I ran into Babs. To my surprise, she smiled, returned my greeting and even said a few words, but she was in a hurry to leave. I noticed she was picked up by the Maggot. So, I rushed home from rehearsal, gulped down my dinner, changed and asked Dad for the car. I don't think he was happy after last week's lateness, but he let me have it. I drove to the dance and – upon arrival – immediately spotted Hep.

The hall was in a seedy area of town, but still was impressive. The building was of solid construction - all stone and decorated with secret

Masonic symbols. Inside, the hall was enormous. There were decorations throughout, and a band was playing up front. The joint was jumping - packed with guys and girls from all different high schools.

There was 'strange' everywhere though the dance had more of a look, don't touch atmosphere. The girls were dressed for bear as we often put it to indicate they dressed up for the occasion. The boys, however, didn't really come to the party. Many had jeans and old shirts on. Some actually had t-shirts despite the winter cold.

I asked a number of girls to dance, but it only amounted to a dance and no follow-up. So, I ended up standing with Hep and his friend Pij from the public school. I'm not sure how to take Pij as he's quite confrontational. He was a bit of a BS-er, but he could spin a good story. After one of his yarns, he asked me for money, but I lied and told him I was broke.

The dance was DJ'd by a local disc jockey from popular station WWTF, John Rubble or Barney - as he was known on air after the 'Flintstone' character. Man was he cool – spinning records in his neat suit and thin black tie. When I get older, I'd like to be a DJ.

While there, I ran into Amy Sing and tried to chat to her, but she was with someone I assume was her boyfriend. Later, she and her partner were crowned queen and king of Mardi Gras. Surprisingly, I noticed Babs with Mirgat. As she had smiled at me earlier, I thought it was OK to talk to her.

The Maggot was with his mates, and they were none too happy to see me. There could have been trouble, but Hep and Pij joined me. With the Negro Pij there, I had no fear. Maybe I should have lent him that money. There was an odd smell throughout the hall during the evening. I asked Pij what it was as I had experienced that smell before. Pij told me not to worry as it was all under control. But under what control?

Babs and I actually talked for a few minutes or as much as one could with loud music being played and cavemen hanging about. I said I'd call her, and she seemed receptive. She even smiled - again. Big trees grow from little seeds, I thought. Soon Hep and I were out of there. For the first time in days, I felt things were picking up.

Cop-u-later.

FEBRUARY 23,
1966 – Wednesday

I'm still without a girlfriend or even any prospects, but things seem slightly better with Babs. She's acknowledging my existence. However, she still sits with that Maggot and the other seniors at lunch. The lunchroom is a real Darwinian social divider. A modern sociologist would have a field day sorting the ins and outs and territorial ownership of the place.

The teachers sit in their own room for lunch, separated from the students by a glass partition. So, there are no teachers in the student lunchroom. Teachers can see the students in the cafeteria from where they sit. I suppose they'd sort out any problems should they arise, but I don't think they'd be bothered unless someone was dying.

The lunchroom moms run the show. Lunch is served in a line strictly patrolled by these matronly Amazons. Some of these women surely were wrestlers or prison guards at one time. They cook and serve what one might call food. Sometimes it's recognisable. After you choose your food and pay, you leave the line and find a place to sit down in the cafeteria.

Lunchtime is staggered. Freshmen and sophomores have one lunch period and juniors and seniors a second. There are no compulsory seating plans, but culturally there is one. And never the twain shall meet! The seniors have their own area and pecking order. Their groups sit farthest away from the teachers. No junior kid need enter the imaginary demarcation without an invite. For the juniors, the rest of the room's seating depends on your status.

The socials or 'cool kids' such as the class president, his cronies and their girlfriends sit in one area. They're always laughing and pointing out the social misfits – probably us. Their ties are askew, and hair neatly combed. The girls are impeccably dressed. Scarves are popular. The hemlines on their school uniforms are slightly below the knee.

The Socials decide who is cool and who isn't, and there's not much you can do to be part of them. Except be cool – whatever that means!

Cool kids tend to gravitate toward each other. They suck up to teachers unmercifully though they would deny this if you pointed it out to them. The Socials are generally smart, good-looking, confident and know it. An invitation is required to join them. Ordinary people need not apply. Jack Cavendish is an example.

Near them are the jocks or the school athletes. You can tell them by their letter sweaters or jackets. The jocks' girlfriends sit at their tables. Selected jocks sit with the cool kids, but most jocks are generally too uncool to sit there. The socials pretend to be friends with the jocks. They pander to them while looking down on them.

The jocks, all male as there are no girl sports at OLPS, are tanned in summer (and winter somehow) and muscle-bound, but generally dumb as dogshit. Jocks often pander to smart girls to get them to do their work, but rarely hang around with them.

One good jock is Rudy Mingo, a star basketballer. Rudy is smart and not stuck up. He actually speaks to the underlings. With the jocks are the cheerleaders. These girls are gorgeous and beyond the reach of any mortals except jocks or older guys. One of my status can only stare and dream.

Near the cool kids are the 'I'm good-looking and I know it' girls. Their school uniform hemlines are usually worn above the knee – school rules be damned. They wear their hair long and straight. Though make-up and jewelry are banned, they often cheat by wearing both. They are street smart. They know what they want and go for it. They will talk to others outside their group, but they usually want something in return.

They often chew gum out of class (and secretly in class) and have their own culture, dress and lingo. They laugh a lot at each other's comments - often at the expense of others both above and below their status. They are generally good-looking (just below cheerleaders), but there are some plain girls in the group that fawn on the others. They often go out with guys older than them. They have a bad reputation – and love it. Janet Voohaus would be in this group.

Then there's the tough guys who wear leather jackets. They act tough, their clothes are often unkempt (not that they care) and their hair has a greasy look to it. They act rebellious and look to James Dean or a young Marlon Brando as role models, but they're not really that tough.

They are spineless and dumb and often avoid any unpleasantness. No doubt they would have cigarettes in their lockers. The Chief can be considered in this group.

There's the plain girls like Katie who sit together and discuss inanities such as movie stars, clothes, accessories, hairstyles and boys. Unfortunately, boys usually avoid them. They're generally smart, but dateless. They dress plainly, often wear glasses, and have dirty hair. They come in all sizes – fat, medium and thin. They're nice, but to be avoided unless you need help with your schoolwork. They're desperate and will do anything for a boy who talks to them.

There's a table of guys we call the eggheads. These guys are geniuses who are socially inept with everyone. They usually wear a vest over their clothes – often in purple or tartan. They are often shunned because they are weird and even a bit scary. They avoid girls like the plague.

You don't want to ask them about schoolwork because you wouldn't understand them anyway. They talk science, math and theoretical problems. Many are into board games. They have funny laughs – even snorts. Racovic is like them, but he's the least objectionable and often sits with us. He's a good guy to ask for help with math.

Finally, there's the average guys like me, Hep, Frenchie and JD. I guess we unofficially belong to a group though we'd never admit it. We do what we have to do and interact with the others, but generally we're not too smart, too athletic or too cool. Conversely, we're not too dumb or too uncoordinated or too uncool. Just average.

There are average girls in the same situation as ours. Our guys and these girls interact, and dating is prevalent between them. Babs is one of this group (though – as mentioned - sitting with the seniors these days).

One last group is the commercial students. These are mainly girls – with one or two exceptions – who are in a secretarial course. They learn typing, shorthand and things like that. They are a bit secretive, and no one really knows them. They are kind of in their own world in their own area of the school. They sit by themselves at lunchtime and don't connect with any of the other students.

They are largely forgettable. So that's it – Fort Pitt (a local beer and advertisement). My world, take it or leave it!

I didn't call Babs tonight because I went to the basketball game. It was one of our last games before the state championship games. We were expected to win against these minnows and did easily 96 – 72. Rudy got twenty-two points. So, we're on our way to the state titles. Three more wins and we're champs.

I took the car to the game. After the game, I said goodbye to Hep, Frenchie, JD and the boys. Walking back to the car, I was punched from behind in the head. The culprit ran off, so I didn't get a good look at the attacker, but I imagine it was one of the Maggot's senior henchmen. This was the second time this week that this had happened, and my head hurt like hell.

I'm pissed off now and may have to call in a few favors from the Chief. I'm sure this was a warning to stay away from Babs. This incident only makes me more determined to win her back. When I got to my car, I found a parking ticket on the windscreen. Just my luck! I better not tell Dad, or he'll go ape droppings. I'll just pay the $2 fine myself.

Cop-u-later.

FEBRUARY 24,
1966 – Thursday

I'm still smarting from that whack across the head. Those dirty sons of bitches! Why don't they do it to my face? They'll get theirs someday. Told Hep about the hit. He said he'd talk to the Chief and see what he can do. I'm not crazy about this idea if only because if he helps me, then I'll owe him a favor. He's a crazy MF so who knows what he'd want me to do in return. I'd rather not take that path. I'll just have to bide my time and see how things unfold.

This morning I got my ride to school with Katie's old man. Katie maybe had forgotten the Sadie snub as she cuddled up to me. I can't say I minded all that much as I hadn't touched a girl in days. Perhaps I don't appreciate Katie as much as I should. What's the saying about putting a flag over a girl's head and doing it for Old Glory?

I had lunch with Katie, though, that's because Babs was with the Maggot. Katie and I talked, but I don't remember anything she said. My mind was on Babs. I hope it didn't show. Anyway, Babs said hello to me in passing, but there were too many seniors around for me to say anything meaningful in return.

After school, I had a 'Brigadoon' rehearsal. There was more dancing with my cousin Vicki. She's not bad. I'd date her, but the horror of going out with a cousin would cause a scandal – and bombard me with insults from all and sundry. I hear in some small villages in Europe this type of stuff and even marriage goes on between relatives.

I didn't catch up with Babs at rehearsal so in the evening I called her. We talked for an hour and a half, believe it or not. I wouldn't have believed it beforehand. We had a great conversation about all kinds of subjects, but not the Maggot.

We laughed like hell talking about certain teachers. Chubs – the Chemistry nun – who doesn't have a clue, though Babs thinks she's cute. And Babs' English teacher – Sister Mary Victorie – who finishes all her sentences with the word 'what.' I think she expects you to finish the sentence. Hence her nickname - 'What-What.' One other thing we didn't discuss was the Sadie or her party and my brother Will. Some things are best left unsaid.

I almost asked Babs if she was going with the Maggot, but I refrained in case the news was bad. The Senior-Junior Prom, the end-of-the year formal dance - is three months off, but I'd like to think I have a chance to go with her. Only if the Maggot does an Elvis and leaves the building.

I asked how her sister was doing. Not very diplomatic on my part, but Babs just laughed it off. I certainly dodged a bullet there. Asking out the Turtle would be the end of Babs and me as a couple. Then again, technically, Babs and I aren't going together.

I had a big algebra test to study for tomorrow, so I finally said goodbye. But man, I felt good. Hope is a wonderful tonic for anything that 'ails you. When I hung up, my heart was beating rapidly, and my hands were sweaty. Sure signs of love. I was back in the ball game. It was the bottom of the eighth inning and, though behind in the score, I didn't intend to lose.

Cop-u-later.

FEBRUARY 25,
1966 – Friday

Despite my long talk with Babs last night, I barely saw her outside of Home Room at school. I managed a quick 'hi' at lunch, but also got hard stares and dirty looks from the Maggot and his Neolithic pals. Talked to Hep, and he told me to expect something happening at tonight's basketball game with Westwood Suburban H.S.

We've already made the qualifiers for the championships, so this game doesn't mean much. The regulars will only play a bit of the game in order to save them for the ones that count. Still, we like to see the boys win.

I wasn't sure what Hep meant by 'something happening' tonight, but I can guess that it has to do with a certain crawly creature. Anyway, Hep told me the Chief would be there in case of trouble. This gave me even more reasons to worry. His presence means there's bound to be problems. We play our first qualifying final on March 7th against Eerie Bishop Van Dorkenburg. We're confident the boys will hold up their end.

Well, I had driven the car to the game where I met Hep who was sitting with his friend Pij. I again asked about the odd smell and strange behaviour of some of the students recently. It's like they're drunk, but without the usual signs. Then I mentioned how Lisbeth, the exchange student, said she had got something to calm down from a student.

Pij again dismissed what he called my rantings. Too easily, I thought. I kind of took offence though held my tongue. After all, the smell was obvious. Pij was so coy that I kind of wondered if he was involved in selling this shit to students. Someone is selling illegal substances at school. Someone I hang around with? Look to my own house indeed. Hep said he knew nothing about such things. I was still curious but decided to concentrate on the game. We won easily and – as always – I 'lent' Pij some money. I wonder if I should charge interest on these so-called loans. The game over, I said goodbye. I didn't see the Chief, but it was a short walk to the parking lot, so I didn't expect any trouble. I figured Hep's warning was an exaggeration.

While walking to my car, I noticed I was being followed by a group of guys. I guessed it was the Maggot and his senior cronies looking for payback for me being seen talking to Babs. I started walking faster, but so did they. Finally, I turned around and confronted them. There were five of them and with no one else within shouting distance, I figured I had little choice but to go down fighting.

The Maggot approached me first and took a swing. He grazed my head as I ducked. This was the cue for the others to move in. Just when things looked bleak, I saw the group break up. Standing near them was the Chief with Hep and Pij. 'Stay away, Chief,' said one, 'Our argument isn't with you.'

The Chief and the others kept walking toward the group. The seniors were pissing themselves but didn't retreat. They foolishly attacked. One guy hit me in the groin (these days my least vulnerable body part). After a couple of swings from the Chief and Pij, the seniors ran away. Despite my misgivings about Pij, I was glad he was on my side

I made a small effort to help, but I wasn't needed. Once again, the Chief saved my bacon. I knew I now owed him and prayed the task wouldn't be too onerous. I just hoped none of the teachers saw tonight's brawl or I could be in big trouble at school.

When I got home around half past eleven, Dad asked me to go out and get some ice cream for Mom. I made it clear I wasn't happy about this and gave Dad some choice words. After all I was bruised, and my head and balls hurt, but he insisted and he's the one who 'pays the rent' and supplies the car. I can't say he was happy about my attitude.

After I had bought the ice cream and returned home, I caught a glimpse of Mrs. Pride's house. There were no lights on. It seemed almost deserted. As I hadn't seen Old Lady Pride for weeks, it seemed awfully suspicious. Especially as I saw Columbus, her manservant, lurking around.

I would investigate further one day. For now, I had a half-gallon of semi-melted French vanilla ice cream dripping on me despite the cold weather. Ice cream at midnight. Mom was forty-six years old if not a day so she couldn't be pregnant.

Cop-u-later.

FEBRUARY 26,
1966 – Saturday

Had to stay home tonight because of my comments to Dad last night. I apologised, but he wouldn't let me have the car. I was stuck at home, but I probably would have stayed in anyway as I was battered and bruised after the fight with the seniors last night. My balls were aching like all hell which led me to believe I had been kicked in that region. I had a hernia repair operation three years ago and didn't fancy another.

In the afternoon, I had a haircut at Herb's Barber Shoppe – commonly referred to by those who've been there as Herb's 'Butchertaria.' Herb was one of the 'old timers' at the barber game. He knew only one way to cut hair – what we called a bowl cut. It looked as if he covered your head with a soup bowl and then cut around it. Although my other friends had long ago stopped going there, my loyalty continued. For one reason.

Herb's comic book collection was one of the wonders of the world. From 'Superman,' 'Batman,' the tough babe 'Wonder Woman' to 'The Justice League of America' and 'Blackhawk,' Marvel, DC. He had all the classics. I used to get to Herb's early just to read as many as I could before my haircut.

Herb had a wooden leg – rumored from a World War II injury – and shuffled weirdly from the chair to his bench where he kept his equipment in a formaldehyde jar (except his electric clippers). While cutting, he breathed heavily on the back of my neck which was unnerving.

He barely said a word throughout the ordeal, though he once broke the silence and asked me about school. My stock answer was 'good' - without elaborating - which he accepted without follow-up questions.

Herb's assistant was Dave Major – a friend a year younger than me who I knew from Fear of the Lord Catholic grade school. He now went to the public high school. Dave's job was to prepare things for Herb and sweep the floor. As Herb often smelled of cheap whiskey – and unfortunately for me would be feeling the effects – he would give the scissors to Dave to finish the job. I never complained about this, but can you imagine a 10th grader cutting your hair?

Herb had an electric cutter, but he mainly used scissors. There was the occasional misstep and scratch, but it was all part of the service I figured. He'd always finish the haircut by shaving the back of the neck with a straight razor which he sharpened on a long strap of leather. I remember my grandfather King had one of those. The haircut only cost $1.50 – a bargain. But as usual, the cut made me look like Little Lord Fauntleroy. Did I mention the comics?

So, I was home for the night and watching 'Gilligan's Island' when I heard a knock on the door. It was Hep and Frenchie stopping by to say hello. We went down to the basement to play pool. As normal, my dad greeted the two in his underwear. I was well past being embarrassed at others seeing this as long as girls weren't involved.

Anyway, Hep said he was told by a friend of a friend (he wouldn't tell me who) that the principal had heard about the fight last night and would be dealing with it on Monday. Hep seems to have his ear to the ground so I was somewhat worried as I was in the middle of last night's brawl. With the musical, the Music Festival and the basketball championships coming soon, I could be in deep shit – if I may borrow one of Columbus' phrases.

Cop-u-later.

FEBRUARY 27,
1966 – Sunday

I'm a bit concerned about the shit hitting the fan when I get to school tomorrow after Friday's fight. I'd hate to miss out on a number of things coming up at school in the next few weeks. I was part of the ruckus, but there's no use kicking myself (pun intended). I didn't start the damn thing. Though my balls were acting up. I'm sure one of those Year 12 scabs kicked me in the family jewels when all this was happening.

I mentioned my unfortunate pain to Dad. Just to make sure my balls were OK; he took me to the emergency room of the hospital. I guess he's looking out for future grandchildren. Anyway, there wasn't much a doctor could do. He performed the usual cough thingy on me that doctors do in these circumstances. He suggested I take some aspirin and call him in the morning if there's still pain. I guess I'm cleared to have those grandkids.

I had hoped to rest a bit when Dad took me home. But Hep called and repeated what he said last night. We were in big trouble, and we were liable to miss the basketball and the music festival. There was no use worrying I figured and, after we finished talking, I settled down for a nap.

I dreamed I was called to the principal's office and was confronted by Father Georgia and Sister Georgakopoulos. They were yelling at me and then laughing. Father pointed at me and said I was out of luck and that I couldn't go to any of the planned activities. I yelled back at them, but that didn't stop them from laughing even more. Then they started to dance around me singing 'nah, no, no, no, no – you can't gooo'!

It was like one of those operas. I was in a clown suit singing 'no, you can't do this.' They continued laughing. I put a rope around my neck and attached the end to a tree branch. They say you can't dream that you die – unless you really do die.

When I woke up, I was sweating profusely and needed to get out. It just so happened that soon after I got a call from Cooey Procco who asked if I wanted to see the Jakstown local professional basketball team called the CJs this evening. He said he would give me a lift. Dad was OK with it as long as I didn't take the car. So, Tom collected me, and we went to the Memorial Arena to watch the game.

The CJs smelled big time. They had only won two out of the past twenty games this season. And they lost again tonight. But Willie Bedford, their star guard, piled on thirty-two points. He was very entertaining with his jump shots and dunks. It's a pity that the rest of the team stunk.

I got home about eleven p.m. and immediately went to bed. My balls were still aching, but I was sure I was in for more 'heartache by the numbers' come tomorrow.

Cop-u-later.

FEBRUARY 28,
1966 – Monday

This time the shit really hit the fan. A group of guys – me, Hep, the Maggot, the Chief and some other seniors – were called into Georgie Porgie's office before school had even started. Someone had seen the fight and the unknown stoolie reported us. We were all shitting ourselves, except for the Chief who lets nothing phase him.

Hep, the Chief and I sat alongside the Seniors in a waiting area outside Porgie's office. We juniors were making nervous jokes while the seniors were snarling and looking super serious. After all they had more to lose than us. Their graduations were at stake.

The principal called us in one-by-one. I was the first one called. His desk was deliberately large with a high seat behind it. Porgie was a small man, but when he told you to sit in front of the desk, you sank into a cushioned chair. You had to look up to see him and he looked enormous.

The Prin got to the point right away. He asked me what had happened on Friday night. I said I didn't see anything as I was walking to my car in the parking lot behind the Arena. He noticed a bruise on my head, but I explained that away with an excuse that wouldn't have made it past a Church Confessional. He asked me if I knew who was there, but I responded in a similar vein as Sargant Schultz in 'Hogan's Heroes.' 'I know nothing.'

After a few more questions and some humming and hawing from both of us, he told me to leave and call in the next 'victim' (my word). When finished with our interview, we were to wait outside the office until all had been spoken to. I felt relieved after the ordeal and hoped my 'play dumb' attitude would keep me from being suspended and missing any or all of the school events.

After all of us had gone through this 'Inquisition', Porgie asked us back as a group to deliver his verdict. Surprisingly, Hep, Maggot, the Chief and two of the Seniors were suspended for three days and were banned from attending the basketball games coming up. I and two seniors

140

got off. I wasn't suspended and was allowed to attend the events, but I had to sit with Sam Signoria – the asshole music teacher - on the bus.

How I escaped punishment I'll never know, but it wasn't as good a result as I would have thought. Most of the others would now assume I squealed on them, and I'd be shunned by friend and foe alike. Porgie might as well have put a target on my back.

But if that was the case, Hep didn't seem all that fussed when I talked to him before he went home. He said that the 'stool pigeon' probably hadn't seen me. Strange, as I was the intended target of the seniors. He added, I was questioned because I was Hep's friend. He said he'd see me on Thursday.

I also saw the Chief before he left. He said he stuck up for me and told the principal I wasn't around at the time of the fight. I doubt if what he said to me was what he said to Porgie, but if it was it saved me. Dad wouldn't have been happy with my suspension. The Chief then reminded me that I owed him one. The way he said it sent a chill down my spine. Perhaps It might have been better if I had been suspended.

Mirgat the maggot and his friends were another story. I was sure to be a marked man. The ones not suspended, crowded around Babs at lunch like some palace guards, but without the Maggot there, I liked my chances with her. Leaving the lunchroom, she took the time to say hello and we chatted briefly.

There was a feeling of relief that I had gotten off with only a slap on the wrist. After school, I had dance practice for 'Brigadoon.' I actually enjoyed dancing with Cousin Vicki. I almost forgot that she was my cousin. As we danced, I squeezed her just that little bit tighter than usual. I did say almost!

Cop-u-later.

MARCH 1,
1966 – Tuesday

They say that if March comes in like a lion it goes out like a lamb and vice versa. Who are these people? Anyway, it was a pretty balmy morning, but there was a wind and a few snow flurries. So, who knows what March 31st will bring?

There's still some fallout over the big fight and the suspension. I feel somewhat guilty for getting off when I was the cause of the fight. I thought about going in and admitting everything to Porgie, but what did Rick say in the movie 'Casablanca,' 'I stick my neck out for no one?' Or as in Porgie's case, 'Round up the usual suspects.' The seniors already think I'm a stoolie, so best I be careful.

The morning was taken up with a scholarship test. Three hours of Math and English. Although I hope to go to college, I'm not one of the geniuses of the school, so my chance of a scholarship was bleak – bleaker than bleak, but Dad wanted me to take the test on the chance of a miracle, so here I was. More to the point, we were all instructed by the teachers to sit the exam. I momentarily wished I was Hep who didn't have to take it because of his suspension.

I didn't get to speak to Babs at lunch although we exchanged a few words during Home Room. Between classes, I got a note from her passed to me by her friend Arua. In it she asked me to meet her after 'Brigadoon' rehearsal. Babs continued to be 'guarded' by the seniors. So, I had lunch with Katie. She kind of grows on you after a while. Maybe she's wearing me down. If only she'd spruce up a bit.

After lunch, I had gym class with PE teacher Big Jack Urethera or 'Old Piss Bag' as we nicknamed him. OPB was a giant of a guy, and we were all petrified of him. In gym, we were doing rope climbing and related athletic stuff that I could give a stuff about - no doubt because I smell at it.

One of the boys, Bob Schultz, aka 'Schultzy', started to climb the rope suspended from the ceiling after Old Piss Bag had left the gym for a few minutes. I called him a fuck'n idiot just as the teacher entered the gym.

Big Jack promptly called me over, told me to bend over and pounded my rear with a big paddle he kept nearby during class. It was a huge green piece of wood shaped like a small oar with a hole in the middle to retard wind resistance and make for a more painful punishment. Man did that hurt! My ass came out red, but I didn't give him the satisfaction of showing any pain. There was no use complaining as no one – including my dad – would take my side.

Part of the 'Brigadoon' rehearsal was dance practice with the lovely Miss Vicki. Again, I thought of Rick from 'Casablanca'.

'Of all the dances in all the musicals in this school, she had to be my partner.' She sure smelled nice though.

Afterwards I met Babs. She said she was concerned about the recent fighting and wanted to talk to me, but not here. I said we could catch up at the Music Festival this weekend. She agreed and then – out of nowhere – gave me a peck on the cheek. 'Here's looking at you, kid,' I thought. That movie really made an impression on me.

I felt so good I decided to skip the bus and hitchhike home, but it started to snow heavily. It took me over an hour in the cold to get a ride. I expect March 31st to be a good day after all.

Cop-u-later.

MARCH 2,
1966 – Wednesday

Got up late and thus got to school late. As my mom wasn't in hospital, I had someone to blame. I had a few choice words for her before Dad, who was also late, drove me to school. I had to get a late pass. There's something about being late that's odd. When you enter the classroom, you automatically become the centre of attention.

Everything stops. Even the lesson. All stare while you get your books organised, settle in your seat, give the teacher your pass, and whisper to the students near you where you were and why you're late. Not that anyone really gives a flying you know what. For the moment, you're a distraction from the humdrum. You are the most important person in the room – until you sit down and the class proceeds.

I had no trouble talking to Babs as the seniors had an assembly at lunchtime. We ate lunch together. Things aren't quite the way they were before, but I think I'm slowly getting Babs back on side. The Maggot comes back tomorrow so I guess I'll be on the outer again, but today is today!

Saw Frenchie this morning. He showed me this article from the rag 'The National Curiosity.' The article was entitled 'Christ's father was a spaceman.' The writer had some bizarre theory that an alien from Outer Space knocked up the Virgin Mary (it didn't mention how) and produced a super creature – Jesus Christ. For evidence, it used astrological signs, alleged reports from Rosewell - where suspected aliens are kept- and selected biblical passages.

Of course, 'The Curiosity' also had stories like 'I Gave Birth to a Fish' and 'The Guy with Two Heads' (wouldn't that be cool?). It's a disreputable, yet popular newspaper sold mainly in supermarkets. Lots of people buy it and – dare I say – believe the stories.

I found the article very interesting despite the poor reputation of the source. It paralleled the story of Christ. I shared it with Father McCracken – our religion teacher. McCracken laughed at first, but quickly got serious and told me it was blasphemous. He implied we'd all go to hell if we read trash like this.

After school, we had yet another dance practice for 'Brigadoon.' Vicki was sick so I was given a fill-in partner for the day - Kathy Wasp. Kathy is kind of cute in her own way, but she smells like rancid cheese. I'm not Fred Astaire, but she dances like she's afraid of stairs (boom, boom!). She kept stepping on my toes. Where's cuz when you need her? I hope this isn't a permanent arrangement.

After dancing, we practiced singing for Friday's music festival rehearsal. We sang some songs from the musical 'Showboat.' Not really my cup of tea. I cringe a bit at the song 'Can't Help Loving Dat Man.' Hep and I would have been in stitches tossing that one around.

Cop-u-later.

MARCH 3,
1966 – Thursday

Thursday, and my ride to school with Katie's dad. I'm on Katie's good list again as she cuddled in the car and touched my leg with hers. For once, I didn't really mind as I can sense the world is slowly turning in my direction. I felt comfortable sitting beside her. Things are going well and I'm not letting her little annoyances get to me.

Hep would be back from his suspension today, as would Mirgat the maggot and the other Seniors who tried to bash me – and in some ways – succeeded. Babs was talking to me again. I thought of Lou Christie's song – 'Lightning striking again' – sung in his falsetto voice. What goes around, comes around. When we got to school, I actually walked Babs to her locker. Screw the seniors.

Hep seemed in a cheerful mood when I spotted him. He said there were no hard feelings about me not being suspended while he was. Even though he couldn't go to the Music Festival and the early finals, he was sure he'd make the championship game. How could Porgie deny a student that privilege?

He asked me about my hurt groin. He added that if my balls weren't functioning, I might have to have them cut off. The only job I could get would be as a eunuch in an Arab harem. Always the optimist, Hep. I told him my systems were working just fine, thank you. He did mention that the Chief wanted to see me after school behind the rubbish dump. I had no choice but to meet him. After all, I owed him.

With everything going on in my life, I messed up an Algebra test. Even that didn't bother me. All I could think of was Babs. At lunch – as always – she was surrounded by Year 12s including the Maggot, but I did get to talk to her briefly before school.

We talked about going to the Music Festival rehearsal on Friday where we'd have a chat to find out where we stood with each other. Unfortunately, part of my penance for last Friday's fracas was to sit in the front of the bus to the city with Sam Signoria – the band supremo.

In the choir, Babs is a soprano and I'm a tenor, so we don't sit together at the rehearsal. I'd have to find time to talk to her. Later that day, I paid $20 for a school ring. It's kind of nerdy, I know, but everyone has one so why not me? Maybe I will give mine to Babs – if that's not too much of a courting cliché.

After school, I met the Chief at the back of the school. I dreaded going to this meeting and now I know why. He was smoking what looked like a cigarette but one that had an odd smell like those I'd experienced recently. It was a similar smell to one I sniffed at the Masonic Lodge dance last week as well as with Lisbeth and at a school dance.

I asked him where he got it from. He told me someone from City High was supplying these cigarettes, but he wasn't a squealer so wouldn't tell me the name. He offered me a smoke, but I left well enough alone.

The Chief said he was cool about me not being suspended but needed me to return the favor. He gave me the instructions. I was to get my car on Saturday afternoon and go down to a seedy section of town where I would meet a friend of the Chief's at a church. He would give me a couple of cases of Steel City Beer. He gave me the address.

I was to keep these cases until the evening and take them to the Memorial Arena. There was a hockey game that night. The Chief would meet me at the end of the parking lot, and I would hand over the cases to him. He said it wouldn't cost me any money. He asked me if I understood, and I nodded. He then took a long drag, threw the butt on the ground, grinded it with his shoe and left.

One eventually has to pay the piper. I risked being caught, missing the big basketball games and the Music Festival thereby earning the wrath of Dad and possibly Babs. That's some hornet's nest I've disturbed!

Cop-u-later.

MARCH 4,
1966 – Friday

I woke up in a cold sweat during the night - thinking about the unpleasant task I had to perform for the Chief tomorrow. If caught, I would certainly have to miss important school events I wanted to attend. Even worse, I could be arrested and kicked out of school. I couldn't sleep, so I turned on the radio and listened to Long John Neville on WNBC out of New York. A number of powerful big city radio stations are able to be picked up from far away late at night.

Long John was interviewing a transvestite or a guy who dresses like a woman. I had no idea people such as these even existed. Talk about leading a sheltered life! Luckily, we don't have them here. Anyway, I finally caught a few ZZZs, got up in time and made it to school.

In the morning, we only had a couple of classes before we left the school for the Music Festival rehearsal in Jakstown. The festival is a big deal music-wise. A number of schools were participating to show off their school's musical talent. This was the rehearsal for the real thing on Sunday afternoon.

Our school was organizing the festival here. Next weekend we would travel to Altona as Bishop McGuillicutty was in charge. It was only a short bus ride to the venue, but I was forced to sit with Sam Signoria and his coterie of suck-ups. I decided not to talk to Sam unless he asked me a question. During the short trip, I silently thought of Babs who was sitting toward the back of the bus.

We sang our vocal cords off during the rehearsal, but Sister Fuhrer, the choir Nazi, wasn't happy about our performance. She went out of her way to praise the kids from other schools. I liked the way we rehearsed, but maybe singing more modern songs would encourage us to produce a better sound, I thought.

Songs like 'Edelweiss,' 'My Favorite Things,' and of course the earlier mentioned 'Can't Help Loving Dat Man' just doesn't cut it with our generation. I considered making a limp wrist while singing the latter song, but without Hep it wouldn't seem funny. In Hep's absence, the whole rehearsal was a dud.

Soon there was a lull in the proceedings, and I finally got to talk to Babs. I really laid it on thick. I told her I liked her and wanted to get back together. I even offered her my school ring when I got it, but she laughed. Whether the laugh was from happiness or pity, I don't know, but I would have taken either.

I laughed along with her, nonetheless. We then joked around for a while without her answering my question about going together again. The rehearsal was about to resume so we farewelled one another for now. Before she left, I asked her if she liked Mirgat, but she avoided the question.

I don't remember much about the rest of the rehearsal. On the way back to school, I rode up front with the teachers. I sat beside Sam Signoria, aka Sam I Am after a character in a Dr. Suess book. SIA smelled of cigarettes and cheap Old Spice aftershave.

It was torture. On the trip, I started to think about tomorrow and my ugly task. Could I pull it off? Would I get sprung? Watch this space!

Once again at night, I had trouble staying asleep. I got up mid-sleep and tuned my radio to Long John's station. He was talking with a guy who had cheated on his wife with another man. Things sure are strange in the big city. I turned it off to go to sleep just as a woman started crapping on about a back-alley abortion performed on her using a coat hanger. There are some things you'd just rather not know.

Cop-u-later.

MARCH 5,
1966 – Saturday

Stayed home most of the morning and afternoon as I was shitting myself thinking about the deed I was to do tonight. When I asked Dad for the car for the hockey game, which I was planning to attend after my task was completed, I was hoping he would say no. Unfortunately for me, he barely hesitated before throwing me the keys. He even asked if I needed money. I didn't but took some anyway!

Around three p.m., I told Dad I was going to the library to do some schoolwork. Instead, I took the car to Cabrero City - a dilapidated section of town with old run-down houses which hadn't seen a paint job since Tom Sawyer. There were many bars and – ironically – churches. When I got to the church designated by the Chief, I spied the Chief's flunky.

He was a thin, wiry guy with a 'Gabby Hayes' beard who looked like he'd seen better days. Drunk perhaps? Anyway, this guy got in my car and took me up a back alley to a darkish corner behind an abandoned house. He told me to wait. We waited for what was probably only ten minutes but seemed longer. The mood was so secretive I kind of expected some spy in a trench coat to appear.

Suddenly, the guy jumped out of the car, carefully looked around, and opened a garage door to the house. He took out two cases of 'Steel City Beer', yelled at me to open the back of my car, then shoved the beer in and closed the trunk. He cautiously looked around again, saw no one was near, lit a fag and told me to piss off.

Before I left, he handed me another package – one wrapped up in brown paper and tied with a string. I said he had made a mistake, but he insisted I take the package and deliver it with the beer. He repeated the Chief's instructions. I was to take the goods to the far end of the Memorial Arena parking lot where the receiver would be waiting. I was to wait for a signal before proceeding. He was pretty vague about the signal.

I was nervous but nodded my head and went home. All the way, I felt I was being watched by some sinister force who would pull me over, search my trunk and discover the booty. At one point, what looked like a police car came near me, but went on its merry way. I was hallucinating, I thought. I drove slowly – too slowly. I finally made it home and parked the car in the driveway. I prayed Dad wouldn't open the trunk for anything.

After dinner – around seven – I headed for the Memorial Arena and the hockey game. While driving, I was suspicious of everything and everybody. I just wanted to get rid of my poisoned cargo. I was almost at the arena when I heard a siren.

The officer motioned for me to pull over. Sweat was pouring down my brow as the cop approached the car. I asked the man what the problem was, and he mentioned that my back brake-light was out. I was sweating profusely, but in the dark he didn't notice. Luckily for me. I managed to keep my cool as he checked my license and registration.

I had only gotten my license last October, so I was a bit concerned he would search the car – particularly as the registration was in my Dad's name. After checking my credentials, the policeman gave me an infringement notice. I was told to report to the city police station next week with the light repaired. I thanked him, then got the hell out of there.

Now I drove to the back of the parking lot at the arena as instructed. All that cop stuff made me late. I looked for the signal – whatever the hell that was going to be – but it wasn't necessary. I saw the Chief standing by a car. So, I drove the car up to him and opened the trunk.

In a motion worthy of 'The Flash,' the Chief took the cases and transferred them into his car. He also took the package. He said he was grateful, but so was I that the ordeal was over. I asked him about the package, but he said it was just some menthol cigarettes he bought from the 'beer' guy.

Strange that there was so much secrecy over beer and fags, but my debt was paid. The Chief offered me a beer, but after all that had happened, I wasn't in the mood. I told him I wanted to get to the hockey game. I was just relieved I'd pulled it off without going to jail.

After all that, I decided not to go to the game, and I got the hell out of there. When I got home, I told Dad I left the game because I wasn't feeling well (which wasn't a lie). A sixteen-year-old with two cases of beer and a package that contained cigarettes would make anyone of my age stressful – and therefore ill. I think I pulled it off.

Cop-u-later.

MARCH 6,
1966 – Sunday

Was called in to serve Mass with my brother Will this morning. It gave me the time and place to thank God for helping me dodge that bullet yesterday. I also asked for Divine Intervention in getting back with Babs. A little bit of help from upstairs would not go astray. I'm still pissed off at Will for his unruly behaviour at Babs' party last month. After all, I believe that it led to my breakup with her. But what's a poor boy to do?

After Mass, I got a frightening call from Hep. He said I'd better be careful because he thinks someone saw me last night with the cases of beer. Hep was banned from going to the Music Festival this afternoon as well as the basketball games so he may be giving me a line of bull.

But how did he know about the beer? Did he know about the package? As this is the second warning, he's passed on to me in a week, I wondered how and where he got his information. I was worried all right, as he was spot on with his last warning.

In the afternoon, I went to the Memorial Arena in Jakstown to sing at the Music Festival. Next Sunday the travelling music show moves on to Altona. Dad dropped me off in the City, as I did not feel I neither needed to drive the car or take the bus where I'd have to sit with the wretched Sam I Am from school. When I got there, I saw Babs talking to the Maggot. He gave me a long stare indeed, but I figured I had the Chief on my side if he started anything. I was hoping I wouldn't require the Chief's services as I wouldn't want to owe him again.

Eventually, I got the chance to talk to Babs. She seemed a bit distant at first, but I eventually managed to crack a smile from her. As for the concert, it was the usual mixture of crappy show tunes and ballads. Bill Gilliam – otherwise known as Sloth for his slovenly dress and manner – sat beside me and bored me with his cheerful and enthusiastic manner. This surely was someone who liked 'Can't Help Loving Dat Man.'

After the concert – as usual our group did everything wrong, and the other groups did everything right according to Sister Fuhrer – I had to wait outside the arena to be picked up by Dad. It was getting late and most of the other singers had gone. As I was standing there, I was approached by the Maggot and one of his pals.

Mirgat put his finger on my chest and started poking me. He told me to stay away from Babs. I was shocked that he would confront me this openly and told him where to go. His friend then threatened to bash me, but Maggot stopped him. Perhaps he thought of the Chief.

The Maggot then told me that bad things would happen if I tried to hang around Babs. I just laughed at his threat although I'm sure the two of them could have taken me as I was alone. This may have come to pass right then and there as I wasn't about to back down, but Dad showed up to take me home and I got the hell out of there.

This incident made me want to be with Babs all the more. The boldness of their confrontation made me think about Hep's warning and whether these guys really had something on me.

Cop-u-later.

MARCH 7,
1966 – Monday

I'm still pissed off at that asshole Maggot and his Year 12 crony who threatened me yesterday. The warning to stay away from Babs made me even more determined to win her back. A good start would be to sit with her on the way to the big semi-final basketball game at Steel City next Sunday. To that end, I – with the help of a $5 loan from Hep – ordered a ticket for next Sunday's game.

The day will go like this. First, we travel by bus to sing at the Music Festival in Altona. Then it's on to the big smoke by the same bus as soon as the concert finishes. Hopefully, I sit with Babs both trips. Finally, we win. In a way I hope I didn't put the cart before the horse. To make the semi of the state championship we have to beat Eerie Bishop Van Dorkenburg, aka 'The Dorks' as we call them, tonight. Most looked on this game as a mere formality.

I told Hep about being bullied yesterday, but he repeated that someone may have seen me with the beer on Saturday. I never know for sure if Hep is playing games with me, but he seemed pretty genuine. He told me he'd tell the Chief what happened to me as I did get the beer (and package) for him. To be honest I wasn't that interested in the Chief's help. I can't hide behind him forever. Though he's big enough!

Worse came to worse in the afternoon when I was called to the office. I sweated this for a half-hour before going there. Thoughts of being banned from the game went through my head. And what about my plans to sit with Babs on the bus? Despite looking guilty as hell when I entered the office, I was only called to receive my basketball ticket for next week. I would have kissed that secretary had she not been old and ugly. Hep's information was wrong.

After school, I dropped the car off at Shark's Service Station to get the brake light repaired. It only took an hour, so I waited. I talked to Crazy Henry in the interim. Henry had just been appointed as 'Save the Tiger' Ambassador at the station. Esso was running a promotion whether to keep the tiger (not to be confused with Tony the Tiger of 'Sugar Frosted Flakes' fame) as its advertising symbol or get rid of it.

Henry sported a badge with a 'Save the Tiger' slogan on it. I asked him about it, and he was tickled pink to be wearing it and supporting the cause. Because he was so happy, I didn't tell him that his colleagues were probably making fun of him by appointing him to this dubious position. What they were doing seemed somewhat cruel to me as Henry was semi-retarded. Henry was a character, but a decent guy, nonetheless. I had a lot of time for him.

The car light repaired, in the evening I drove to the basketball game and met Hep and the boys. Hep also bought a ticket for next week's game, but he'll be on the regular school bus and not the music bus as he's banned from the Festival.

I'll meet him at the game - assuming he's allowed to go. I wouldn't bet against him. As expected, we beat the Leprechauns (a stupid nickname for a team) easily 80-58. I could say we were too tall for them, but I'd only get and deserve a long groan.

Now we play the Steel City Holy Ghost (or for us the Caspers) Rollers next Sunday at the Steel City University Arena for the western championship. We're only two wins from the state title. I saw Babs with the Maggot at the game but decided to stay clear for the time being. No use forcing my hand too soon. Go Cruisers!

Cop-u-later.

MARCH 8,
1966 – Tuesday

'It's déjà vu all over again,' as Yogi Berra of the New York Yankees would say. Someone squealed about the beer on Saturday night and now we're in trouble. It was probably the seniors who ratted to get even with us juniors. The Chief was suspended once again which means three things.

One, Hep, a suspected partner in crime of the Chiefs, would also be accused of one thing or another - even though he wasn't within shouting distance of the place. Two, I could be next. Three, with the Chief away, I have no protection from the seniors. Four, Hep was right after all.

I only hope the unwritten no squealing code is followed, and mouths stay shut. I'd hate to miss the game and – to a lesser extent – the Music Festival. Then again, if the Chief stays quiet, I might owe the Chief another favor. My heart can't take it!

Hep is already banned from riding on the music bus to the game and could be banned from going altogether. Frenchie and JD are riding on the regular school bus. So that doesn't leave me with anyone interesting to be with. Except Babs! The Senior secret service detail has her covered tightly, but they won't be travelling on the music bus.

I saw Babs in class and slipped her a note to meet after lunch. I assume she's going to sit with the Maggot at the game, but I'm hoping I can change that. I could be with Babs on the bus If only I didn't have to sit with the teachers. I'll see if I can get out of this situation. Anyway, saw Babs after lunch at the back of the school. I told her I liked her and wanted to get back together. I held her hand and did everything I could to sweet-talk her.

Babs said she liked me, but I was too unpredictable and unreliable. Mirgat was more her style. What could I offer her? She then gave me a peck on the cheek, and said she'd sit with me on the way to the game if I could get out of being with the teachers. A small victory, but I'll take it. This could be my chance to get her to go with me. I was as happy as

Larry – and you could throw in Moe and Curly for what it's worth. I couldn't wait until Sunday.

So, I was in a better mood when I got home only to be told by Mom to pick up Dad downtown. After a long day at school, it wasn't what I wanted to hear, but I grudgingly performed my duty as a son. Before I collected Dad, I dropped into the City Police Station to have my backlight checked by the policeman who pulled me over on Saturday. The whole procedure only took a couple of minutes. I passed the audition.

Now I proceeded to get Dad. I found him at the Royale Hotel – his usual watering hole across from his place of work - where he had been drinking. Dad was in good spirits when I got there and asked if I wanted a drink. I'm not sure if he meant an alcoholic one, but it was irrelevant as the barkeeper only served me a Coke.

Meanwhile, Dad had another shot of vodka. He introduced me to his fellow drinkers as 'the handsome one' before we left.

Naturally, before we went home, we bought a ½ dozen Coney Island Hot Dogs – delicious, but lethal on your breath. Dad told me I was a great son, which made me feel good. He's a pretty decent dad – all things considered. He wondered if Mom would be upset at his drinking. You can count on it, I said. It was terrific just being with my dad in a father-son situation. Such times were few and far between. As Deano sang, 'Memories are made of this.'

Cop-u-later.

MARCH 9,
1966 – Wednesday

Hep survived the 'big stink' on Saturday and wasn't suspended. Considering he wasn't there, justice was served. He said he'll be going to the game on Sunday, but as expected, on the school bus. He didn't tell me about his ban, and I didn't ask. We celebrated by stealing Eggy's lunch and rigging his locker. Considering we're inches away from suspension; this probably wasn't a wise move. We just can't help ourselves.

We're only two wins away from winning the state championship, and b-ball fever is high. The school is decorated to the hilt, the teachers are talking up the western final on Sunday and the school song ('Succour Forever') is being played and sung ad infinitum and then some.

Oddly, though, the school routine is much the same with classes and lunch. Only we're all in festive, non-learning mode. The Chief has been suspended, some say expelled, so I've got to tread lightly. Once again, I escaped punishment without a scratch – bodily or mentally. I must live right. Saw Babs in class and told her I'd like to see her at 'Brigadoon' practice. I soon got a yes reply via her friend Arua.

Saw Lisbeth for the first time in a while. The term is almost over as is her exchange. She'll be going back to Argentina soon. In broken English she thanked me for being her friend. She said she'd be leaving after the basketball games. I'll miss her absolute beauty, but certainly not the hassles associated with her. In another dimension, things might have been different. I won't cry for her in Argentina.

Collected my school ring. It has a fake ruby stone embedded in the setting. The stone is surrounded by the letters OLPS - initials of the school's name - and a picture of a crying cross. Pretty crappy I say. One can only take so much doom and gloom on a ring. Anyway, I decided to give my ring to Babs at musical practice – as corny as this seemed. Hep laughed and wanted to know if she was going to wear it on a chain around her neck.

After school, I had 'Brigadoon' dancing with my untouchable cousin Vicki. I kept thinking as we danced that second cousin isn't that close – genetically speaking. In some European countries, cousins often marry cousins. We're getting much better at our dancing routines. Poor Hep has been saddled with the 'five-left feet' Wasp for a partner.

After practice, I caught up with Babs. I asked her if we could speak privately. We moved to one of the band rehearsal-rooms where I offered her my school ring. She laughed, but said it wasn't at me, but at the situation. She said she wasn't sure she wanted to go with the Maggot or me but needed time to decide.

I told her to take the ring and – if she decided otherwise - give it back to me in a week. She accepted. I told her I really liked her, and she gave me what now is the safe kiss on the cheek. I may live to regret giving her the ring without a commitment, but love does strange things to a guy. Love and basketball – a lethal combination.

Cop-u-later.

MARCH 10,
1966 – Thursday

This is the day before a momentous weekend (knock on wood). I'm going to rehearse with the choir at Altona tomorrow. On Sunday, a bus will take us to the Festival in Altona, then we'll hightail it to Steel City for the western championship basketball game. God willing, actually teachers willing, I'll get together with Babs on the bus.

So, I was on a high to say the least. Even the trip with Katie's father - and Katie rubbing against me on the way to school - didn't seem a drag. I smiled at her once or twice, but not enough to encourage her.

The day was uneventful. Saw Babs at lunch briefly, but she's still sitting with the Maggot and the other seniors. It seemed as if they were giving me dirty looks, but maybe it's all in my head. They can't do anything to me. Another black mark against some of them and they may not be allowed to graduate. Then there's the Chief to consider.

Toward the end of the day, I found a mysterious note in one of my books. It said to meet me out back of school at the end of the day. It was signed Babs, but the signature looked suspicious. I should have ignored the note, but any chance to see Babs had to be taken. That's love for you.

After school I went to the designated meeting spot, but no one was there. Perhaps I was early. When I waited ten minutes more and she didn't arrive, the warning bells went off. I looked up and saw Mirgat and his senior henchmen coming at me from different directions.

The Maggot came up to me and pushed me. He told me to stay away from Babs. I made some smart-ass reply only to be punched from behind by one of his henchmen. The others aggressively joined in the punching and – when I fell – kicking. I tried to respond, but it was no use.

The best I could do was protect my head. After a couple more kicks, and a 'stay away' shouted at me, they were gone. I was bashed up badly and was not a little bit sore – cuts, bruises, pride. My face was relatively untainted. It would have been good to have an unsuspended Chief around.

I managed to make it inside the school to the boys' toilet area where I cleaned up the best I could. I didn't want to call home, as I would have some explaining to do. So, I caught a local bus, a City bus, then slowly and painfully walked home the short distance from the bus stop to my house. I told Dad I had fallen down some steps. Who knows if he bought it? He offered to take me to the hospital, but I told him I was OK.

So, the day that started with such optimism ended disastrously. After being attacked by the Maggot and his thugs, I now wanted Babs more than ever. As for the creeps who did this to me, their day of grief would come. I would bide my time until it was the right moment to pounce. Forgive and forget. I think that's a biblical phrase. When it comes to those assholes, I will do neither.

Cop-u-later.

MARCH 11,
1966 – Friday

I was feeling sore this morning, but I couldn't miss school. I had to go to Altona to sing at the local Arena with the choir. It was a rehearsal for the concert on Sunday. We had a couple of classes in the morning. In one of them I managed to talk to Hep to tell him about the bashing I got yesterday from the Maggot and his soft cocks.

Hep wouldn't be travelling on the music bus, but he would go on the student bus to the game on Sunday. I didn't think he was allowed to go at all, but Hep has a way of getting around these restrictions.

I only caught a glimpse of Babs and didn't tell her about the beating yesterday. I still felt like shit, but I was able to hide any bruises and bumps. It's tougher to hide pain. At lunch, I saw the dicks who did this to me. That's three times I've been hit recently. I'm tired of being a punching bag.

I wasn't about to tell the teachers or Principal as my reputation would have been shot. Maggot and his cohorts looked at me and laughed while I stared at them. I don't know when or where, but I'd get back at them. Revenge would be sweet. Hep said I should talk to the Chief, but it would have to wait, as I felt like death warmed over this moment.

I was in major hurt. The worst thing was I couldn't sit with Babs on the bus as I was still forced to sit with Sam I Am – my bus buddy. This kind of suited me as I needed a chance to recuperate from my injuries on the trip to Altona. It would do me good to rest despite the fact the bus had to go over rugged mountains and the roads were pretty hairy. I was hoping to sleep on this hour-long journey, but it was a toss-up as to whether I'd be able.

We made it to Altona in no time as, just as I had hoped, I slept. I got out of the bus and hobbled to the auditorium. Babs sat with her girlfriends. The Maggot squad hadn't travelled with the choir, so I wasn't worried about another attack. We had a lot of time before the rehearsal, and I decided to walk over to Babs.

After some small talk – I often joke about her mom who's not bad at age thirty-five, still old, but not ancient like my mom – I asked her about the ring. She said she wasn't sure if she wanted to keep it. She seemed a bit standoffish, so I didn't press the point. Perhaps I was pushing it too much.

Now it was time for the rehearsal. We sang our songs including a medley from the musical 'Showboat.' The Egghead Racovic told me how he loved 'Can't Help Loving Dat Man.' Am I the only one who thinks that song is for homos? Note to myself – watch him! The other schools then did their thing. Finally, the combined choirs sang 'The National Anthem.' I found my voice stretching for some of those high notes. How Francis Scott Key wrote this song with bombs 'bursting in air' I'll never know.

Afterwards – following a caning from the Fuhrer who praised the other schools' performances at our expense – we left on the bus to return to school. Babs and singing had made me forget my pain, but once again I felt terrible. I was hobbling to the bus when a senior girl who I didn't know from Adam, stopped me.

She had a message from the Year 12 bullies. She said they would finish the job if I didn't stay away from Babs. I told her what I thought of her message in no uncertain words. Unfortunately, Sam-I-Am heard me and told me off. The return trip took forever as I didn't sleep. For the moment I could only think of Oliver Hardy of Laurel and Hardy – a comedy movie duo of the 1930s – who said, 'This is another fine mess you've gotten into.'

Cop-u-later.

MARCH 12,
1966 – Saturday

I'm really hurting. The bashing I took Thursday has come back to haunt me. I have pain on top of my pain. I'm in luck, as the concert and game aren't until tomorrow. I called Hep and told him how I felt. He told me the Chief had been informed and had a plan he was working on. Hep and I discussed what the Chief had in mind, and it had possibilities, but the bite might be worse than the bark, I thought. I told Hep I'd see him tomorrow at the game.

I also called Babs who can't seem to make up her mind about going with me. She said she would talk to me on the bus to the music concert tomorrow – assuming I can get away from Sam-I-Am. The time for talk is over, but I can't force her to make a decision.

So, I resigned myself to living with my pain, uncertainty and self-pity. Particularly the latter. I had a lot of work to catch up on anyway. I asked my mom to help me with my French. I appealed to her vanity as she fancies herself a Francophile - even though she's probably never been to France. She would never admit she couldn't understand the work, so she's bound to do it. That's less for me to do.

While home for the day, I couldn't help noticing Mrs. Pride's house next door. I had almost forgotten about not sighting Mrs. Pride and the mysterious comings and goings of her chauffer Columbus. My room was opposite her house, and I noticed the covered furniture.

I tried to catch a glimpse of the old broiler but saw neither hide nor hair of her. Every so often, I saw Columbus. He seemed to be enjoying himself with a beer in his hand and what looked like a woman – not Mrs. Pride – by his side.

Despite still hurting from head to toe, I decided to have a closer look in the afternoon. I went outside and peeked through a house window. Sure enough, there was Columbus, a strange woman, alcohol and no sign of Mrs. Pride. There was snow all around, so I was getting cold. That didn't stop me from moving around to the back of the house for a better view.

In the backyard there was a strange mound of dirt which I hadn't noticed before. It looked like someone had dug up a section of the yard and then covered it over. I peeked through another house window. Columbus appeared to have the run of the place. Where was his boss? Well, I only had a brief look so maybe I didn't get the whole picture. I would check out the situation another day. For now, I had more serious shit to wipe.

Tomorrow morning, I have to get to school to catch the music bus to Altona and, afterwards, Steel City. It would be a long day, so I decided to call it an early night. I would likely see those criminal seniors tomorrow, and they wouldn't be happy as I was determined to sit with Babs. Sometimes a man's got to do what a man's got to do.

Cop-u-later.

MARCH 13,
1966 – Sunday

This was one of the longest days of my life, but also one of the more memorable. Anyway, I was feeling a lot better after the bashing I took the other day. It's amazing what a long sleep can do for you. I had to get to school to catch the bus, so Dad gave me a ride.

Before we left, I briefly caught up with Babs, and looked forward to sitting with her on the trip to the concert and the basketball game. I begged, no, cajoled him to let me sit elsewhere, but that despicable Sam-I-Am wouldn't have a bar of it. One good thing. I didn't have to cope with the Maggot and his fools as they were going directly to the game on the later school bus. They wouldn't be around for the concert.

We got to the Altona and performed the usual pap. I thought we did a good job considering the selections, but the ever-critical Georgakopoulos thought otherwise. There's no pleasing that penguin. After the concert and a quick lunch at the arena canteen, we boarded the bus for the trip to Steel City for the Western Championship game. I took a chance and asked Sam-I-Am if I could sit elsewhere. The heart of stone turned into a heart of gold. He agreed and I eagerly shared a seat with Babs.

The trip to the big city took two hours, but it passed in a flash as I don't think I ever had a better conversation with Babs. We laughed, told jokes, related our life stories (from our exaggerated points of view naturally) and talked over things. We were serious at times, not so serious other times.

I felt a real connection with her and hopefully she with me. Before we got to Steel City, I again asked if she would go with me. This time she said yes. I don't think I'd ever known real happiness before this. She said she would break it off with Maggot that very night.

When we got to the Steel City University Arena, I saw Babs go off to talk to the Maggot. I went to get something to eat and then find Hep. While looking for Hep about a half-hour later, I suddenly noticed five senior boys surrounding me. I thought here we go again, but this time I was determined to take them on. I was tired of being a Palooka. I ran around to the side of the arena to avoid the teachers.

I was ready to go fight when I saw the shadow of a big man-child named the Chief. I wasn't about to ask him how he was allowed to go on the bus after being suspended, but his presence was a godsend. He was with Hep and some other Juniors.

The fight didn't last long as the boys got stuck into the seniors. Despite my previous injuries, I wasn't about to miss getting my revenge. I joined in whole heartedly. They were going to get back what they'd dished out to me. Our boys did us proud and made a meal of Maggot and his crew. After a number of well-landed punches, the seniors had had enough.

Before they left with their tails between their legs, the Chief said if any one of the Year 12s squealed to the principal, he would get his friends from town to give the seniors a 'talking to.' We all knew what he meant and who he was referring to. I was never so glad to see the Cavalry as when I was surrounded. I couldn't thank the lads enough.

Anyway, these events took us right up to the start of the basketball game. I couldn't find Babs, so I sat with Hep. It was a great game. Rudy Mingo – our 11th Grade hero – got eighteen points and had ten rebounds. The game went right down to the wire.

We were behind by one with twenty-five seconds to go when Rudy got the ball at the top of the key and swished it through the net. The last seconds were tense, as the Caspers threw everything at us. Once again Rudy was the star as he blocked a last second shot. We won 59-58. Now it was on to the State Championship game next Friday.

We were in euphoria on the bus trip home. I sat with Babs, although she was strangely quiet on the return trip. I was too excited and exhilarated to analyse it, though. It had been a long day. And what a day! We won the game; I got my girlfriend back and – like in the Western movies – the bad guys were admonished. If I was a betting man, I'd put some dough on the Irish Sweepstakes. The planets had finally aligned for me.

Cop-u-later.

MARCH 14,
1966 – Monday

Despite getting home at 1.30am (Dad reluctantly picked me up from school), I hardly slept last night. I still got up early, as I wouldn't dream of missing school with everyone basketball crazy. Indeed, when I got there, it was bedlam. We're playing for the state championship this coming weekend. There was a euphoria I hadn't seen in ages. Even some of the Senior boys were friendly although, after yesterday's events, I had doubts this would last.

The brawl at the game inevitably means there's always the chance someone squealed, and I could miss the ultimate game on Friday. I found out we'll be playing Bishop Goldthump from Harristown for all the marbles. We'll be going there by bus. Anyway, no one was called to the office by the principal, so perhaps even Porgie's caught up in the pure joy sweeping the school. Or the Chief's warning hit home with the seniors.

I did manage to see the Chief to thank him for saving me from a severe thrashing. I knew one day the bill would have to be paid. That's what happens when you sell your soul to the devil. The upside is that with the Chief on my side it wasn't obvious I'd have to worry about the seniors.

I ran into Hep. I thanked him for helping me out yesterday. Hep had told me what the Chief had in mind when I talked to him on Saturday. Although I was skeptical about its success, it had worked a charm. I'd owe the Chief a favor, but I was happy as a pig in shit to be in his debt.

The whole getting even thing had been planned by the Chief and it worked to perfection. We both laughed our asses off at the seniors getting some of their own medicine. The fighting was a good tonic for my injuries. Whoever said revenge was sweet knew what they were talking about.

Hep said he found out he was allowed to go to the game with the school this week (of course his ban didn't keep him away on Sunday).

He wondered if we could sit together on the bus to the championship game, but I was hoping to sit with Babs, so I put him off for now.

Speaking of Babs, I searched for her, but – other than Home Room – didn't catch up until lunchtime. She was subdued on the bus home last night, but I thought it was because she was tired. However, she still seemed chilly toward me. I finally asked what was up.

She said she didn't like what happened at the University Arena last night (she obviously had heard about the fight – probably from the Maggot). She decided not to go with the Maggot or me. She sat with her girlfriends away from the seniors. Just when I thought my life was a big go, it turned into a big no. I was again without a girlfriend. Just like the person in the 'Beatles' song, I was a real 'Nowhere Man.'

To compound my grief, we had 'Brigadoon' dance practice after school. Cousin Vicki wasn't there, so I had to dance with Kathy 'Twinkletoes' Wasp. I'm not exactly Fred Astaire, but Wasp is a far cry from Ginger Rogers. I hope she's not my permanent partner. What started as a great day ended up in Mudville. At least I got my health!

Cop-u-later.

MARCH 15,
1966 – Tuesday

Beware the Ides of March! I'm still sweating it out about being able to go to the game. Rumors are that the guys who had been fighting Sunday have been identified (probably by one of the Seniors' cohorts) and will be banned from this weekend's state championship. In the Chief's case, it may mean expulsion as it's his third time. So far, I've escaped twice from trouble, but maybe the third time's the charm.

Babs didn't sit with me at lunchtime, but for that matter neither did she sit with the Maggot. She did say 'hi' to me this morning at Home Room, however this frostiness isn't what I expected when I sat with her on the bus, and we again became boyfriend/girlfriend. Didn't she take my ring as a sign of her fidelity?

Ran into Lisbeth. The term finishes on Friday and she'll be going back to Argentina. Friday's game will be her swan song. She's still as beautiful as ever, but she's trouble as well as a temptation, so I've avoided her recently.

In broken English, she thanked me for helping her. I couldn't help noticing she was a bit disoriented. She wobbled when she walked and slurred when she talked. As this wasn't the first time, I wondered if she had taken some substance. Who was selling this shit?

Lisbeth said she had a going-away present for me because I had been so nice to her. *I didn't want to be nice,* I thought, it just happened. She had a farewell gift she wanted to give me later this week. I insisted it wasn't necessary.

Just knowing her was enough for me. Who said I couldn't lay it on when I had to? She insisted. I was curious as to what she could possibly gift me. I said goodbye, and soon forgot about her present or the way she acted just now. I had other things on my mind.

After school, I went to a meeting of the school newspaper 'The Perpetual Press.' I thought I could use some extracurricular activity to help me get into college next year. So, I signed up as a reporter for the paper.

I was immediately asked to write a story about the bus trip to Friday's game. It sounded like a lot of work, but I pictured myself in a trench coat and fedora - with the word 'press' written across the brim - and agreed. Asking questions and writing crap. Right up my alley.

The rumor mill turned out to be almost right. On one hand, no one was suspended. On the other hand, because of the happenings at the last game (read the fighting), it was decided that the buses taking the students to the championship would be segregated – boys only and girls only. You'd better believe we were pissed off, as no one really wanted single sex buses.

The socials finally were of some use, as they started a student petition to get signatures to get this ghastly single gender bus edict overturned. Our Student Council Reps were then going to show Porgie the petition and see if weight of numbers could change his mind. My plan to sit with Babs – if she wanted me to – on the long trip to Harristown was temporarily on hold. Hep could ride on the same bus and sit with me, though I was still holding out for Babs.

Got home and stayed up late doing schoolwork. I want my work to be caught up by the end of the week, so nothing stands in the way of the big game. Imagine – Our Lady of Perpetual Succour – State Champs. It had a nice ring to it that lingered with me until I fell asleep.

Cop-u-later.

MARCH 16,
1966 – Wednesday

We play Bishop Goldthump (the Vultures) this Friday in Harristown. They beat the Libertyville Catholic Librarians (aka the Bookworms) by ten points to reach the championship. They have done well to get this far. We've been told they're more of a one-man gang with a gun player in Steve Care who averages over forty points a game, but we're a team and we're going to kick their asses.

Excitement was really building at school, and Hep and I were determined not to be left behind. We paid our $5 for a ticket this morning to reserve our place on the bus and a seat in the arena. And our prayers were answered.

Our Student Council Reps persuaded Porgie that only the freshmen and sophomore buses needed to be segregated by sex. The junior and senior buses would be mixed. Our Reps came through big time. So, I have a chance to sit with Babs – if she's not still mad at me.

As mentioned, the whole school is experiencing basketball fever. Rooms are decorated in team colors (yellow and red), players are adored (I admit I shook Rudy's hand damn near a dozen times) and cheerleaders are leading cheers during lunch, between classes and – depending on the teacher – in classes. You'd think classes had been suspended. I wish!

A pep rally was held at lunchtime that included an introduction of the players (not that we didn't know them). Each player's name was followed by riotous cheers. There was also theater (a group dressed in our colors pounding a Vulture – representing them) and mock games. We won every time.

Other activities included singing songs (our school spirit song 'On You Succour was popular), hanging effigies of the other team from the gym rafters and spreading general goodwill amongst all of the student body. A couple of seniors – but not the Maggot – actually shook my hand. Even Lisbeth gave me a peck on the cheek. She said that wasn't my present, but a preview. I was more intrigued than ever as to when I would get that gift and what it would be.

So, we were one big happy family – except for Babs. I wouldn't say she was unhappy, as she was laughing with her friends at the rally, but I'm sure she had other things on her mind. Then, maybe not having a boyfriend was a load off her mind. I have to remember to talk to her before the game.

After school we had 'Brigadoon' practice. We rehearsed the songs from the musical. Later we had dance practice. Once again, I had the Catherine Murray-want-to-be Wasp. My cousin had another partner which wasn't good news for me. I hope it's only temporary.

We tried on costumes after practice finished. The fittings were checked, and the kilts were to be returned at the end of the rehearsal until needed for the production next month. I got my kilt and all the crap that went with it. Hep made a crack about my big ass sticking out the back of the kilt skirt. He couldn't talk as he looked like Liberace in his outfit.

Hep also inquired as to what I was wearing underneath. 'A gentleman never tells,' I replied. I also got my bartender uniform for my big bar scene. But all this was just minor league stuff. In two days, we'd be going to Harristown for the big game. If there is a God, we'll win.

Cop-u-later.

MARCH 17,
1966 – Thursday

I can hardly wait. I'm so excited I'm busting (or is it bursting?). Whatever, only one more day and we'll be off to Harristown for the state championship game. After I got dressed, I went downstairs. My father, who normally sleeps in on Thursday, was dressed in green for the big St. Patrick's Day festivities. He insisted I wear a shamrock pin which I dutifully put on, though I don't really feel the connection to the Irish like the old fools who dress up do.

I got my usual ride with Katie's old man. To my surprise, both Aldo and Katie were dressed in green. She even had her hair streaked with the color - though I doubt she or he, for that matter, had Irish blood. As always, Katie sat right next to me. I asked her if she was going to the game. Sadly, she said no. I briefly felt a little bad about that, but not for very long to be honest.

At school, Mo Glink – a kid in my history class and always the rebel – wore the Protestant Irish orange. He was making fun of Mr. Ranan who has a strong Irish Catholic background. Doc really got stuck into him when Mo started to make fun of the Irish.

Mo asked him what a seven-course Irish meal was. The answer was a six-pack and a potato. I actually thought Doc was going to kill him.

Talked to Babs at lunch. She seemed pretty friendly and happy to see me. She said she wasn't ready to go steady with me or anyone else. She said she was going to the game but would sit with the girls. She would be on the same bus with me, Frenchie, Hep, (and probably the Maggot) so I'd see her.

Oddly, a couple of seniors said hello. Jack Hammon, the star football player for our school and his mate John Balog – a tough guy, but a jokester and one of the few year 12s I got along with – both knew my dad and asked me to give him their best on St. Pat's Day. Perhaps these guys talking to me means the worst of my battles with the seniors were over. Maybe last weekend's fisticuffs did some good. We should fight more often!

The bus was leaving at three p.m. tomorrow so I would have time to go home before returning to and taking the bus from school. We'd be coming back early Saturday morning and dropped off at OLPS. I wanted to get home quickly today to have a rest before my long day began. When I got home, I laid down and slept from four p.m. to eight-thirty. I was surprised no one woke me up for dinner. When I went downstairs, I saw Dad passed out on the kitchen floor.

He was wearing all his Irish St. Patrick's Day paraphernalia. I helped him up to get him to bed when he started to sing Irish songs like 'Too Ra Loo Ra Loo Ra' and the ever popular - and overdone - Irish ditty 'Who Put the Overalls in Mrs. Murphy's Chowder?' Mom was still recovering from her gall bladder surgery and Kitty was in her room. Will was watching TV. So, I ate a bowl of Wheaties and retired to my room.

After my long sleep I wasn't tired. Knowing I had a full day tomorrow, I tried to sleep, but couldn't. So, I listened to Long John Neville on radio until 1.30am. More aliens and a government conspiracy to keep flying saucers a secret. Finally, I went to bed. It took me a long time to get to sleep as I was too excited about the big day coming up. Bring it on!

Cop-u-later.

MARCH 18,
1966 – Friday

Had a couple of classes this morning, then we were allowed to go home to change and pack a small bag with food and incidentals. I said goodbye to Mom and Dad, who were there to drop me off at school. We had to be at school by two-thirty p.m. to catch the bus to Harristown for the big game.

I saw Babs briefly before I boarded the bus and asked her again to sit with me. Ask is probably too tame. I begged her to sit with me. She turned me down with a thud. She wanted to sit with her girlfriends. It hurt not being with her, but I was happy to sit by Hep.

Frenchie and JD were also close by, so I expected an interesting trip. Eggy was there as well with some of his nerdy friends. Also, on the bus was Lisbeth on her last school function before returning to Argentina. Before we left, I said goodbye to her. She again mentioned the present she had for me. I laughed and nodded my head. I didn't expect anything. Still, she said she'd have it for me later.

We left school around three p.m. for the three-and-a-half-hour trip. We were pretty confident our team would prevail but knew the Vultures would be tough. The key was to keep their star player – Steve Care (we referred to him as their 'Care Package') – to a reasonable number of points. We felt we had the better overall team. Rudy told me yesterday we would win and if he was that confident then how could we be any less.

On the way there, we bullshitted, rated the girls and made fun of Eggy. The Maggot was in the back of the bus, so he wasn't near Babs. We also played cards – ace-deuce – for nickels and dimes. The nature of the game meant there were some big pots.

Each person was dealt two cards. After throwing in an ante in the middle (the middle being the floor of the bus), a person could bet all or part of the money from the pot. The object was to bet whether the next card would fall between the two cards you held. If it wasn't, you matched

176

the pot. If you got an ace, you could call high or low.

Anyway, the pot became huge when Joe (aka PS) Croyle (the initials were after a girl we tried to get Croyle to go with named Prissie Sarp) bet the entire pot holding the king and a two. A two was pulled out of the deck and he had to match what was in the pot. When it came to my turn, I had a Queen and a four, went for it all, got dealt a five and won $10.

This money came in handy when we made a pit stop on the way. At a Howard Johnson's rest stop, I got a large coke and a couple of packets of chips. While here, I saw Babs talking with the Maggot which made me somewhat jealous, but the game was the thing. My problems with Babs could wait.

We got to Harristown around six-thirty p.m. – about an hour before the start of the game. Hep and I both got a hot dog. He chatted with Mason – his Sadie date – who wasn't allowed on our bus as sophomores had their own bus transportation. At seven-thirty p.m. – after we got to our seats and the National Anthem had been played (yawn) – the team came out onto the arena. The cheers were deafening. We were ready to play ball.

Cop-u-later.

MARCH 18, 1966
Friday – The Game

What a game between the Jakstown Cruisers of OLPS and the Harristown Vultures. The lead ebbed and flowed all evening. We were on the edge of our seats throughout as we watched our boys do their thing. Rudy was fantastic and chipped in ten points in the first half as we took a four-point lead.

But the Vultures were not finished. They came back to take the lead by three at three-quarter time. Steve Care was as good as advertised and put in shot after shot. It came down to the last few minutes.

Down by a point, our Jim Gruce decided to shoot the ball from outside the key. We had to wonder why he would attempt such a low percentage shot. Miraculously it went in, and he was fouled to boot. He nailed the foul shot. We led by two. Rudy then stole the ball from his unsuspecting opponent with a minute to go, put in the layup and made the subsequent foul shot. A five-point lead to us.

Still, the Vultures wouldn't be denied. The 'Care Package' dribbled the ball the length of the court and scored. Then he stole the in-bound pass and put in another two. We had a one-point lead with thirty seconds to go. Care again stole the ball from our guy.

It looked curtains as he dribbled down the court and took a shot from the key. The ball rolled around the rim for what seemed like an eternity before bounding away. We got the rebound with 15 seconds to go. They had to foul. We made the two foul shots, then put the icing on the cake with two more foul hoops with two seconds to go. We won 88-83. The 'Package' had forty-five points, but we had the title.

When the buzzer sounded, we all went berserk. The Cruisers were the state champs. We hugged each other and jumped up and down. We sang our song and cheered our boys – continuously. Even some of the seniors got into the hugging action. All I needed to make the day complete was a hug and a kiss from Babs, but I didn't spot her. Later I saw her hugging the Maggot so it kind of soured the moment – if only temporarily.

We got on the bus later for the long journey home – yelling and screaming out the bus windows. 'We're number one', we shouted to no one in particular and to everyone. This lasted quite a while. The teachers did nothing to curb our enthusiasm as they were as excited as we were. It took a long time for the bus to settle down, but eventually we got on with our journey home. Our group went back to our ace-deuce.

I had won a couple of bucks when I heard a commotion from the back of the bus. Everyone seemed to be looking there so I decided to check things out. When I pushed to the back, I couldn't believe my eyes. Lisbeth had her shirt pulled up and her bra off. She was showing her boobs to all and sundry.

When she saw me, she smiled. 'I told you I had a going-away present for you,' she said with a mischievous grin, 'In fact, I have two.'

Cop-u-later.

March 19,
1966 – Saturday

Things happened so fast last night I can barely make sense of it. Lisbeth flashed her tits at the back of the bus. Although they were magnificent and extremely compelling to look at, no make that stare at, I felt a bit like a peeping Tom. My big brother instincts kicked in, so I took my jacket off and covered her rather enormous breasts. Naturally, that act made me quite unpopular with the other guys and maybe even the girls.

The teachers in the front of the bus heard the ruckus and rushed to the back. They whisked Lisbeth to the front, then told us to shut up the rest of the trip. They took some of our names and said they would talk to us on Monday. So, the rest of the trip was pretty quiet.

As it was late, most of us slept. I sporadically dozed off, with periods of wakefulness. I kept seeing Lisbeth in all her glory. I doubt if I'll ever see that Argentinian student again, but she certainly made an impression on me. In addition, she managed the impossible. She temporarily put our State Championship on the back burner.

We got in at three a.m. I found a pay phone outside the local hospital and called Dad to pick me up. I had to wait 20 minutes before he got there. Strangely enough, Babs had just finished a phone call and was waiting for her ride. It was cold outside as I realised Lisbeth still was wearing my coat.

We chatted about the game – avoiding that 'unfortunate incident' on the bus. We were both tired, but Babs was upbeat. I got the impression we still might have something going. I told her I'd call her, and she didn't object. Her ride came first followed by mine a few minutes later.

On the way home, Dad and I chatted about the game. It's still hard to believe – State Champions. Of course, I avoided mentioning the other incident. Then he dropped a bombshell. My sister Pippa and her boyfriend Ennis were getting married. I suppose it was inevitable and I guess it's a good thing. It may curb his philandering. May! If they want to live with each other and have kids, marriage makes sense.

It's just it seemed a bit sudden. Pip only turned twenty-one two months ago, and both En-ass and she were still going to college. All kinds of thoughts went through my mind. Did they have to? There was never an official engagement. All things considered; I was happy for her. I guess congratulations were in order when next I saw her.

I went to bed about four a.m. but had trouble sleeping with all that had gone on. The trip, the game, the championship, the boobs, Babs, Pippa getting married. I finally dozed off, but the morning came quickly. I had to get up earlier than I wanted as I had 'Brigadoon' practice in the afternoon.

Once there, I went through the motions of singing, dancing, and reciting my bartender lines as I was otherwise preoccupied with thoughts of the events of yesterday.

Cop-u-later.

MARCH 20,
1966 – Sunday

If I wrote a novel and included the events of the past few days, readers would consider it too outlandish to be credible. It would not be believable. I don't know which was more memorable – winning the State Championship basketball game or seeing Lisbeth's bazungas. I had to write a story for the school paper about the bus trip and the game. How would I clean this up?

Then there was Pippas's shotgun wedding. And my older sister Biddy and her husband-to-be DD are having their traditional wedding next month. I'm supposed to be an altar boy. Things are moving as fast as a runaway freight train. Too fast to digest.

I decided to stay in and do some homework as I was somewhat jaded from all the events of the past two days. I was able to finish a clean version of the game for the school newspaper. After that, I found doing work near impossible as my mind wandered. Around four p.m., Hep called and said there was a victory party for the basketball team at a primary school beside OLPS.

By staying home and doing a limited amount of homework this afternoon, I earned some 'brownie points' from Dad. So, he said I could take the car to the party if I was home by midnight. I didn't really like this Cinderella scenario, but if I wanted the car in the future, I'd best be home by then. I also didn't want to turn into a pumpkin!

I picked up Hep at 6. When I got to his place, his public-school pal Con and Fido were there to be taken to the party. I wasn't happy as Hep hadn't told me about the two freeloaders. Especially Con. I smelled trouble brewing! Anyway, the party was great. The basketball players were there as well as some of the cheerleaders and – of all people – Babs.

Babs had gone to the party with her friend Richard – a senior. I didn't look on Richard as a threat as rumor had it, he liked guys. This bothered others more than it did me. Live and let live I say. I was more concerned that the Maggot was there. Babs was with him for a while, then at some point came over to me. It was great. We talked, we danced, we smooched, we acted like boyfriend/girlfriend.

One could hardly call this gathering calm. Students and friends were going all basketball crazy. Naturally. At different intervals, each of the basketballer's names were called and everyone cheered wildly. Later on, the party started to get rowdy as I suspected alcohol and perhaps something else got the crowd going.

That strange odor again. Could Con and Fido have anything to do with this? Lisbeth had mentioned a student had given her something to calm her down. The Chief had mentioned that he got his 'funny' cigarettes from a student at City High. Con went to City High. Eventually the yelling got out of hand and the caretaker ordered us out by 11.

I told Babs I'd take her home, but unfortunately, I had Hep, Con and Fido with me. Hep and Fido I knew from school, but Con was more of a mystery. When Con and Fido got into the car, they started swearing and yelling at the top of their lungs. I was OK with that. Then Con started to insult Babs about her outfit, hairstyle and even her sexual proclivities.

At this juncture, I pulled over to the side of the road and told Con and Fido to leave. Con got aggressive and called me out to fight. But when he and Fido got out, I took off. Hep was pissed off, so I took him home right away. I drove Babs home where we made out just outside her house. I knew that Con and maybe Fido would want their revenge, but that was for another day. For now, it was Babs and me and nothing else mattered.

Cop-u-later.

MARCH 21,
1966 – Monday

Surprise! When we got to school this morning, Home Room and 1st period were cancelled for a pep rally to honor our champion basketballers. Each of the guys were introduced at an assembly by the principal. Every one of the boys got a huge cheer when his name was called. The juniors really rocked the gymnasium when Rudy Mingo was introduced.

There were yells, catcalls and whistles galore before the coach talked about each individual hero and his contribution to the winning team. The rally continued for an hour, and included a speech from the team captain, presentation of the State Championship trophy, and many spirited songs including 'On You Succour' – our fighting theme song. And then of course the school song Succour Forever

When the rally was near its end, the principal stood up for what we thought would be a boring speech. Porgie thanked the guys, the coach and the students. He then surprised everyone by giving us the rest of the day off. You should have heard the cheer. The noise was jet airplane-like!

We were all revved up and ready to run for the hills until I remembered we had 'Brigadoon' practice scheduled. When we got to the music room, we discovered the Fuhrer had called it off. Chalk one up for our side. Just to make sure, in case she changed her mind, we got the hell out of there pronto.

Anyway, I looked for Babs, but I couldn't find her. I did run into Hep. He told me that the principal accepted that Lisbeth was solely to blame for the incident on the bus on Friday. As she was leaving to return to Argentina, nothing would be done to her or to the others. I was sorry that Lisbeth left without a proper goodbye, but under the circumstances, what did I expect? I did know I had given her my coat on Friday, and it hadn't been returned.

Hep also told me that Con and Fido weren't happy about being dropped off in the middle of nowhere (well, not really – I was under the impression it wasn't all that far from their homes). I didn't need any more enemies. I told Hep I'd make this right.

I saw Fido as we were leaving. I apologised and said I'd buy him a dozen hamburgers next time we're at Stuver's Hamburger Place. He liked that idea, and we shook on it. Now if I can only avoid going to Stuvers with him. As for Con, Hep told me he often skipped school, but it wouldn't be hard to find him.

After a short search, we discovered him on the bridge over the Stringybank River. When I saw him, I said I was sorry and put my hand out in friendship. Con smiled, then came up to me and gave me a good one in the gut. I fell down, once again, sore, then got up to continue the fight.

Con laughed and put his arm around me. He held up his hand, then said all was forgiven. I'd had so many hits recently I felt like a Mohammed Ali sparring partner, but who was I to hold a grudge? Besides, Con was one of those bulky Eastern European types and had fifty pounds on me – maybe more.

We walked along the river and smoked Lucky Strikes. I wasn't much of a smoker, as I didn't get much out of that vile habit. I smoked one, but didn't inhale, as a peace offering. I looked for evidence of those crazy smokes going around school, but I didn't see or smell any remnants. I'm still not convinced Con's innocent of being the supplier.

We then raided a convenience store where the chocolate milk was sitting outside unattended. Our next stop was the Boro, a poor run-down section of town where Con lived, to hang around. I saw Pij in the distance and decided to make my exit – stage left - as Pij always hits me for money.

Besides, I can't get my dad's words out of my head about Negroes. What if he's right? My dad would call Pij 'uppity.' I suppose that means he doesn't know his place. And yet Pij has helped me get out of jams. It's a conundrum alright. It was getting late. I hitchhiked home.

I wanted the car as I was hoping to see Babs. Dad wouldn't give me the Buick or the VW as I was out past midnight last night. I asked Will if he could get a friend to take me to Babs' place only to be rebuffed in a rude manner. I didn't feel he made much of an effort. This pissed me off as I had taken him many places in the past months.

So, I called Babs and had a wonderful conversation about Porgie giving us the day off and what each of us did. I fibbed and told her I stayed in and did homework. I then asked her if she would be my girlfriend. Once again, she said she'd think about it. After an hour talking, I had to get going as Dad interrupted the conversation and said he wanted to talk to me. I told Babs I would see her at school tomorrow.

Dad didn't seem himself when I saw him. I wondered what was up. His two daughters were getting married, so I thought he'd be happy. It turned out I was right. Something was amiss. He told me he needed to take a trip to Washington D.C. tomorrow, and he wanted me to go with him. He was a bit mysterious about the reason. The plot thickened as I felt obligated to accept.

Cop-u-later.

MARCH 22,
1966 – Tuesday

Dad kept his cards close to his chest about this little trip to D.C. It's about a two-and-a-half-hour drive from here. He didn't tell me a thing until we got over our state line. Then the bombshell! Pippa was pregnant by Enass and had to get married soon.

Since the baby was due in November and it was the end of March, the math didn't add up. We had to go to a place in West Virginia to get a back-dated wedding certificate, in order to give the baby the appearance of legitimacy. It seemed like a lot of phooey to me, but Mom was a stickler for that stuff and Dad wanted some company.

The trip was anything but nice. The roads were narrow and over steep areas. Cliffs were prominent on the one side of the road. It got a bit hairy when another car passed us from the opposite direction. The weather was OK, not snowing, but the roads were wet and slippery from melted snow.

Then there was Dad's incessant smoking. Because it was cold, he kept the windows up. I tried to sleep, but how could one under these circumstances? Besides, Dad needed someone to talk to so he would not fall asleep, drive off the road and kill us.

Eventually, we made it to this plain building that looked like it was made of cardboard. After meeting this guy (there's always a guy in these instances), we were taken to a back room of what supposedly was the Courthouse.

You're kidding me, I thought. The guy was right out of the TV show 'Green Acres.' But this person was no rube. He played that role, but indeed, he was quite the wheeler-dealer. He held all the cards and knew it.

Custis, of course it is, was his name. He called us friend, but – believe me – he was no friend. He wanted $1000 for the fake marriage certificate. Dad offered him $500. They agreed on $850 in cash. The guy saw us coming, all right. The certificate was indeed a magnificent piece of forgery. It had the official-looking titles and artwork on the front. It was signed by the appropriate people I gathered.

It stated that Siobhan Philippa Gaughan and Ennis Patrick Lysaght were married at Podunk Centre, West Virginia on 21 January. Of such things honor is maintained. My mom would be able to keep the family name respectable. En-ass was far from respectable and would sleep with anything on two legs. I think everyone in our family knew this, but Pippa. If that's love, deal me out!

Anyway, soon we finished our business, paid the man, and got the bogus certificate. Now for the long drive home. I was anxious to get back as I missed Babs and there was still celebrating to do over our championship. On the way home, Dad decided to stop at a local bar and have a celebratory drink or three. Straight vodka with a beer chaser. He offered me a beer, but I declined as I was hoping he'd let me drive.

It wasn't to be. When Dad was ready to leave the bar, he insisted on driving – forgetting about the mountainous roads and his condition. I could only cringe as he went from one side of the road to the other – at times getting perilously close to the edge of the cliff. It was a relief when he finally reached the highway. But here there was no improvement in his driving. I asked to take over, but he said he wouldn't let a sixteen-year-old drive 'on such treacherous roads.'

To my relief, he was stopped by a cop. Dad used every trick in the book to try and persuade the officer to let him go with a warning. He even invoked the name of his brother – Andy – who has some political clout in this region. The cop let him go with a warning, but only if he let me drive. Before we got home, we stopped for dinner. We finally made it home around midnight. Luckily for me, Dad slept most of the way.

When we got back, who should be waiting, but Pip. 'We got it – Yatze boo,' Dad said in his bastardisation of an eastern European phrase, 'How about a nitecap?' 'Nos krovya,' he shouted as he poured straight vodka into a glass. He offered me one, but I was too tired to do anything.

Drinking was not on my mind. I went to bed but heard Dad and Pippa toasting their success multiple times before I drifted off to sleep.

Cop-u-later.

MARCH 23,
1966 – Wednesday

After my bizarre trip to West Virginia yesterday, I was only too happy to get back to school. I missed Babs, and I finally felt we had something going between us. Unfortunately, I saw the dreaded Maggot talking to her. I need to trust Babs and vice versa, but that still didn't stop me from seeing 'green.'

The euphoria at school had continued unabated in my absence. Everyone was as high as a kite as one would expect of students at the state champion school. I really can't say state champions enough. It seemed a might lonely on the eyes not seeing Lisbeth, but her contribution to the school is now legendary. We will never forget you, Lisbeth! Indeed, I finally submitted my story of the bus trip and the big game to the school newspaper. Without being specific, I thanked Lisbeth for her contribution to the school and wished her well. I'm not sure how that will go over with the editor.

Speaking of whom, Rich Casey had his tail up that I handed it in so late. He said he wanted it Monday. I told him school was cancelled Monday and I was away yesterday. That didn't wash with him, as he went on about deadlines and responsibility. He accepted the work anyhow, but with no promise of future assignments. I only hoped my journalistic career wasn't over before it had begun.

Anyway, next week is the annual 'Future Teachers Day'. Each class is to be taught by a selected student instead of the teacher. Doc Ranan nominated me to teach his History class. I can't see myself as a history teacher, but it might be fun bossing around my classmates.

I wonder if I can give homework and detentions. Hep gave me a bit of shit and said he was going to be naughty during the class, but I told him where to go. I figured Ranan would be there to stop any miscreants.

Nominations for class president and other officers for next year's Senior class have to be in next week. I'm kind of interested. I'd have to get thirty kids and five teachers to sign a nomination form. There would be an election later. I may try for class president, though the socials usually have a lock on the class officer positions. F--- them. You've got to be in it to win it!

After school, had 'Brigadoon' dance practice. I'm back with Cousin Vicki. Down boy, I thought. It was good having a partner who knows the steps (and can carry me). Kathy Wasp is nice enough, but... Let's just leave it at that. Practice went well. I'm actually looking forward to this production.

Well, today's the first day of spring; spring has sprung, the grass is ris, I wonder where the birdies is. When I got home, I thought I'd check out Mrs. Pride's house to see if she had returned. With the beginning of spring, the snow was melting, and you can see bits of the yard now.

I walked over to the house and peaked in the window. All I saw was an empty shell with covered furniture. It looked as if no one had been in there for the longest time. I tried looking in another window, but again saw no sign of activity. Where the hell are you, Mrs. Pride I thought?

Suddenly I felt a tap on the shoulder. It scared the bejesus out of me, but it turned out to be Columbus. 'Now why you be looking in that window, Gussie?' he said. He always referred to me as 'Gussie.' I hate that name. I stammered and reached for a credible answer, but eventually stuttered a weak and incomprehensible one. I then boldly asked him what was going with the covered furniture.

'None you mind, young 'en,' he answered, 'You best be on your way'.

He didn't seem particularly angry, but the whole thing bewildered me. I was too scared to ask about Mrs. Pride and slowly moved on. As I was walking to my place, I again noticed the mysterious mound of dirt near the back window. This was worth looking into at a later date.

When I got in the house, I noticed Dad lying on the couch. Mission accomplished yesterday; he was asleep. I briefly saw Pippa who didn't look all that pregnant to me, but what did I know? I didn't say anything to her as I felt a bit awkward knowing what I knew. She might have a bun in the oven, but I was more interested in having a bun to eat before dinner.

Cop-u-later.

MARCH 24,
1966 – Thursday

Katie was especially perky this morning during our weekly ride. As usual, she sat beside me. I was OK with that, but then she started talking about some shopping trip she went on. I nodded politely but tuned out. She was cuddling up to me again. With her father driving it's awkward being in this position.

I have a theory that Katie's encouraged to do as she does by her dad and my dad who want me to ask her to the Prom. I'm not interested in that scenario. I want to ask Babs, of course, but our relationship is such that who knows where we'll be in two months? Anyway, I lied when we got to school and told Katie I had to study for a test so I could quickly get the hell away from her.

Meanwhile, Doc Ranan is giving me the shits. I have to teach the History class next week for Future Teachers Day. He's making me do all kinds of crappy things in preparation. I'm still thinking homework and detentions!

As for my political ambitions, I got the five teacher's signatures without hassles, but I'm having trouble getting thirty kids to sign my nominating petition for class president. It looks good if you're a class officer when applying for colleges, which I'll be doing next year.

As expected, Jack Cavendish is running for president. Regis Hoss, our current junior class president, isn't interested. Cavendish is one of the socials who mocks everyone not in their group. My friend Donny Munchkin is going for vice president. Donny is one of the ordinary students like me, but he's going up against Josh Shalich – the popular school drum major. I wouldn't give him much of a chance.

School baseball is starting soon, and I have the musical 'Brigadoon' to think of so who has time to be President? But as they say about our country's President, LBJ all the way!

During French class, Racovic – the Egghead – bounced his superball against the wall when Sister Mary Cheree briefly left the class. Racovic is president of the honor society, so this seemed out of character. He put the super bouncy ball away just as the nun walked in. He was lucky to get away with it. This made me think that maybe he's an all-right guy after all. We often tease him even though he tries to fit in with our group. Maybe I can get the others to lay off him.

School ended early to enable us to see the annual varsity-teacher basketball game. The school is still on a high after our sterling state championship victory last week. To us the players are gods (small g). So, there was lots of booing when Mr. Rockoff – the coach – refereed in favor of the teachers.

Fouls not there were called on the varsity team, and the benefit of the doubt always went against them. I know it was a fun game, but we don't like our boys to be beaten by anyone. At the final buzzer, the cheating got the teachers home 66-64. I briefly saw Babs at the game, but she wanted to sit with her friends. At least she wasn't with the Maggot.

When I got home, I caught up with Pippa and her future hubby En-ass, who are temporarily staying at the house. Pip asked me about the trip to West Virginia. I told her that the deed had been done. She would no longer be considered a loose woman. Her reputation was intact, and her child would be legitimate. I don't think she appreciated my sarcasm and she told me in no uncertain words that I could put those comments where the sun don't shine.

Cop-u-later.

MARCH 25,
1966 – Friday

It's all happening. The school production of 'Brigadoon' is only three weeks off. Pippa and En-ass are preparing for a secret wedding next month (their wedding certificate will say they were wed in January) though I don't know when or where. Biddy and Duane Oss are having a real wedding in Steel City in a few weeks.

There are still the signatures to get for class Prez. I have a history class to teach next week. And baseball is right around the corner. If this was a TV show, I'd have just the given the viewers a preview of future shows, and I thought things were hectic last week with the basketball.

Then there's Babs – an on-again, off-again saga. Is she my girlfriend or not? On one hand, she's been quite affectionate with me lately. On the other hand, she continues to talk to the Maggot. Since our brawl and the Chief's threats to the Seniors, they have laid off me. So, things are in flux with Babs, but overall peachy. Perhaps not a ripe peach just yet. I saw Babs and told her I'd visit her tonight at her home.

As for 'Brigadoon,' I still don't know who my dance partner is going to be on the night of the production. Will it be Cousin Vicki or 'two left feet' Kathy? Had practice after school with the Wasp. Sweet Mother of God! I'm close to getting the thirty signatures needed to nominate for class president. I need them by Monday. I keep asking myself why I need this aggravation.

When I got home, I saw Pippa again. I'm expecting a big announcement soon about her 'sham' marriage. Let's hope it gets done before she starts showing her bump. As for Biddy, she's going to have a lavish wedding at a big cathedral in Steel City. She officially confirmed Will and I as altar boys for the wedding Mass. The wedding rehearsal and the ceremony conflicts with some of the 'Brigadoon' performances so arrangements will have to be worked out.

After dinner, I found out I couldn't get either of the cars. I asked Will if he could get one of his friends to take me to Babs' house. He's only fourteen, but there are drivers within his social circles. You'd think that with all the times I took him places, he might have done me this favor. I

193

didn't even ask for a ride home, but he said he had to go somewhere right away and couldn't spare the time to do as I asked.

I was pissed off and called him every name in the book, and even a few that hadn't been invented, yet still he wouldn't make the effort to get someone to take me. 'Get a cab,' he said.

Revenge will be sweet when it happens, I thought, and it will somehow, somewhere.

So, I walked to my Grammy Gaughan's house (about four blocks away) to beg her sister – my Great Aunt Edie who lived with Grammy – to let me use her car. She said I could use her '52 Ford if I put gas in it and bought her a carton of cigarettes. She certainly likes her smokes!

This was easy-peasy as the gas was cheap and I got Pip – a heavy smoker – to get the fags. I told her I'd do something for her if she made the purchase (with my money of course). She agreed. Her requests couldn't be any worse than those of the Chief's.

By the time I got to Babs' place, I discovered Babs had gone out with her mom. I knew I should have phoned her first. The Turtle let me in the house and said I could wait until Babs came home. I sat down on her coach and briefly petted the dog, Milly. The Turtle then sat close to me – a little too close for my mind. I didn't want to go where she was taking me, so I told her to tell Babs I had been there, and I left to pick up Hep.

I collected Hep and we went to an amateur (non-school) basketball tournament at the school gym. Here Hep met his friends Con and Fido which to me spelled trouble – with a capital T. I suspect one of them is selling some weird crap at my school and who knows where else?

But, except for abusing some of the players, they were pretty much well-behaved. I didn't notice any untoward activity by them, especially Con.

If anything, Con treated me like a real pal – which made me nervous. We stopped off at Stuvers after the game to pay Fido those twelve burgers I had promised. At Stuvers you order then bring your food to the car to eat. I was relieved the guys didn't make a mess of my aunt's car. When we finished, despite protests from all of the group, I took them home early and got the car back to Aunt Edie. She was already on her second pack of cigs.

Cop-u-later.

194

MARCH 26,
1966 – Saturday

With the production of 'Brigadoon' getting closer, practices are more intense, and on a Saturday afternoon! Once again, I'm dancing with my 'cuz. I admit I look forward to being with her. Perhaps I need a cold shower!

I did my dances, then rehearsed my short role as Frank the bartender. I talked a bit with Babs, but in keeping with our hot/cold relationship these days, she wanted to hang around mainly with her girlfriends. At least she's staying away from the Maggot.

Anyway, Sister Fuhrer took us through the grinder with mixed results. She wasn't happy and labelled the whole musical 'sick.' I hope the reviews of the show are better than hers. I'd hate to embarrass ourselves on the night of the performance.

While here, I told Hep I'd meet him tonight at the Canteen. I don't know why I go there as it's so ho-hum. Maybe I go because you get to meet girls from the public schools. I'm sure Hep will bring Con and Fido along with him. That could mean trouble, but as I told him I'd go, I thought I'd better see it through.

At the canteen, things looked pretty bleak the first hour. Then I ran into Amy Sing, the daughter of the local Chinese laundry owner. Her father's business always cracks me up as could anything be more stereotypic? Amy seemed glad to see me. We danced, then went outside and made out.

I'll tell you one thing – Babs is good at the smooching thing, but she has nothing on Amy. I have to be careful as there may be spies from our school and this could get back to Babs, and I think Amy has a boyfriend. But as much as I like kissing Amy, I'm hung up on Babs. Amy invited me to her house for dinner and although I hate Chinese food (I hear it's made of dog or cat), I accepted. I gave her my phone number and told her to call when ready to have me over.

Once again, there was that ungodly smell. I noticed it as we arrived, so I'm not convinced Con, and Fido are the suppliers of this mystery substance. I dare not call it a drug as I don't know much about it, but it appears to be widespread among high school students.

Even if I caught them selling this shit, what the hell would I do? Squealing on the guys would label me for life as a dog. The word would get out and I would be ostracized by all schools from here to kingdom come. For now, I would keep my cards close to my chest.

Things being piss poor at the canteen – meaning no luck for the others with the babes - Hep, the boys and I left. We split a quart of DuBois Budweiser Beer compliments of Con. It quickly went to my head though I only had a few swigs since I was driving. I felt woozy. We went looking for girls to pick up, but I was less optimistic than the others that we would succeed.

For one, what kind of girl would get into a car with four guys who had been drinking? Two, Con was embarrassing to be seen with. We would stop by some girls walking along the sidewalk. Con would ask them if they wanted a ride. His tongue would be sticking out and he would be licking his lips. When they inevitably turned down his invitation, he would insult them by calling them sluts and worse.

This farce went on for an hour before I could take it no longer. I pulled the plug and told the boys I would drop them off where they wanted before I went home. They did persuade me to go to the Coney Island restaurant for hot dogs. CI is an institution in Jakstown and has been serving drunks for fifty years.

They also have the worst looking dogs – smothered in onions on a soggy bun with a relish whose contents I defy anyone to figure out. On top of that, the frankfurter is covered in a type of meat sauce (repeat the same defying as with the relish). Top all that crap with ketchup and mustard. Though less than appealing by appearance, the hot dogs taste fantastic.

One of the cooks/servers is called 'Pickles.' Who knows his real name? He lines up six hot dogs in buns on his hairy right arm and puts all the extras on the dogs with his left. It's quite amazing how he balances the dog, the bun and all the condiments and toppings even if the process is borderline unsanitary.

Our usual waitress is Irene – or Sweet Irene to us. She's fifty, if not a day, but quite fun. We joke around with her by telling her she won't get a tip if she doesn't treat us right. To which she always replies, 'again' in a sarcastic tone. The routine has been done to death, but it always makes us laugh. The old routines are always the best.

Cop-u-later.

MARCH 27,
1966 – Sunday

Got my aunt's car again to go see Babs. Dad was PO'd about me staying out past the witching hour last night so I couldn't use the family cars. Wasn't he young once? Once more, I had to buy Aunt Edie a carton of cigarettes. That means I have to use the services of sister Pippa to buy the fags. That means I owe her again. That means next time I'm going to try to buy them myself.

Before I left home, I got a call from Hep telling me that the Chief wanted to see me. It took me less than a second to realise what he expected. I owed the Chief a favor for rescuing me from the Seniors at the game. When I met Hep at his house, he and the Chief were waiting. What he wanted to do blew my mind. He said he needed my car to do something and that he would bring it back in an hour.

Of course, I was less than happy with this arrangement because my aunt treated the car like the child she never had. I wanted to be able to show my face at family functions – something I wouldn't be able to do if the car wasn't returned in one piece. Even worse, suppose it was involved in something illegal? Or involved in an accident? But what could I do, but agree? This would make us even.

The Chief dropped us off at the local basketball tournament where Hep and I met Fido and Con. I suspected those two were up to their old shenanigans and maybe selling those foul substances. I kept an eye on them, but they spent most of the time giving the raspberry to all-state star Dick Smith who was playing for one of the amateur teams.

About an hour and a half later, I went outside the venue to check for the car. There was still no sign of the Chief who was supposed to pick us up there. Hep reassured me the Chief was a safe driver and that there was nothing to worry about. I thought of General Custer. Famous last words!

We were tired of waiting, so we walked to a local hamburger joint where I was so nervous, I could only eat 3-15c burgers (18c with cheese), fries and a chocolate shake. While we were eating at a table, Con started to make cracks about Fido's girlfriend.

Whether it was in fun, I don't know, but Fido obviously took offence. Soon the two were going at it tooth and nail. Both were big and brawny lads who knew how to handle themselves. Each one got in their licks. However, Con knew all the tricks and soon had Fido subdued in a head lock.

I was tempted to stop it, but Hep told me it would be better to stay out of it. After trading punches, both guys suddenly stopped brawling. Despite the sheer anger they had exhibited moments before, they immediately made up and were asshole buddies again. Who can figure? Hep said this was a normal occurrence. They were really good friends who couldn't stay mad at each other for long. So, they got cleaned up and finished their food.

After two and a half hours, the Chief still hadn't shown up with Aunt Edie's car. I feared the worst. I wouldn't know what to tell my aunt so I suggested we go back to Hep's place by bus and maybe I could spend the night there to avoid the atomic bomb sure to be detonated when my aunt found out her car was missing. We said goodbye to Con and Fido who went on their merry way to who knows where! Hopefully not to sell anything.

When we reached Hep's place, the car was parked in the front of the house none the worse for wear. I looked at it carefully and marveled that there wasn't a scratch to be seen. There was no sign of the Chief, but the keys were in the car under the seat. Hep somehow knew where they'd be.

There was an odd smell like some tires had been burning. And I found a funny looking cigarette and a used rubber in the back seat. Disgusting, but a small price to pay to get the car back in one piece. I never really asked the Chief why he needed the car. Frankly, I didn't want to know.

It was late so I went into Hep's place to phone Dad to tell him I'd be home soon. When I came out fifteen minutes later after chatting with Hep's parents, I discovered two hubcaps missing from the car. Stolen, I assumed. This would cost me, I know, but a car in the hand was worth two hubcaps in the bush.

Cop-u-later.

MARCH 28,
1966 – Monday

Aunt Edie was distressed that her hubcaps were stolen last night and made that clear to me and Dad. Dad was unconcerned, but glad when I said I'd pay for them. But, as the car is vintage 1952, they're not going to come cheap. I doubt she'll ever let me drive that coupe again. I was just happy there was no damage. Who knows where the Chief went when he took the car?

Unfortunately, it's still important I have some backup with the seniors in case they come after me again. In that case, I'm glad the Chief is on my side even if I do pay for it with my 'pound of flesh.'

It's Monday, so I got to see Babs. Love can be a wonderful thing, but it's illogical. I don't know which way the wind is blowing with Babs, so I wing it and pray I get it right. Today she was OK – not too affectionate, but willing to talk to me. She seems to want to be with her girlfriends a lot. And she's still talking to the Maggot.

I think I have a truce going with the seniors. I hope so, as my mental health won't allow many more favors owed to the Chief. I heard that the Maggot has a new girlfriend, but that's only a rumor that I hope turns out to be true. Then maybe I'll have Babs to myself.

I have other concerns. I signed up for the baseball team. We have tryouts the next few weeks. The snow is more or less gone and, though it's wet outside, the ground should dry out soon and training will start.

Then there's Doc Ranan, the history teacher, who is on my back. I have to write an introduction and a lesson plan for the History class I'm taking on Wednesday. Who would want to be a teacher anyway? Low pay, crappy kids. I always wanted to be a cowboy or fireman. Perhaps it's not too late.

Now there's the class presidency. I turned in the required signatures to be nominated. But on second thought, I'm of two minds whether to continue with my candidacy. If I go on, I'd have to campaign, give speeches, kiss babies. Well, maybe not the latter.

If I won, I'd have lots of work to do. On the other side, Dad would be very pleased, and it would be look good on my college application. I can't pull out of the race without being branded a chicken. I'll have to think of a cunning plan if I decide to withdraw from the race.

Finally, there's the big musical 'Brigadoon' in a few weeks. My worst nightmare has come true, as I've been permanently assigned Kathy 'I Couldn't Have Danced All Night' Wasp as a dance partner. We've been moved to the back row to hide her lack of rhythm. I'll have to leave right after the performance on the first day of the production to get to my sister Biddy's wedding rehearsal anyhow. I'll totally miss the Saturday performance.

Two pieces of good news. I finally got my jacket returned to me. I had put it over Lisbeth on the bus to the big game when she revealed her melons. It took a good ten days for it to arrive back at school. This leads me to believe it was sent from Argentina. I wonder if it has her scent on it.

And the school newspaper came out with my story of the game. Unfortunately, the reference to Lisbeth had been deleted. Still, it felt good to see my name above the storyline, and the story read well. Perhaps I should think of being an ace reporter for some big metropolitan newspaper. Like Clark Kent!

I found out from Mom that Biddy, Pippa and Kitty went to Steel City yesterday for Biddy's shower. The wedding is on April 16th. It's interesting that Pip hasn't announced her back-dated wedding (with the bogus license). She needs to get a move on as she's pregnant and will be showing sooner rather than later.

As you can see, I'm a busy SOB. On top of it all, Will – my brother – is giving me the shits as he keeps 'borrowing' my clothes. I'm still annoyed he didn't ask a friend to take me to Babs' place last week. 'O what a tangled web we weave when first we practice to deceive.' How's that? Two Shakespeare references in one day.

Cop-u-later.

MARCH 29,
1966 – Tuesday

Doc Ranan's giving me the shits with all the stuff he's making me do for this crappy History class I'm taking tomorrow. I'm teaching about the French Revolution. I thought it would be interesting if I demonstrated the use of the guillotine - preferably by using a teacher as the aristocrat. Sacre bleu! Seriously, I'm pretty much prepared. I figure things will be OK. Maybe I'll impress Babs.

Speaking of Babs, she sat with me at lunchtime. I think I'm making progress on this girlfriend/boyfriend thing. Babs still talks to the Maggot, but I saw him with another girl. Perhaps the rumors are true, and he's going with someone other than Babs. Maybe for this reason, the seniors have backed off me. A few have even talked to me. Then again, it could be due to the Chief.

After school, there was baseball practice. We're having tryouts for the team. The first session was torture. Leideman, aka PP for Porky Pig the fat baseball coach, put us through a fitness test. We ran laps, we ran sprints, we had two-person piggy-back races.

Dave Griffiths and I were partners. We almost won the p-b competition, but he dropped me in the semi-final and that was that. I'm hoping we actually throw some balls and get a few hits soon. I'm trying out for catcher because I figure it would be the easiest way to make the team. Understandably, no one really wants to catch.

After school, I stuck around with Hep to see the movie 'The Cardinal.' It was dull as dishwater – about a guy who went from priest to cardinal over his lifetime. We spent most of the time talking to some Sophomore girls as Babs wasn't there. Let's hope none of her friends saw me or I could be in big trouble if she finds out.

I got home late because of the movie. Once again, I noticed Columbus pottering around in the garden. There was still no sign of Mrs. Pride. And once more, there was that mound of dirt in the back yard. I need to investigate further now that the snow's pretty much gone.

Perhaps Mrs. Pride went away to Florida or somewhere warm for the winter. But it seems strange she's been away for so long. And what about her furniture?

When I got home, I saw Pippa and overheard her talking about a wedding. She's going to have to do something soon before someone notices the battle of the bulge. The big thing now is Biddy's wedding to Duane Oss in just over two weeks.

As mentioned before, Biddy asked brother Will and I to be altar boys, but 'Willy' and I are not getting along. I saw Will wearing one of my shirts and went bananas. I guess I wouldn't mind lending him some clothes if he asked, but that's not in his vocabulary – obviously.

Cop-u-later

MARCH 30,
1966 – Wednesday

I finally got to teach the long-awaited History class. I was a bit concerned after seeing some of the other efforts. In Chem class, Mo Glink was mixing some chemicals together to show us a chemical reaction. He got one all right in the form of a gaseous cloud that smelled of rotten eggs. For the second time this year, Chubs had to evacuate the classroom.

And Bonnie Rasza got more than she bargained for in English. Her translation of Chaucer included some very bawdy words indeed. We asked her numerous questions in that class.

But I think my History class went well. I did a bit on the French Revolution. As part of my lesson, I explained how the guillotine worked. I had the class eating out of my hand as I made Hep put his head into a fake guillotine. I was pretty gory with my description and made sound effects that even scared Hep while he was in my mock device.

I think Doc was fascinated with the demonstration and, dare I say, the class. He didn't have to do much. Still, it was good he was around as I'm sure the knuckleheads would have given me shit otherwise.

I tried to give a detention to one kid who shouted some half-ass comment about boobs in the guillotine, but Doc shook his head vigorously from side to side. He gave the clown a very hard stare which shut him up. He did let me give homework, but I have to do it as well. What's the point?

Anyway, the whole day was without our regular teachers, so it was pretty damn easy. At lunchtime, I ate with Babs. She seems OK being with me. I don't think the Maggot's interested anymore though during the day I saw Babs talking to him. I wasn't happy, but I trust her more now that I know the Maggot is seeing another babe.

There was no baseball practice after school, so I told Hep I'd pick him up to watch the amateur basketball tournament at school. Despite the presence of Con and Fido, no problems occurred here. Afterwards, Hep persuaded me to take him, Fido and Con to Stuver's fast-food joint.

On the way home, Con asked me if he could drive. I thought of all the stress I had with the Chief the other day and told him no way. Con wasn't going to take no for an answer. He grabbed the steering wheel as I was driving and started turning it from side to side. This wasn't cool as he turned my car into the other lane where a truck was oncoming. I grabbed the wheel back from him and got out of harm's way just in the nick of time

Everyone was laughing furiously at his antics, but I was pissed off and made myself clear on this matter. Con reacted as he always did when he didn't get his own way. He wanted me to pull over and fight. I managed to defuse the situation by making some dumb joke.

Then I took the boys home. Con is more bother than he's worth and getting on my nerves. I'm going to tell Hep I don't want to hang around with Con anymore. Fido's OK. I still wonder if Con's the one selling drugs to the students though I have no evidence he's doing so. I'd have to say it's doubtful as he's too damn dumb to organize such an undertaking.

Biddy's wedding is a little over two weeks away, and she's working furiously on those last-minute details to make it a success. Pippa is still living at home. I would hope her wedding announcement is soon. Otherwise, her reputation will be shot as people will wonder when she was married.

Anyway, both Dad and Pip were having a few drinks (Pip ill-advisedly). When I got home, they started giving me shit and teasing me about going with Babs. Will, my brother and the one who blabbed about her to them, joined in. Well, I got angry and started wrestling him. No blows were attempted and Dad broke things up quickly. He scolded us and sent us to bed.

Pippa and the Old Man continued on their merry way once we left. There's some ill-will between Will and me which I hope ends soon or it could get out of control. As I was going upstairs to my bedroom, I could hear the strains of 'Danny Boy' coming from the living room. Could 'Mrs. Murphy's Chowder' and those dastardly overalls be far behind?

Cop-u-later.

MARCH 31,
1966 – Thursday

Got my weekly ride with Katie and her old man. Katie seemed pretty upbeat. As usual, she sat by me and rubbed her leg against mine. I pretended to ignore it, but I decided to go with the flow. It wasn't an unpleasant feeling by any means. I was happy to see her not gloomy.

I too was upbeat upon reaching school. I got compliments about my teaching from some of the students – mostly the girls – and from Mr. Ranan. Just as well I didn't give detentions. Maybe I could be a History teacher when I get older.

I was PO'd when report cards were handed out later in the day. I was hoping to make the honor roll but missed out by getting a C plus in French. Why not a B? All my other subjects were B plus or better. I guess I'm not going to Harvard, and definitely not on a scholarship. Worst of all, I lost my honor pass.

Results of the scholarship exam were released. I didn't get one. Not that I expected it. I'm sure some did well and will be rewarded, but I'm not curious enough to find out who they are. I guess if I go to college, it will have to be the old-fashioned way – paid for by my parents. Still, I wasn't all that down. I'm now eating lunch regularly with Babs, and not a Maggot in sight.

After school we had a 'Brigadoon' performance from the start to the finish. I'm now permanently dancing with Kathy 'I Can't Dance' Wasp. Perhaps I'm being cruel cause Kathy's a nice girl and not all that bad looking. She's smelling better as well, but I was 'hot to trot' with my cousin Vicki and I miss her. Now Hep's with her – the lucky dog!

I also practiced the bar scene, which occurs toward the end of the musical. If nothing else, this role gives me a chance to act and say a few lines – as short as the scene may be. Our first performance is on the day of my sister Biddy's rehearsal. So, something will have to be worked out if I'm to be an altar boy. I'm sure brother Will would be happy if I wasn't, as we've been crossing swords lately. Our wrestling match last night is still hanging over our heads.

The weather has improved with the beginning of spring. It's a bit cool, but the sun is shining, and the birds are singing (why did I say that drivel?). March really is going out like a lamb. The old wives' tale is true.

Once home, the improved conditions gave me a chance to get a better look at Mrs. Pride's house. I peeked through a window to look inside. Some furniture was missing, and the ones still there were covered. I could see her chauffer Columbus and he seemed to have people coming and going. And that mysterious mound of dirt in the backyard? Sinister thoughts entered my mind.

I decided to check out the dirt to see if I could come up with something to explain why the ground had been disturbed. Thoughts of Mrs. Pride buried there entered my mind. Suddenly Columbus appeared and chased me away – though in a kindly fashion. Columbus is nothing if not diplomatic. So where is Mrs. Pride?

I'm going to investigate further this weekend. Let the chips fall where they may. The die is cast and I'm going to find out what. How's that for another Shakespeare reference?

Cop-u-later.

APRIL 1,
1966 – Friday

First day of April, and we're just full of hijinks or maybe we're just full of it. The boys and I submitted an announcement to the office from a fake teacher asking the secretary to page Freddie Fudpucker. She butchered the announcement just as we had hoped – much to the amusement of the students.

Whether the brass liked it is another story. We didn't stick around long enough to find out. Hep suggested we try and get the secretary to page Mike Hunt, but this is a Catholic school and I figured we better not push our luck.

Then we left a message for a teacher asking him to phone Mr. G. Bear. Naturally, we gave the zoo's number for the return call. I'm not sure if this call was made by the teacher, but the idea sounded good, and I could picture it clearly in my mind. So, I was in good spirits at lunchtime when I sat with Babs. She invited me to her place tomorrow night. I said yes but couldn't help thinking this may have been her April Fool's joke.

Had baseball practice after school. We're still in the tryout stage, but I was in Nirvana as I was practicing with Rudy, Stan Rock and Jim Gruce from the champion basketball team. It's heady stuff, let me tell you.

As mentioned, I'm going out for the catcher position, but also second base. It would be fantastic if I made the team. I got a hit in a practice game, but also missed a grounder. I'm not sure when the team will be announced.

At night I got the car, although I'm not quite sure why as I didn't ask for it. Never look a gift horse so it's been said. Or something to that effect. Drove the boys (Hep, JD and Frenchie) various places looking for babes. The basketball tournament was a bust, so we left early, then, we had a quick stop at the Canteen. Hep had a look but insisted after ten minutes we could do better elsewhere. This was followed by the now futile search for girls walking on the sidewalk in town.

As expected, (from my end) no luck! What girl in her right mind would get in a car with four guys who ask if she wants to go to a party? What planet are we on? Why do I participate in this piece of street mayhem? I guess it's on the off-chance we might be successful in our girl quest.

The whole night was dullsville, as the beatniks would say so I decided to drop the boys off early. On the way, a cop stopped us to warn me that the car was overloaded. He let us off with a warning. This wasn't an April fool's joke.

When I got home, I decided to have another look at Mrs. Pride's place. There was a light on inside, but no activity I could see. I decided to check the mound of dirt in the back again. The atmosphere was quite eerie – something that wouldn't have looked out of place at Halloween. I was determined to get to the bottom of this mysterious scene.

I grabbed a shovel from our garage, snuck in the back and dug. The ground should have been hard after winter, but it was obvious someone had dug previously as the digging took little effort. I soon got a result from my shoveling. I came across a number of bones imbedded in the damp dirt.

It was hard to tell as it was dark, but it looked like human bones. Just as well I didn't find a head, or I would have freaked out. This whole exercise was getting a bit scary. I had visions of finding Mrs. Pride's body if I dug further.

Soon, I heard sounds from people leaving the house. I covered up the objects as best I could and made like Speedy Gonzales to get the hell out of there. From behind my garage, I had a clear view. I didn't spot Columbus, but I noticed another guy – the latter looking the worse for wear.

A big guy with huge muscles, he wore tattered clothes and had that unusual smell that seems to be dominant these days where kids hang out. He looked mean and ugly. I sensed danger and got out of there lickety-split. I really didn't know what to think of this. It certainly wasn't an April Fool prank.

Cop-u-later.

APRIL 2,
1966 – Saturday

I'm still shaking after last night. Something's awry at Mrs. Pride's house. Were those Mrs. Pride's bones I saw? If not, where was she? And what was Columbus' role in all of this? Who was the big guy? I thought about calling the cops, but the local guys are more like Barney Fife, so there was no point. I would return and get to the bottom of this.

Saw Pippa and Biddy this morning. Pip seems to be living with us these days. I worry her reputation could be shot if there's no announcement about the bogus wedding soon. She's put on a little weight (wink, wink).

As for the Bidster, well, her wedding in Steel City in two weeks will be a C.B. DeMille production with the blockbuster 'cast of thousands.' I'm confident the conflict with 'Brigadoon' can be worked out and I'll be there.

Pippa was smoking this morning along with Biddy and Dad. Surely, Mom wasn't far behind. Considering the Surgeon General put out a warning two years ago about the dangers of smoking, you'd think Pip would consider her condition more carefully. My parents and siblings all smoke. I often wonder how I escaped the horrors of the demon weed.

Anyway, in the afternoon I went to 'Brigadoon' rehearsal. I got the car and drove Hep. Things seem to be falling into place. The Fuhrer seems happier with us. Kathy Wasp is finally getting the hang of the dancing and only occasionally steps on my toes. Hep is the lucky one, as he gets to dance with my cousin Vicki. Just as well, as my attraction to her was confronting.

While there, I told Babs I wouldn't be able to go to her house tonight. I said I couldn't get the car which was a white lie. I had a date at Mrs. Pride's house. Babs said she didn't expect me anyway, which is something I didn't care to hear. Too much information.

Visions of the Maggot and her entered my head, but she said she was going to a movie with her friend Dave. Quite safe, I figure if what I hear about his attraction to the same sex is true. This doesn't matter to me as long as he doesn't ask me out.

Dad was amazed when I told him I was staying home for the evening. I told him I needed some home time - whatever that means. I don't think he was suspicious. At dinner all the talk centered on Biddy's wedding. Will and Kitty knew nothing of Pip's bogus one, so it wasn't brought up.

After finishing dinner, I told everyone I was going to study. I temporarily went to my room instead. When everything had quieted down, I snuck out of the house and watched Mrs. Pride's house from behind my garage.

After a very cold hour waiting, I noticed some stirring. A big truck backed into Mrs. Pride's driveway. There was no sign of Columbus, but some other guys started to load the truck with her possessions, e.g., chairs, a couch, dressers, etc.

Still no sign of Mrs. Pride. There were references to the 'Old Lady' followed by much laughing. There was drinking and smoking, not tobacco I surmised, as evidenced by the clanging of bottles and that odd smell I had encountered before.

Finally, having loaded the truck, they all took off – some in the truck and some in another car. This was my chance to finally see what craziness was happening in the house. Visions of the movie 'Psycho' and Tony Perkins (who played the psycho old lady) came into my head. I thought about what happened to Janet Leigh. I was about to walk over and peek in the window when I heard a noise.

It was Dad. He was taking out the garbage when he saw me. I told him I was getting some fresh air. I'm not sure he believed me. I would have been very suspicious, the way I was acting. If he was, he didn't let on. He told me I'd better get into the house as it was cold.

I was sprung so there was no way out. I did what he asked. Thus, I missed my chance to discover the Pride secret. I'm eager to find out more than ever what is happening. If that sounds dramatic, so be it. I'll get to the bottom of it - come hell or high water.

Cop-u-later.

APRIL 3,
1966 – Sunday

I was determined to get to the truth of the Mrs. Pride mystery. Where was she? Who was taking the furniture? What was in that hole? Were those human bones that were buried? Where was Columbus? I would check things out when it was dark and see for myself.

I picked up my report card this morning. The school sends it to the local parish to check and the parish priest distributes them to the students in their area. As the FOTL Parish pays for the education for their student parish members, I guess it makes sense that the parish priest gets to look at and comment on the report. I was happy with my results except French, and even that was good for me. It should get Dad and Mom off my back.

During the afternoon, I went to 'Brigadoon' rehearsal and then to the final of the amateur basketball tourney with Hep, but my mind was not on these things. After the game was over, we went for a burger or two at Stuvers. I then said I wasn't feeling well and took Hep home.

When I got home, it was getting dark. After a light dinner, I excused myself and went to my room. Following a short interval, I quietly snuck out of the house and immediately took my position behind the garage. I made sure no one saw me leave the house.

Things were quiet, so I went and got the shovel to dig where I saw the bones the other day. I dug a bit. This time I didn't find any bones. Then I dug some more. Still no bones. Something was up, but what?

I'd had enough of digging. I snuck around to the side of the house and looked in the window. I saw nothing. Now I noticed that a side door was partially open. I decided to walk in. Once inside, I looked around and saw no sign of Columbus, Mrs. Pride or the sinister-looking men I saw yesterday. I checked things further. It was so dark I could hardly see my hand in front of me. I walked around the downstairs. Most of the furniture was missing.

Dare I go upstairs, I thought, where I would be trapped like the character in Hitchcock's 'Rear Window' if someone was home? But I just had to know what the deal was with Mrs. Pride. Was she dead? Did those bones belong to her? I slowly walked upstairs – one silent step at a time. I was nervous as I didn't know what to expect.

In fact, I didn't even know what I was looking for. Some clue as to Mrs. Pride's disappearance? I thought of that detective in 'Psycho' who was murdered when he went snooping around. Another Hitchcock reference. If I had heard screechy violin music, I would have been out of there in a flash.

I peeked into a couple of rooms and saw nothing. Although it was dark, the moon was spreading some light. In one of the rooms, I noticed packages similar to the one I had encountered the last time I had completed a task for the Chief. Small packages in brown wrapping paper and tied up with string. Cigarettes? Odd, I thought. I had seen enough. No sign of the old lady. It was time to make like a tree and leave.

I was now scared and vulnerable. Suddenly, I heard footsteps coming from downstairs. What was I to do? Run, hide, fight. It was then that the light went on. I turned around slowly only to see Mrs. Pride herself staring at me. I nearly jumped out of my skin.

I was in Mrs. Pride's house for no obvious reason. She probably thought I was stealing something. She whacked me on my shoulder with an umbrella. She was good for another whack, but when she saw who I was she stopped. She looked me up and down for the longest time. Finally, she said – in that creaky old voice – 'Gustav, what the hell are you doing here?'

I had to think fast before she called Columbus and perhaps the cops. I told her I heard noises coming from the house. I was worried someone had broken in to steal things. The door was open, and Columbus wasn't around, so I thought I'd better check things out. Just then Columbus came in the front door and, from the floor below, asked if everything was all right. Mrs. Pride and I went downstairs, and I repeated my fake story once more.

Columbus then set me straight. Mrs. Pride was getting new furniture and was getting rid of some of the old stuff. He mentioned the truck and the men removing the items. I told him about the bones I had found. Columbus said he didn't know of any bones, but they could have belonged to a dog Mrs. Pride owned which had died years before. As they weren't there when I dug today, I really had no proof the bones existed.

As for Mrs. Pride, well, she couldn't stand the cold and had been in Florida. She just had to return as the baseball season was beginning soon and her beloved baseball team, the Buccaneers, would be playing. While she was gone, Columbus was watching the place.

As they seemed to accept my explanation for being in the house, I was forced to accept Columbus' explanation. I was given a cup of cocoa and told to come back anytime. I gulped it down quickly, despite it being hot, as I was anxious to leave this awkward situation. I was just happy the police hadn't been called, and that Mrs. Pride was alive.

So, the mystery was solved. Or was it? Where was Columbus when the moving van was collecting Mrs. Pride's furniture? If the dog died years ago, why were the bones so close to the surface in a freshly dug hole? What happened to the bones? I don't remember Columbus or Mrs. Pride ever having a dog. They certainly didn't look like dog bones. Why were there people drinking and doing whatever in the house while she was away? Who were the men I saw? Why would Mrs. Pride come home now before her new furniture arrived?

Things just didn't seem to add up. I was going to keep my eyes and ears open until I found out the truth about Mrs. Pride. Now the only thing missing was my own pride.

Cop-u-later.

APRIL 4,
1966 – Monday

I was kind of tired after all that happened at Mrs. Pride's last night. I was just glad I wasn't arrested. Or worse! There's more to this story than meets the eye. I'll need to become Sam Diamond to get to the bottom of things. For now, the solving of this riddle will have to be placed on the backburner.

Saw Babs at lunch. I told her I was sorry for not seeing her yesterday. I couldn't tell her the real reason. Instead, I said I had to work on my science project. She accepted my fake story quite reasonably. Perhaps too reasonably.

The line about the science project wasn't totally false. I had told Chubs I would submit an entry for the City Science Fair. My science project is due this week and I haven't started it. I'd better get my ass in gear, as the work is due to be displayed in the City this week at the Memorial Arena.

I'm making a representation of a volcano - out of paper mâché - that actually erupts. This will work by putting a series of chemicals, some baking soda, and red and yellow food coloring in the cone. When acid – the last piece of the puzzle is added – boom! Fake lava coming out of the cone.

As we aren't able to give demonstrations and the use of acid is dangerous and banned from the fair, my effort won't be so swift. Anyway, it looks like a volcano, and there will be some information that shows what makes it tick. Actually, the whole project is pretty crappy, but that's the best I can do on short notice.

Had another 'Brigadoon' rehearsal after school. 'Five Left Feet' Kathy – my dance partner – is now down to two. She's improving, so I don't think we'll be all that embarrassing on the night. Who would notice us in the back row anyway? I can't help but pine for my cousin Vicki, who's now with Hep. Maybe Vicki feels the same as I do and wants to stay away from me. Maybe there is a tooth fairy. I admit I'm a little jealous of Hep.

I also practiced my bartender scene with the actor who plays 'Tommy.' There's not a lot to it. I get to wear a neat bow tie and stand behind a bar. Less than two weeks till the performance. After rehearsal, I didn't have time to talk to Babs, as I had baseball practice. I haven't made the team yet, but I'm in with a chance. I had a good practice and hit the ball hard.

This evening, I had dinner with Amy Sing at her place. She had called me on Sunday to invite me. I didn't tell Dad as I'm not sure how it would go over that I'm dining with a Chinese family. Amy was born in the USA, but I'm not sure Dad would make that distinction.

From the time I arrived at the Sing residence, I felt welcomed. The atmosphere was pleasant and not nearly as formal as I had expected. Mr. Sing has a very nice house. Very colourful and full of Chinese knick-knacks. He and his wife seemed generally happy to see me. We had a great conversation about how he came to America. He asked me a lot of questions about my family and myself which I gladly answered, though I wasn't about to disclose my dad's attitude toward non-whites.

Soon we were called to eat. The food looked excellent. Amy showed me how to use chopsticks. Although I was offered a fork, I thought when in Rome, do as the Romans. I made a hash of it, but it was worthwhile. I'm not sure what I ate, but it tasted fantastic.

Before dinner, I quietly put the question to Amy about the food content. She laughed and told me we were having grilled puppy and kitten before telling me she was joking. She assured me I wasn't eating dog or cat.

I'm glad I didn't ask about the food content in front of her father, as he might have been insulted. After dinner, I was given a fortune cookie. The fortune said, 'Things don't just happen, they happen just.' I really didn't understand it, but was I supposed to? Very cryptic, I thought.

Afterwards, we had lychee nuts for dessert (not really nuts) and some Chinese tea. I stayed for a couple more hours chatting with the family before it was time to go. I had the best of time. The visit gave me a much greater appreciation of another culture. Mind you, the Sings were American through and through.

Before I left, I thanked Amy's dad and mom profusely. I wouldn't mind returning, and someday even asking Amy out, but there's Babs to think of. Besides, I've seen Amy with a boyfriend, so why would she want to go out with me? Then again, we made out recently. Food for thought!

Amy walked me to my car, and then gave me a goodbye kiss. Man, that babe can pucker up. Before I left, I told her I'd see her at the canteen sometime. I really like Amy. I could see myself asking her to our house for dinner - if it wasn't for Dad.

Got home and saw Pippa. She still hasn't announced her wedding despite now being semi-obvious. Reminds me of the joke – what's black and white and red all over. A pregnant nun in a confessional. (Boom, boom!) Despite having tests this week and the dreaded science project due soon, I called Babs. We talked for over an hour and then did the 'you hang up first, no you hang up first' routine. I can't believe I participate in this corny exercise.

The Prom is coming up in May. I'd better ask Babs pronto before the Maggot gets in first. I've heard he's seeing some other girl. I hope so, but I can't be sure. While I was talking to Babs, Will wasn't happy as he wanted to use the phone. He interrupted me a number of times demanding I hang up. When I didn't, he called me an unmentionable name. I'm getting tired of the way he's acting. We're going to have it out someday and someone is going to get hurt. You mark my words.

Cop-u-later.

APRIL 5,
1966 – Tuesday

This week is like the lull before the storm. It's all happening next week with the 'Brigadoon' production, Biddy's wedding and Pippa's much-delayed nuptial announcement (if it doesn't happen soon the cart will definitely be put before the horse). Talked to Babs at lunchtime. No point mentioning my dinner with Amy. Babs and I have started to really enjoy each other's company. Dare I say – like girlfriend/boyfriend.

Also saw Katie for the first time in ages (not counting the Thursday drives). She's making an effort to look better but has a long way to go. Maybe I'm being a bit cruel. She's a very nice girl with a great personality (the kiss of death for a girl by some guy standards), and am I such a prize? Do wild bears shit in the woods?

After school, went to a wheelchair basketball game. The wheelchair team easily beat our state champions who had no experience playing ball in wheelchairs. How do the 'wheelers' do it? After that came baseball practice. With Easter approaching this coming weekend, there's all kinds of musical and baseball practices scheduled outside of school hours. There goes the neighborhood!

Anyway, I was totally exhausted when I got home. I went to bed very early, first after eating dinner, then second after watching 'F-Troop' on TV ('I'm warning you, Dobbs'). It took no time for me to fall asleep. I had the weirdest dream.

I saw Babs at school and went to talk to her, only to see her with Mirgat. I was quite upset as she was laughing at me. I was in my pajamas, so everyone was laughing at me. Except Katie. She ran up to me and smothered me with kisses.

To make matters worse, Babs said she was asked to the Prom by the Maggot. Then Katie asked me to go to the Prom with her. I told her I'd think about it. Then Amy showed up and I kissed her. Katie started crying. Then my brother Will came at me with a knife. That's when I shouted out as I woke up.

I don't know what my ID, ego, or superego were trying to tell me. Then again, my bad dream might have been the result of that only one taco I had for dinner reacting badly in my stomach. Just the same, I figure I'd better ask Babs to the Prom soon or I'll miss my chance. I will do so as soon as 'Brigadoon' and Biddy's wedding are over.

As for Katie, she's very nice, but I'm just not attracted to her, and Will's violence toward me in my dream? Freud could have written a book analyzing that one. For now, I obviously went to sleep too early as when I awoke around two a.m., I found I couldn't get back to sleep. Time to listen to Long John interview someone about wife swapping.

Cop-u-later.

APRIL 6,
1966 – Wednesday

This is the last day of school before the Easter break. Unfortunately, I have to go to school on Good Friday and Easter Monday for final musical rehearsals, as the production is the following week. I have baseball practice tomorrow and Saturday as well. I'm still trying to make the team, so I don't dare miss any of those.

To make matters worse, I've picked up a pesky cold. Thus, the next few days, while sick, I'll have to sing, dance, bat, throw, and – hopefully – kiss while ill. I'm an all-rounder! Had lunch with Babs. I shouldn't be so insecure, but I can't help thinking the Maggot wants to go to the Prom with her.

When I got home, Biddy was having her second wedding shower – this time for the locals. All her crazy friends were there. One got a laugh at my expense by kissing me when I came in the house. I made the mistake of wiping my mouth, giving a disgusting look and crying out a loud 'eew.' It was like offering free drinks at a stag party.

Naturally, the other guests made a beeline for me to get a similar reaction. I got the hell out of there tout suite. Hopefully, I provided them some entertainment away from that dreary shower. Biddy's friends are all soused old cows – age twenty-three maybe twenty-four. I hope the one that kissed me catches my cold.

Anyway, later I called Babs with the intention of asking her to the Prom. We got talking and had a good old chat about this and that. I don't rightly remember as I was more focused on the asking part. That didn't happen as I chickened out and didn't pop the question. Perhaps I was worried about getting a negative response. Surely, she wouldn't turn me down, I thought, unless she's already accepted another invite.

When I finished the call, I went to my room only to find Will with my piggy bank. All right, so I save money in a piggy bank. Shoot me! Well, I was totally pissed off and told him to stay away from my stuff. He said he needed the money and planned to pay me back in a few days.

We were close to blows when Dad suddenly appeared at the door of the room. This had the effect of breaking things up. He told us off before Will left piggy-bank free.

I hadn't checked the bank for quite a while. It was damn heavy as I tend to put only pennies, nickels, and dimes in it. I counted the contents and found I had $21.42. Not a bad haul. Heck with saving it. I've got to find something to do with my money other than splurge on my brother.

As I hid the dough away in a new spot, I heard one of Biddy's drunken friends downstairs yell, 'Where is that cute kid? He has gorgeous eyes.' I nearly threw up when I heard that old bitty say this. Secretly, my ego was happy to hear this compliment. Then again, my reaction could be because I'm sick with a cold and I'm delirious. Are my eyes really gorgeous?

Cop-u-later.

APRIL 7,
1966 – Thursday

The Easter holiday started, but I had to go to school for baseball practice. It's still up in the air whether I'll make the team. I decided to concentrate on the catcher position. Not many want this piss-ass job thus it will be worth all the hand bruises if it helps me make the squad.

At practice, I had some good hits, but my catching needed to improve. I had trouble catching pop-ups and was given the dubious name 'Radar' as a result. Soon it started raining so practice was curtailed which was all right with me. My heart wasn't in it during a free day. It's a long walk from the baseball field to the school, so I got rather wet.

As I had the car and $21.42, I decided to blow it on something. I went to Hep's place to see if we could score some beer. As we were underage, Hep told me to call the Chief. He's also underage, but he knows people who can get it for us. I hate to owe him for reasons already made apparent, but I agreed.

I got the number from Hep and gave the Chief a ring. Well, he told me he'd meet us in town and see what he could do to help us. I was happy with that, as I needed to go to the public library to get some magazine articles for an English assignment.

When we met him, the Chief asked what we wanted. I asked him to get us 4 quarts of Dubois Budweiser Beer. It's pretty cheap, and I didn't want to blow my whole wad. The Chief asked for ten bucks, but I'm sure would rather have had bills than only pennies, nickels and dimes. Nevertheless, he took the money and said he'd get the beer. He would contact Hep tomorrow as to when and where he'd pass us the brew. Hep approved of the plan, so it was full steam ahead.

The Chief then asked for another $10. This seemed extravagant as it should only have cost $10 for the beer. But I dutifully counted out the dough and gave it to him. That left me with $1.42 – hardly even gas money. I had blown almost all of my booty.

After a quick trip to the library, I decided to see Babs. I couldn't be bothered taking Hep home, so he came with me. When we got there, she was with Richard – the guy who likes guys, so they say. He was kind of cool with colorful clothes, a snazzy car and a way about him that at once was flamboyant, but also friendly and down to earth.

Hep warned me not to talk to him because he was a 'homo,' but he seemed OK to me. He hadn't asked me out or anything, so I was good with his choice of lifestyle. Soon, Richard departed.

Babs seemed happy to see me. I tried to get Hep to go for a walk or even catch a cab home, but he stayed there and played with Babs' dog Milly. Nevertheless, Babs and I flirted, and spoke to each other in that goofy boyfriend/girlfriend talk that those not in love can't stand. Making out was out of the question, as Hep was with us as were her parents in an adjoining room. The best we could do physically was hold hands.

Her dad is quite a big bloke – a stereotype steelworker. Quiet, but friendly. Not tall but built like an NFL lineman. Her mom is good-looking for her age – about thirty-five I'd guess, and there was the Turtle who ignored Hep, and tried, unsuccessfully, to flirt with me. After a couple of hours, we left. Since Hep was there, I didn't ask Babs to the Prom. What a mouse I am!

And what a chump. I can't believe I gave the Chief $20 for beer!

Cop-u-later.

APRIL 8,
1966 – Friday

Good Friday. Supposedly a day of prayer and reflection, but I have my own crosses to bear (only kidding, Jesus). It always seems to get dark from noon to three p.m. on this day, which makes it appear like the end of the world is just around the corner. However, we all know that won't happen until the year 2000, so I have well over 30 years to go.

Had 'Brigadoon' practice this morning. As if we haven't had enough rehearsals, why another on this sacred day when Jesus died for our sins? Have we no respect. There's no school. We should be at home reflecting on the sacrifice He made. Did I sound convincing?

The rehearsal went well. Kathy Wasp is getting better all the time as a dancer. Of course, she has a good partner! I've almost forgotten about Vicki King – my Year 12 heartthrob cousin. I delivered my bartender lines perfectly.

Saw Babs briefly. BS'ed for a while, but we really didn't spend all that much time together. I'm still nervous about asking her to the Prom. I also saw the Chief and reminded him about tomorrow and the beer. He told me to 'keep my shirt on.' I assume that means not to worry. He had it under control. Great! But it cost me $20 – half of which I should get back. These favors from the Chief will be the end of me.

After rehearsal, I tried to go to the library, but it was closed on this Holy Day. Instead, Hep and I went to the local pool hall. On Good Friday this seemed almost sacrilegious. I could hear Professor Harold Hill telling us that we got 'trouble, trouble, trouble...'

Anyway, I clobbered Hep in 8-ball, then won some dough in 9-ball. After that, we went to Stuvers to spend some of my ill-gotten gains. As it was GF, my conscience got the best of me, and I had a fish burger. It cost twenty-five cents, and they skimped on the tartar sauce. Still, some fries and a chocolate shake made up for my disappointment.

Hep laughed at me and got his usual three hamburgers. 'To hell with it,' he said when I pointed out that Good Friday was a meatless day. He'd better be wrong about the hell part. It was also a fast day, he reminded me. Then he added that if you were under eighteen, the rules didn't apply. I hope he knows what he's talking about.

I then took Hep home, as I thought I'd spend some time with my family. When I got there, it was a veritable beehive of activity. Biddy was making last-minute touches for her bridal entourage. The wedding is a week from tomorrow. Pippa was smoking despite her condition. She's really starting to show. She needs to announce her wedding soon to avoid a scandal. If she's not worrying, why am I?

Dad was sitting in the living room drinking his favorite beverage – beer with a shot of vodka dropped in it (shot glass and all). He calls it a 'Korean Bombshell' as he had some connection to that war. Very slight, says Pip. Even Mom was out and about. She was sitting beside him with her highball and her ever-present cigarette. She chain-smokes Bette Davis style – not bothering to inhale.

Will and Kitty were also having a fag in their rooms. Kitty was reading a fan magazine about Cary Grant. I don't know what Will was up to, and frankly didn't give a stuff.

After dinner – fish of course – Dad organised a family Bridge game. Our Bridge games are like no other. We drink, we swear (Mom tells us off to no avail), we complain, everyone but me smokes and occasionally we play a bit of Bridge. Dad, who plays by the seat of his pants (or should I say shorts) often wins because of some outrageous play.

Duane Oss fancies himself a Charles Goren level player, but never wins with us. He often complains about our inconsistencies and lack of knowledge of the rules. It is to laugh!

We played until two a.m. As usual, Dad won. Most – including me – got shit-faced in the process. Perfect practice for tomorrow with the guys.

Cop-u-later.

APRIL 9,
1966 – Saturday

Not much to write home about in the afternoon. Had baseball practice which I think went well. Still haven't heard if I made the team. Then I picked up Hep and we went to the library (not that I got a hell of a lot done with Hep there). Had dinner at Hep's house (macaroni and cheese believe it or not). Then followed the night we had planned.

I picked up JD and Frenchie, and we went to the canteen as per the Chief's instructions to Hep conveyed that afternoon. About ten p.m., we walked behind the Canteen building to meet the Chief. He duly gave us four quarts of Dubois Budweiser Beer before he left. I always wondered how it could be called 'Budweiser' as there already was a beer with that name. I guess that's a story for another time.

As the beers total cost couldn't have been more than $10, the Chief made a nice profit at my expense. I noticed he didn't give me any change, but there's no use crying over spilled beer. The sight of this 'liquid gold' for now made up for my financial loss. Luckily, Hep brought a 'church key' to open our prize so we were able to down the dear liquid.

The beer had a bitter taste at first as we drank it right out of the bottle. The more we drank, the less we noticed, and the smoother it went down. We spent damn near forty-five minutes drinking in the cold, but man it felt good.

As we drank, the noise level went up. The conversation got slurred and probably unintelligible. We laughed at the slightest comment – funny or not. Soon we were all alcohol affected. JD was the first to throw up (outside the car), but the rest of us felt great.

Before we were finished, we all decided to go to the canteen to pick up some girls. I'm not quite sure what we would have done had we been successful in this endeavor, as the beer was more than we could handle. We were obviously pissed – not the type of guy a normal girl would go out with. Not that this mattered to us. We were confident in our ability to score. It really didn't matter if the girl was normal.

Somehow, we kept our composure long enough to get past the guy at the door. We had been stamped from a visit earlier in the evening so there was no drama. Once inside, we split up to look for 'snatch.' It didn't take long for any girl to realise our condition. She would have to be as desperate as us to follow our lead and go out.

I ran into Amy Sing for the first time since the dinner at her house. I was a bit embarrassed for her to see me in this way – swaying back and forth and spitting my words. I told her what a great time I had at her house. Then I told her a few corny jokes. She laughed – probably more at me than with me. I'm not sure, but I think I asked her out, but was turned down. I hope she let me down easy.

When it appeared we were all going to strike out, I suggested we leave. The boys wanted to go to Rachael's House of Ill-repute on the Hill. Rachael's was the town bordello – an institution that had serviced the town's males for generations. Many a young lad sewed his wild oats there for the first time as well as quite a few respectable male citizens. I was curious about the place, but I wasn't sure we should go as I really wasn't in any great condition to drive or, more realistically, perform.

Hep confidently said he could take us there. He – like someone who knew what he was talking about, but probably didn't - said it cost $50 for a half hour. He added that the whores would do anything. Well, who would carry that much cash other than the Chief? And I'll bet Hep had never been there anyway.

I persuaded the others to save it for another day. Instead, we went to the Coney Island Hot Dog place for a bite to eat. Here we saw the usual crew. 'Pickles', the guy who can balance six hot dogs on his arm, and Irene, the sassy waitress. Frenchie turned his full water glass upside down on the table without spilling a drop to make things humorous for us, though difficult, for her.

We finished and went back to the car. Once there, JD and Frenchie passed out. I then threw up – away from the car. By now I didn't think I was ready to drive. Hep and I heard the church bells and decided to go to the Easter Vigil midnight Mass at the Cathedral across the street. Tomorrow was Easter Sunday, and the Mass was starting.

I figured if I rested for an hour in the church, more than one person would be resurrected this night. I then would be OK to drive. Now it was time for prayer. I prayed for my parents, I prayed for my family, I prayed for my friends. I prayed for Babs. I even prayed for world peace. And I prayed that the $10 the Chief had conned me out of would be returned.

Cop-u-later.

APRIL 10,
1966 – Easter Sunday

Didn't get home until after two a.m. After Mass, had to wake up JD and Frenchie, both of whom had slept in the car, and take those two and Hep home. Dad and Mom were asleep – although in recent times, Mom has been staying up at night and sleeping during the day.

My head had barely touched the pillow when Dad came into the room to wake Will and me. It was the ridiculous time of six a.m. I silently cursed Dad, but knew I had to get up. The tradition at home is for everyone to get their Easter basket at once.

My head was throbbing and my stomach churning. My breath smelled like a lion had slept in my mouth. But upon wakening and going downstairs, I duly followed our family yore and searched for my Easter basket.

Our parents like to think they hide our baskets where no one can find them, but I found mine in twenty seconds. After this, we had our annual Easter photo. This time it was Kitty, Will and me posing with our baskets for this inane ritual. I can see myself at fifty holding a basket with chocolate eggs and getting my photo taken.

The Easter 'loot' was fabulous: chocolate and white chocolate bunnies; a big crème-filled egg; jellybeans; marshmallow chicks; candied eggs with a super sweet substance inside that only a scientist could identify; smaller eggs; and assorted little things like Hershey kisses. It was a zit-maker's paradise.

Unfortunately, with my stomach out of sorts, I was in no mood for chocolate. Dad asked what Mass I was going to. I could hardly tell him I had already gone. Thus, I had to attend another Mass which – like all Easter services – last forever.

Before we left, I made an excuse to go outside (it was cool, but the snow was long gone) and threw up in Mrs. Pride's garden. No one noticed. After Mass we all went to Grammy Gaughan's for those dreaded kisses, a bit of chit-chat and yet more chocolate. I was still feeling rat-shit but weathered the storm without further vomiting.

I was feeling so bad when we got home, I decided to cheer myself up by calling Babs. I wished her a Happy Easter and we talked for a bit, but her family had their own Easter traditions. So, we said goodbye. Once again, another chance to ask her to the Prom went begging. I secretly derided myself for being such a coward. Before I hung up, I told her I'd see her tomorrow at choir practice.

The day was pretty much taken up with feeling sorry for myself. I stayed home and watched basketball and the Masters golf tournament. Around five, Dad asked me to pick up Gran-King for dinner. Dad had cooked a turkey (Mom cooked all the other stuff), so we were going all out this year.

I still felt like hell and asked Will to come along with me, as I wanted someone to knock on GK's door because I didn't want to get out of the car. He said he was busy which pissed me off more than ever. He's really getting on my nerves.

The distance to GK's house is only a hop, skip and a jump from ours by car, but the return trip home was long and tedious. She obviously had a few drinks beforehand and was in her usual nasty form. She spent most of the trip putting down Jews and Negroes. I wonder what Columbus would have thought.

The dinner consisted of all this food that I had to eat, otherwise Dad would have wondered what I was up to last night. I had to force it down. After dinner, it came right back up, but I excused myself beforehand. I think I got away with Dad not knowing about the drinking. I doubt if I would have gotten the car again otherwise. I said to myself that I'd never drink again. Until the next time!

Cop-u-later.

APRIL 11,
1966 – Monday

Easter Monday. No school, but as we open 'Brigadoon' this week, we had rehearsals from ten-thirty to five-thirty. We ran through the musical first, then had another go around after a break for lunch. It was pretty tedious, as there were periods where I had little to do. I hung around with Hep and made a lot of jokes at the expense of others. The Fuhrer wore the brunt of many of these, but few were spared.

At lunch I sat with Babs. We had to bring our lunch with us. Mine consisted of hard-boiled Easter eggs and chocolate bunnies of course. I still haven't gotten the nerve to ask Babs to the Prom. Maybe psychologically I don't really want to go. Yes, I do. It's just a matter of finding the right time to ask her.

Babs and I are on stage at different times, so I have to take advantage of our togetherness anytime I can. Indeed, I didn't see her as much as I would have liked. Anyway, I sat with one of the other cast members – Donny Muncine (or the Munchkin or just Munch).

Donny is a short, fat kid with thick glasses and light brown hair styled in a crewcut. He likes to make corny observations and irreverent jokes. When one of the cast members was at the bride-to-be's house he started to sing 'Standing on the corner watching all the girls go by'. When the girls sang 'Jeannie's packing up.' He sang 'Jeannie's Shacking Up.' Funny, but corny.

Munch, one of my social status at school, and I had a nice chat consisting of making fun of 'Brigdoon', its characters and its outrageous plot. It was a laugh a minute until he told me he was running for class president instead of vice-president as he had earlier indicated. Like me, he didn't give himself much of a chance. Jack Cavendish – one of the socials – is the favorite though us average Joes prefer someone else win.

As I've given much thought to backing out of the race despite getting the nominating signatures, I suggested to Munch we pool our resources. We would both try to get some support and – when the time is right – the candidate with the lesser support would drop out. He seemed to like the idea. I said we'd talk later. I'm hoping he has more support than me.

I was just getting over the effects of our big booze fest of Saturday when who should I see but the Chief. I thanked him for getting the beer. Then I asked him about the money I gave him for it. I told him he owed me $10. He said he'd pay me after rehearsal. The rehearsals went well. Kathy Wasp was much improved as my dance partner. Even my brief bartender scene went through with nary a flaw.

Afterwards, I went looking for the Chief to collect my money. I didn't see hide nor hair of him, so – after screaming bloody murder to no one in particular – I decided to go home. When I went to start my car, the battery wouldn't turn over.

After trying quite a few times, it still wouldn't start. I was ready to phone Dad. Just as I was leaving the car to call, the Chief showed up. He asked what was wrong. When I told him, he opened the hood and had a look. He said he could fix it – for a price.

Well, I knew what was coming and feared the result would not favor me, but I let his little production continue to its conclusion. He went to his car and grabbed a piece of metal the likes of which I'd never seen before. He monkeyed around with the car and in seconds, he fixed the problem.

The car started right away. He then declared it would cost $10 for the part that he put in the car – the piece of metal that he just happened to have in his car. He declared us even.

I wasn't happy about this obvious scam, but I wanted to get home. I was in no mood for an argument and perhaps a fight. It's not good to antagonize the Chief as you never know when you might need him. So, my money was gone. I had become the number one sucker of the day. I just hope the Chief and I are even. With friends like that, who needs enemies?

Cop-u-later.

APRIL 12,
1966 – Tuesday

Well, it's only a few days until Biddy's wedding, but Pippa managed to upstage her. There always was this rivalry between them. Pippa finally made herself an 'honest woman'. En-ass, Mom, Dad, his parents and she went to University Town for the 'unofficial' wedding.'

In this convoluted universe, it actually was the real wedding, but not the one that would be announced to the rest of the world. Even I have trouble following this sleight of hand. All I know is that she was well past midnight in keeping her condition quiet. She was starting to show her wares.

The secret ceremony was conducted at the University by a priest, but the wedding certificate shown to anyone will always be the one dated 21st January which states the marriage was in West Virginia. The bogus certificate that I picked up with Dad last month confirmed this charade. So, when the baby is born in November, he or she will be legitimate. Kind of!

I could hear the sigh of relief from Mom all the way here. It's all done with hocus-pocus and mirrors if you ask me. Anyway, Mom and Dad left me in charge of Will and Kitty – not that W & K would ever listen to me. Will, especially, challenges me on everything. It's getting mighty annoying!

We're back at school after the long Easter break. I had 'Brigadoon' practice followed by baseball. For the former, we had yet another run through (after two yesterday). The first performance is Friday. We have a dress rehearsal tomorrow, so we tried on our kilts. I admit I looked rather good in a skirt. Best I keep that opinion to myself.

I hardly saw Babs during the production but caught up with her at lunchtime and after school. I really think we can be a couple as things have finally settled down. There's no hassles and no Maggot to get in our way. We joked around and enjoyed each other's company.

After the musical rehearsal, had baseball practice. I'm still trying to make the team. Someone will be dropped after tryouts, so I'll make sure my rabbit foot's available. Had a stint as catcher and did alright – although I'm still referred to as 'Radar' for dropping pop flies in front of the plate. Had some good whacks when batting, though. After school, went home to cold pizza courtesy of Will, who walked extremely slow when picking up the pepperoni pizza and bringing it home. I put it in the oven to warm.

It was the first day of the big-league baseball season. I could hear Mrs. Pride's radio up full blast – due to poor hearing – as she listened to her beloved Steel City Buccaneers. The team was one of her real pleasures in life, and she never missed hearing a game.

The Buccaneers had a successful start to the new baseball year by beating Atlanta 3-2 in thirteen innings. I thought I heard her cheer when they finally won. I tried to get excited about the new season, but frankly I have bigger fish to worry about. Whether fried, baked or fricasseed.

Cop-u-later.

APRIL 13,
1966 – Wednesday

Heard Dad and Mom get home in the wee hours of the morning after their trip to University Town for Pippa's wedding. Pip and En-ass, students at State University, stayed there. Of course, the charade of the two being married in January remains. That's their story and they're sticking to it. Thus, their child – due in November – will officially not be a bastard. The only one of those is En-ass who got Pippa in her predicament in the first place.

Since the parents were in no condition to do anything this morning, I got Will and Kitty ready for school. Then I had to catch a public bus myself. At school, I started to talk to Babs in POD class when Sister Donuts yelled at me. She gave me a punishment assignment.

I had to write an essay on the ups and downs of a ping pong ball. I wrote it during a lull at our 'Brigadoon' practice ('the ball went up and over to the other side of the table, then down to the first side after being hit, then up and over'). You get the picture.

During the day, we got time off from afternoon classes for a dress rehearsal. The show runs Friday afternoon, Saturday night, Sunday matinee and Monday night. I'll leave for Biddy's wedding rehearsal right after Friday's performance. I'll have to miss Saturday's show, but I'll be back for the rest.

I thought I did well at today's rehearsal. I nailed the bartender scene. The music was good. The dances suck. Although improved, Kathy Wasp still could use a double foot transplant. Hep doesn't seem much better despite being with Cousin Vicki – a dream dancer.

I worked on that stupid essay during the time between the market dance and the wedding dance. For most of the play I'm a townsman and wear a kilt. Toward the end of the musical, I put on my bartender outfit for my brief New York scene.

I like the 'Brigadoon' songs, but the whole thing about a town appearing only once every 100 years is a bit hokey. You'd think that in something like 4066 AD someone in a spaceship would notice the town by using the advanced technology of the time.

I did manage to have a talk with the Munchkin about the class presidency. I've kind of lost interest in the position (look at all the trouble President Johnson gets into) but hate to drop out, as I told Dad and got him all excited. But is the Munchkin the right person to challenge Cavendish? All he does is make those crazy jokes and observations. Then who's to say I would be any better? I just don't want that social guy, with his ass ten feet higher than his head, being elected.

Sister Georgakopoulos, the Fuhrer, as usual was not happy with the rehearsal because she ordered another one tomorrow on what was supposed to be a rest day before the big event. Now I have to choose between baseball and the production. I'm not on the team yet. So, I wasn't all that happy when I got home. And in a shit-ass mood.

When I got there, Will reminded me we were going to Steel City on Friday for Biddy's wedding. I told him to piss off and went to stew in the bedroom. I have enough to do to have to be reminded of the bleeding obvious.

Cop-u-later.

APRIL 14,
1966 – Thursday

Got my Thursday ride with Katie and her dad. As usual, she cuddled up to me. Yuck! I hope her father doesn't blame me if he notices she's being too familiar. Who am I kidding? I'd be sure to get blamed. Fathers can be mucho protective of their daughters. Katie asked me about the musical and my sister's upcoming wedding, but I answered her queries in as few syllables as possible.

Anyway, as soon as we got to school, I rushed away as quickly as possible as I was anxious to see Babs. Unfortunately, I only saw her to say hello in the morning although we had lunch together later. The Maggot is still around as the Seniors don't finish until the end of May. I'm not as worried as before because I heard on the grapevine, he's going out with someone else. I should have Babs to myself. Now to find a good time to ask her the $64,000 question.

I had to choose between baseball and 'Brigadoon.' As it was the final, final dress rehearsal (unless we have one in the wee hours of tomorrow morning), I felt obligated to go with the musical. I guess I'll have to miss tomorrow's baseball practice as well, so my chances look bleak as far as making the team.

I worked out some arrangements with Dad about tomorrow. I'll do my thing during the matinee performance for the students. Then, I'll quickly change and rush outside to catch a ride waiting for me to take me to Steel City for Biddy's wedding rehearsal on Friday evening.

The timing will be tight, but I'm sure we'll make it – barring a five-car pile-up on the freeway. Thanks to the Bidster, I'm going to miss a photo session. I'm sure Hep will love taking my place – he's such a ham!

The Fuhrer was outwardly happy, well satisfied, with the dress rehearsal - though she didn't say anything. What could she say? To quote Bugs Bunny, 'there's no rehearsing or nursing our part, we know every part by heart'. I can't believe I just quoted a cartoon character. I feel we're as ready as we're ever going to be. After school, I had to rush home to pack for the trip to Steel City. We'll be staying in a hotel there for two nights.

As I walked by her house, I heard Mrs. Pride listening to the Steel City Buccaneers baseball team. They were beating the Braves 6-0 and you could hear the old girl cheering her head off. I saw her through the window and waved at her. I swear she winked at me. At her age? And with Columbus handy?

Said hello to the folks, but they were still recuperating from Pippa's 'wedding' on Tuesday. Pippa – Biddy's maid of honor – will meet us tomorrow night in Steel City. It's weird to think that the folks married off two daughters in one week. I spotted Will and hoped to have a truce. I felt a bit bad about shouting at him yesterday. After all, we are both altar boys on the big day.

But when I went to the room to apologise, I noticed Will wearing one of my shirts. I was super pissed off and came close to directing some choice words toward him, but in the spirit of tomorrow's occasion, I decided to let things ride. I know it's just a little thing (I really like that shirt though), but since I rescued him at Babs' party, he's doing all these things to annoy me. We haven't been getting along. I hope we can work things out this weekend.

So, I'm all set for tomorrow. Before I go to bed, I thought of calling Babs and asking her to the Prom. No, I decided to let sleeping dogs lie. I have too much on my mind at this time.

One piece of good news. Kathy 'All I Want for Christmas is My Two Left Feet' Wasp broke her toe dancing and won't be able to be my partner in the production. So, Sister G. bumped in Rita Rousseau – one of the commerce girls - as my partner. My prayers have been answered. Although I only had one run-through with Rita, I could tell she knew what she was doing. Louie, I think this could be the start of a beautiful friendship.

Cop-u-later.

APRIL 15,
1966 – Friday

The day started out well, but later it took me on a strange path that I'll never forget. The afternoon 'Brigadoon' performance went well. The matinee finished, I changed and rushed to a waiting car to take me to Steel City for my sister Biddy's wedding rehearsal. We – my parents, Will, Kitty and me – arrived there about five-thirty.

Soon after, the rehearsal for tomorrow's wedding went ahead. Will and I were told where we should stand as altar boys and what we should do during the ceremony. The other attendees were told same by the priest. Everything went smoothly without a hitch.

The whole group and a number of Biddy's hangers-on then went to the hotel where we were staying for dinner. Kitty, Will and I ate with 'the kids.' When we finished, we went up to our rooms while the other diners stayed on in the restaurant. When we got there, I turned on the TV. I wanted to watch one program, Kitty another. She called me a name, so I got mad and threw a glass ashtray at her. It missed but hit the wall and broke up into many pieces.

Will didn't like how I treated Kitty and angrily came at me. I picked up one of the pieces of broken glass and stabbed him in the stomach. As soon as I did, I felt awful. Will and I hadn't been getting along, but that was no reason to hurt him. How could I do that to my brother?

Anyway, blood came gushing out of the wound. I told Kitty to get Dad as I applied pressure to the spot where he had been stabbed. Will was crying and screaming out that he was going to die. When Dad came to the room, he took a look and immediately phoned an ambulance. After a short wait, the medics came to the room and took Will to the hospital. I had no idea at the time if he was going to live or die. I prayed and for once meant it.

As Dad and Mom went with the ambulance, I was left alone in the room. About a half-hour later, a cop knocked on the door and I let him in. He asked me some questions about the incident which I truthfully answered. He then told me to come with him to the police station.

I was ready to face the consequences of my action. It was what I deserved. Just then, Dad returned and told me to lock myself in the bathroom. I'm not sure how long I stayed there, but it seemed an eternity. I'm not sure what Dad told the cop, but he finally persuaded him to leave. I was able to leave the bathroom.

At this point, Mom came into the room, and I told her the story. She said I needed to see a psychiatrist. I also had to tell Biddy and Duane the news on the eve of their big day. I felt about two inches tall. They said the right things to make me feel better, but they had to have been concerned about my behavior. Dad then went back to the hospital for about an hour. When he returned, he said Will was OK and would be able to serve Mass at the wedding tomorrow with me.

I couldn't think of a worse punishment for me as Will's presence would be a reminder of my stupidity. I caused what could have been a fatal injury and perhaps ruined a lovely occasion.

Will returned a few hours later from the hospital. The doctor sewed the wound up with some stitches. Dad said Will would tell non-family members who might have seen him in the ambulance that he had to go to the hospital because he fell and hurt his shoulder. What can I say? I embarrassed the family by stabbing my own brother on the eve of what should have been a time of celebration. Maybe I should see a psychiatrist!

Cop-u-later.

APRIL 16,
1966 – Saturday

Today was the Bridget Gaughan and Duane Oss wedding. I hope I didn't ruin it with my untimely brain fade last night. Will was patched up OK as if nothing had happened. There was no fight and no stabbing. That's what the 'world' thinks, but I know better.

I told Will I was sorry, and I hope he accepts it, but I wouldn't blame him if he didn't. I can barely look him in the eyes. I'm going to try to forget any differences we've had recently, but who knows if things will ever be the same?

Anyway, Biddy's wedding was beautiful. Duane (I suppose I should give up the 'Dorky Duane' reference now that he's one of the family) and she were married in Campbell's Chapel on the Steel City University campus. It's a very large chapel which gives the illusion of looking small on the outside, but somehow big on the inside.

Will and I performed our altar boy duties for the Mass that was part of the ceremony. Dad looked great in his tux as he gave Biddy away. Mom looked wonderful in her long brown and gold dress. Right up until the wedding began, she was still smoking the ever-present cigarette.

Everything went like clockwork. Will and I each got a wallet for our meagre efforts.

Afterwards, there was a reception at the Steel City Cricket Club. I doubt if cricket has been played by that Club for generations, but the members obviously like the name because they've kept it. It's quite a prestigious organization. The building where the reception was held was grandiose.

There was a huge reception hall in the building. Inside there were round tables, each seating ten, scattered around. There were whiter than white tablecloths covering the tables which were decorated with flowers. A name tag indicated where the guest should sit. There was a souvenir menu in front of each place. Well-dressed waiters in fancy garb took care of our every need. Real class!

Everyone seemed to be having a good time. The food – I think we had duck with some gooey sauce, potatoes with cheese, and vegetables smothered in another type of sauce which made them almost bearable to eat – was to die for. Of course, wedding cake for dessert. Champagne, beer and wine were plentiful. The whole meal was superb.

I sat at the same table as my cousin Joey from Steel City who's a year older than me. Joey's always been a bit crazy, but – after last night - I may now be in the running for that tag. After the speeches and the champagne toasts to the happy couple were completed, Joey encouraged me to have a few more glasses of champagne. In my mood, it didn't take much encouraging.

I had five or six glasses of the bubbly (maybe more, maybe less - I kind of forgot) so I got somewhat tipsy. Joey spotted a couple of older unknown girl cousins in their twenties and suggested we pick them up. I admit they were quite the lookers.

I told Joey I was only sixteen. He told me to lie about my age and tell the girls I was eighteen. I wasn't in shape to do anything after all those drinks, so I begged off. In reality, I didn't have the balls to talk to them, and I still had what I did to Will hanging over me. I soon lost track of Joey, so I never found out if he succeeded in his conquest.

After all was over and the married couple was off, I spoke to my brother. I again apologised and told him I loved him. It was a bit soppy, admittedly. I started to cry with real, not fake tears. Will said to forget about it, but whether our relationship would ever be the same was problematic. They say time heals all wounds, but it also wounds all heels. The latter is me.

All I know is that I couldn't wait to get back home to Babs, 'Brigadoon,' baseball and the familiar. The more familiar the better.

Cop-u-later.

APRIL 17,
1966 – Sunday

It was good to get back to the hometown after the forgettable circumstances of the weekend. I still don't know what came over me. Maybe I'm jealous of Will. He's much better at sport than I am. He has this way with girls that I wish I had. I'm going to treat him better and show more patience when I feel he's annoying me.

Anyway, we had a matinee performance of 'Brigadoon.' I had to rush home after a night in Steel City and a long car trip in the morning. Then, quickly to school only to be smothered in weird makeup and go through some singing warm-up exercises. Now I had to get my kilt costume on for my role as a townsperson. In addition, I prepared my bartender outfit – consisting of a white shirt, black pants, a black bow tie and an apron – for my 'big' solo piece later.

The dancing is going well. Although I feel bad about Kathy Wasp who practiced for weeks before getting injured, her replacement – Rita Rousseau – is a real pro. Her dancing is faultless. If anything, I'm now in the role of Wasp. Rita is with me for our dances, but also dances with other girls in the 'Bonny Jean Ballet'.

I have a dance towards the beginning of the show with the guys in the town square. I appear in the rain scene, the chase and the funeral. Rita and I are together for the wedding, and we do the glen dance. I have to quickly change after the funeral for the bartender scene. It can get somewhat hectic at times. But I'm really into it.

I'm not sure who took my place for Saturday's performance. I do know that Hep got in all the photos that were taken before Saturday's show so his picture will be in the student Yearbook and not mine. The guys get a kick out of the 'Go home with Bonnie Jean' song and dance in the town square.

One of the perks of the production is being close to Sue Doddle – one of the best-looking Seniors (non-cheerleader of course) – who plays the role of Fiona. In the show, Fiona is the girl who wins Tommy's heart.

We joke that we'd like to go home with Bonnie Sue – not that she'd ever give us the time of day.

Afterwards, I asked Babs and some of the others if they wanted to come to my place. Hopefully, my dad would be dressed and not prancing around in his underwear. Babs said she told her parents she'd go right home so we took the party to her place. Here we had chips and soft drinks courtesy of Babs' parents.

Babs' dad is big and bulky – someone you wouldn't want to meet in a dark alley. Her mom is about as gorgeous as a housewife her age could be. Hep talked about doing things with her, but of course it was all talk. For one, he wouldn't have the nerve. Two, he wouldn't know where to take her. Three, he wouldn't know what to do anyway. Four, what about her husband?

The worst part of the night was when Babs' sister tried to cuddle up to me. The Turtle was OK to look at, but she was no Babs. I did my best to avoid her – hoping Babs wouldn't get upset. The way I look at it – why have boiled candy when you can have chocolate?

We listened to 'Mamas and Papas' music. I can relate to the words of the song 'California Dreaming.' Anything to hide from the terrible deed I inflicted on my brother and the humiliation incurred. 'I'd be safe and warm if I was in LA. California dreaming on such a winter's day.'

Cop-u-later.

APRIL 18,
1966 – Monday

Tonight, we had our final performance of 'Brigadoon.' I'm going to miss the rehearsals probably more than the actual performances. It was a great experience and lots of fun – though I'll keep that news to myself as I have a reputation to protect. I will have to do more musicals in the future. During the day, the cast had school despite having a show in the evening.

Had baseball practice after school. With the end of the musical tonight, I can now concentrate on making the team. Unfortunately, I missed practices on Friday and Saturday due to the wedding. There's a practice match tomorrow. I hope the coach puts me in. Either way, I'm not confident of making the squad. Still, I thought things went well. I had some good hits, and my catching was much improved. Fingers and toes crossed.

After training, I stayed at school to get ready for our final performance. The production went well this evening. Mom and Dad were there to see me as was Kitty. Will was absent, but who could blame him after last Friday's fiasco?

Today was our best effort and – at the risk of blowing my own horn – my best performances as a Scotsman and as the bartender. Mom and Dad were happy. Even better, the Fuhrer, praised us. Will wonders never cease?

Afterwards, we had a big cast party in the gym. There was heaps of food, good music and girls out of uniforms! Sue – the lead – was as tough a girl as could be. I teased Hep, who was salivating at the sight of her, and told him to ask her out, but he was a chicken so didn't even talk to her. I saw my cousin Vicki – also tough – but sadly off limits. Then again, I was with Babs and didn't consider asking any other girl out.

With all that has been going on, I still haven't asked Babs to the Prom. I was thinking this would be my chance. There was plenty of fast dancing where I made a fool of myself. I try, but I'm dreadful. I was waiting for a slow dance to dance with Babs.

When it finally came – 'Unchained Melody' by the Righteous Brothers – I was all set to pop the question. Instead, someone cut in. I couldn't believe it. It was the Maggot, who had crashed the party, dancing with Babs. I thought he had a girlfriend and was out of the picture.

It was hard watching Babs and the Maggot together. They were laughing. They were flirting. They were dancing awfully close, but I was determined to be cool about it. I wanted to be near the couple, so I asked Katie to dance. Katie – who had worked on the costumes – was overjoyed. Dancing with her was far from unpleasant despite the sweat. I'm not sure if it was hers or mine.

While dancing with Katie, I stared at Babs. I was praying she wasn't being asked to the Prom. After what seemed the longest three minutes in history, the music finished. Babs came back to me. I thanked – more like dumped – Katie and things were as they had been. Or were they? All I could think of the rest of the night was Babs with the Maggot. Perhaps this was on Babs' mind as well, as she was distant the rest of the evening.

Cop-u-later.

APRIL 19,
1966 – Tuesday

Babs was again aloof after last night dancing with her old beau Mirgat the Maggot. Maybe it's already too late to ask her to the Prom. We talked today at lunchtime, but mostly about trivial stuff. She didn't want to hold my hand. I really can't stand it. If this is Babs' idea of love, she has a strange way of showing it.

I'm getting paranoid. I think I see the Maggot in every corner, under every rock, behind every tree. I thought I'd better ask Babs' friend Gretel about Babs, Maggot and the Prom. Gretel couldn't or wouldn't tell me anything -which was a bad sign.

Anyway, to get my mind off this revolting development, I decided to talk to the Munch. There's still no resolution about who's going to run for class President for next year. We both don't want Cavandish – one of the Socials – to win. One of us needs to withdraw from the race or we could split the vote against him and guarantee his victory.

At first, I thought I'd drop out as I really can't be bothered running for and performing the duties of president. All that sucking up doesn't appeal. On second thought, should I go ahead with my candidacy? Dad would be mighty dazzled if I won as the Gaughans are political animals in this town. I hoped Babs would like it as well. The election is in ten days, and we're supposed to deliver a speech a couple of days before at an assembly. Decisions, decisions!

After lunch, I found Munch and we discussed our election strategy. He didn't directly say it, but I think he expects me to withdraw and give him my support and my supporters' votes (although I couldn't tell you how many, if any, there are). I was deliberately vague about what I was going to do when Munch and I talked.

Even I didn't know my plan. I've really got to stop procrastinating (I heard this word used as an answer on the TV quiz show 'Jeopardy' and it fits me to a tee). The Munch asked me when I was going to withdraw from the race. I winked which conveyed no answer and every answer –

depending on how you interpret the gesture. For me it meant f--- all. It did give me some time to think.

After school, I went to the baseball practice game. Tim Adams – my biggest rival to make the team – got to play ahead of me probably because I missed so many practices. I'm not all that optimistic about my chances. We won the game 2-0 over a public high school team.

Adams didn't get a hit. I felt bad for wishing he'd do poorly. Or did I? All's fair in love and baseball. I wonder if the Maggot feels that way about the former. There's a game on Friday that I was told by the coach I would play. The final countdown!

Got home and saw Will. It was just him and me. Once again, I told him how sorry I was. He said all was forgiven, but his body language told another story. This was an event that wouldn't go away easily. Then again, with my guilt, I don't think I'd want it to.

Cop-u-later.

APRIL 20,
1966 – Wednesday

I had the weirdest dream last night. I was driving around with Will when suddenly someone jumped in front of the car. I slammed on the brakes. Will went flying through the windshield and was impaled on a piece of glass.

The persons who ran in front of the car were Babs and the Maggot. This seemed very strange, so I got out of my car and asked them if they saw anything. The two then kissed passionately. The Maggot showed me his and her Prom tickets.

They both started laughing their asses off and pointed to Will who was staggering around holding his stomach from his wound. All I could do is shake my head and wonder about my ill-fortune. Then I woke up. It was morning and I had slept in. Dad couldn't drive me, so I was late. I had to take a City bus and only made to school during the first period.

As a result, I didn't see Babs until lunchtime. Once again, she seemed cold towards me. My first thought was that she had been asked to the Prom by the Maggot. My second was that I would not be going with her. Hep tried to cheer me up by saying something about their being lots of fish in the sea. In my mood, I didn't need some irrelevant nautical advice.

Hep also told me he was stepping up a notch from the Sophomore Mason and was going to ask the toughest non-cheerleader in the Junior class to the Prom – Janet Voohaus. Tall, blonde (peroxide, not that there's anything wrong with that), leggy, vivacious, beautiful hair and eyes and built like what my dad would call a 'brick shithouse.'

I was totally impressed. I had totally underestimated Hep. He told me we could double. I nodded but was pessimistic about this outcome as I hadn't asked Babs.

Not being in the best of moods, I went to baseball practice after school. We had a practice game – seniors vs. juniors. I thought I did a reasonable job behind the plate (though I did drop a pop-up hence more

'Radar' jibes). I had a bat but didn't get a hit. Selection day is next Monday. I only hope I get a chance to impress on Friday when we have a practice match against City High School. For now, it's not looking good!

Got home and saw the old man with a vodka. He says he drinks this beverage because it doesn't smell, but he's not fooling anyone. Mom was smoking like a fiend and nursing a highball. Kitty – all of eleven years old – was cooking dinner. What a family!

I went upstairs to my room and spotted Will in our room. I meekly said hello and he responded likewise. He didn't seem particularly upset. He told me that he had the stitches removed and showed me the damage to his tummy. That scar will be with him until the end of his days. My scar – the memory of the incident – would be with me until the end of my days.

Cop-u-later.

APRIL 21,
1966 – Thursday

Got my Thursday ride with Katie's dad. When I got in the car, Katie was smiling like the proverbial cat that ate the canary. For once, she didn't cuddle up to me. We rode in silence for about half the trip. She continued to smile. Finally, I couldn't stand it any longer and took the bait by asking why she was so jolly. Just as she obviously wanted me to.

'Why are you so happy, Katie,' I asked. I didn't need a sledgehammer to get her to spill her guts.

'I have a boyfriend,' she semi-shrieked. Her tone got everyone but old man Aldo – her dad – to look at her.

I nearly fell out of my chair when I heard her news – or I would have if I hadn't been sitting on a car seat. My first impression was who the hell would go out with her? And then – unbelievably – I got jealous. Although I sometimes treated her unkindly, alright like dirt, I had a soft spot for the girl. I could always count on Katie to pander to me through thick and thin. Now I was being replaced.

'May I ask who?' I inquired.

'Stan Lopata,' she said in a way that only a girl in love could speak.

Stan – a junior – was a student who I didn't know very well. He played clarinet in the band, but kind of kept to himself. He was often referred to as Stan the Man after a famous baseball player. Still, it was good that Katie had met someone who liked her. I think it was.

Anyway, with the momentous news conveyed to me and our trip to school completed, I told Katie I was happy for her and went off to live my own life. I looked for Babs – my 'girlfriend' (my quotes) so to speak. Babs was once again cool toward me. That's how I perceived her attitude.

I had more or less given up going to the Prom with her. I was convinced she was going with the Maggot. To make sure, I decided to ask Hep if he could find out. The lucky dog was going to ask Janet Voohaus to the Prom – I should be so fortunate. He said he'd look into my request.

The rest of the day was the usual mixture of tedium mixed with a large dose of crap. In religion class, I was put on a panel supporting teenagers in religion. As I don't think churchgoing is that important, it was a chore thinking up arguments.

I mean I go to church, but I'm not really sure why. I've mostly thought of it as an old person's activity that I'll take seriously when I'm forty.

When it came time for me to argue, I came up with the 'Wrath of God' argument why teenagers should be religious – always a strong point when discussing the Supreme Being in a Catholic school. I threw in the 'Fires of Hell' for good measure. Our side carried the day even though I thought the negative panel had the easier option.

Perhaps we had Divine Intervention on our side – as ironic as that sounds. This win made me feel good in one way, but also made me think that it was a worry if the 'Wrath of God' really meant I'd be punished for my cynicism – not to mention the episode with my brother.

After lunch I was invited to go golfing with Hep and a classmate LBH – Little Bob Hannon. As he was small, we referred to him by those initials – not that he liked it. After school, I stopped off at home to change and grab my old Wilson clubs. Hep picked me up. When we got to the course, we saw Sam Mitchell – a Senior Hep knew – and made a foursome with him.

As the worst golfer, I was teamed with Mitchell who, from the start, knew his way around the links. I shot a dreadful sixty – about twenty-four over par but won money from the others (about $1) as Mitchell was my partner and carried me throughout the nine-holes. I had to sink a four-foot putt to clinch the win. I did – just as Arnie Palmer would have.

Later, all but Mitchell went to my place where I won at a game I knew well – pool. It had been a long day which oddly ended with me thinking not about Babs, but Katie and her new boyfriend. I can't put my finger on it, but I really was jealous.

Cop-u-later.

APRIL 22,
1966 – Friday

Today was crunch day for baseball. We had a big practice game against City High School after school. I was nervous during the day. Once again, Babs wasn't particularly close towards me. I sat with her at lunch, but she might as well have been in another dimension. I thought I spotted her looking at the Maggot more than once.

Hep reported back to me about Babs and the Prom. He said he didn't think she'd been asked. He had checked with some of her friends, but they were pretty much all tight-lipped. He suggested that I ask her asap, but I'm resigned to not going.

Anyway, the Prom costs a lot and who knows if Babs would get along with Hep's hyper-date Voohaus? I suppose I'm trying to convince myself. I still can't believe Hep's going to the Prom with Voohaus as she's miles out of his league. The rumor is she dates college guys. I also saw Katie with her new boyfriend Stan 'The Man' Lopata. Why does this bother me so much?

It was with this background swirling in my head that I went to the baseball game at the local park – Roxborough Park – after school. As informed by the coach the other day, I started as catcher. I felt I performed quite well in this role. I wasn't going to be the first-string catcher even if I made the team. But I was going to give it everything I got.

Anyway, in the third inning, I finally got a bat. I hit a long fly ball to left field that was caught deep. I felt good about this swing even if it was an out as it gave me confidence that I was doing things right. In the fifth, I came up to bat again. There was a man on third with two outs and we were losing 1-0.

I connected and hit a little dribbler to the right of the infield that just eluded the pitcher. The first baseman grabbed the ball and underhanded it to the pitcher running over to cover first base. The pitcher received the ball but was slow getting to the bag. He decided to tag me, but I slid into the bag and the pitcher missed the tag. I was called safe by the umpire. I drove in the tying run.

Later, I was told by the coach one doesn't slide into first base, but he congratulated me for my effort. I was stranded on first base. Then I was substituted, but the guys told me I did OK. Coming from some Year 12s, this was an unbelievable pat on the back. Unfortunately, we lost the game 2-1, but I was on a high the rest of the day. Dare I believe I could make the team? Monday I'll find out.

I was feeling very good when I went to the school dance that evening. Babs didn't go, but that gave me a chance to brag – read exaggerate – about my baseball exploits of the afternoon. Without Babs, it wasn't the same, so I was inclined to leave the place early.

It was noticeable that there were a number of teenagers who were not quite right. They could be drunk, but more likely they're on that shit being peddled in schools. Who is the source? Rudy said to look to my house if I wanted answers to this riddle. Didn't the Chief say he got the shit from someone at City high? That rules out Hep and the boys.

What about Pij? He seemed eager to deflect my questions when I mentioned the foul smell at a dance. He acts suspiciously at times. His manner fits the 'out there' dealer you see on TV and the movies. Didn't Dad tell me to watch those of Pij's race closely? I'll keep my eye out.

Afterwards, I went to my house with Hep, Racovic (the boys and I no longer refer to him as Egghead), Frenchie and JD to play pool. Even an appearance by my dad in his underwear couldn't embarrass me or make me feel bad. Things were finally going my way after a dreadful week. Was it possible there was a future Prom for Babs and me in the works?

Cop-u-later.

APRIL 23,
1966 – Saturday

I had that dream again last night. I was driving around with brother Will when all of a sudden someone jumped in front of me. Will went flying through the windshield when I slammed on the brakes and was impaled on a piece of broken glass. The people who jumped in front of me were Babs and the Maggot.

When I got out of the car, those two started kissing. The Maggot held up Prom tickets and both started laughing. They pointed to Will who was staggering around holding his stomach. I stood there and shook my head. Then I jumped out of bed in a cold sweat.

The dream shook me up more than I imagine. I'm not feeling good about myself. The optimism I felt last night was a mirage. With Katie going with Stan the Man, she mercifully has a date for the Prom. I really have no one to go with me. Babs appears to be going with Mirgat the Maggot. I'm resigned to being alone and date free.

In the afternoon, I decide to get a haircut. Once again, I went to the same barber I've been going to since I was a little kid. Herb the Butcher. He cut my hair as he always did as he only knows one way. As he cut the hair, he snorted and belched. His breath stunk and I swear there was booze on his lips.

On this day, Herb outdid himself by giving me possibly the worst haircut ever. As always, his assistant, a guy near my age, Dave Major, finished cutting my hair before sweeping the floor. I vowed never to go there again, but I knew I probably would anyway. I liked the homey atmosphere of the shop and the uniqueness of Herb despite all his idiosyncrasies. I think I mentioned the comics before.

After this, I joined Hep in the City as I had to return some magazines to the library. He made a snide comment about my haircut, but I told him to f--- off and we carried on with what we were doing. He said he had good news for me. He found out from a friend of a friend that knew Babs' best friend that Babs hadn't been asked to the Prom.

It was a longshot, but maybe I still had a chance to go with her. Hep said we could double (of course he'd expect me to drive my old man's Buick Wildcat). Just the thought of being in the same car with Janet Voohaus gave me goose bumps, but I was undecided. In truth, I had put the question off for so long, I had lost the nerve to ask. I told Hep I'd think about it.

So, I went home 'singing the blues' as the song goes. As I was going into the house, I heard Mrs. Pride listening to her beloved Steel City Buccaneers. They were ahead 5-4, and I could hear her cheering away. This reminded me that there was still something weird at that house. With all that's been happening with me, I'd almost forgotten.

Mrs. Pride saw me and invited me in for a lemonade. When I looked in her house, I noticed she had new furniture, but I'd had enough of her. I made an excuse about dinner or homework or whatever reason was handy. She didn't need me for company. Columbus, her manservant, was nearby if she got lonely.

Cop-u-later.

APRIL 24,
1966 – Sunday

Last night I, again, had that dream where someone jumps in front of the car, and I slam on the brakes. Brother Will is impaled on the broken glass. Babs and the Maggot are the ones who had jumped in front of the car. They're laughing while the Maggot holds up Prom tickets and they kiss. Will is staggering around while I just stand there shaking my head.

Then I wake up in a sweat. Man, I'm messed up. Either that, or I've got to stop eating spicy Italian meatballs for dinner. Perhaps I should consult Freud who would attribute my procrastination to an Oedipus Complex – as gross as that may be.

In any sense, I can't let this situation go on much longer. Pippa and Ennis (I suppose now that they're officially married, I should can the En-ass reference) are finally revealing their marriage (the fake one) at a fancy country club do this afternoon, and not a day too soon as Pip's bun in the oven is rapidly cooking.

The invitations to the lunch at the exclusive Sasquatch Country Club read that my parents were announcing the marriage of Siobhan Philippa Guaghan and Ennis Patrick Lysaght in West Virginia in January. So, the trip I made with Dad to pick up the bogus wedding certificate had a purpose.

Of course, the real wedding took place about two weeks ago. One didn't have to be a mathematician to work out things would not be kosher if that April wedding was announced. Mom insisted we keep up the pretense of a January wedding so the baby – due in November – wouldn't be called the 'little bastard' (my words).

As mentioned, the announcement took place at the local country club. They had it there thanks to my Uncle Andy – a prominent lawyer and mover about town. Dad once tried to get into this club but was blackballed – probably because of his drinking.

As Groucho Marx once said: 'I wouldn't want to belong to any club that would have me as a member.'

The whole affair was a big deal. All the family members from far and wide attended. Biddy and Duane cut their honeymoon in Florida short in order to be there. There was the usual: toasts, booze, band, presents and bad dancing. The only thing missing was the ceremony, but no one seemed to care.

Dad made a stirring speech, did the bridal dance and then proceeded to get stoned. Mom was the picture of propriety. She wore a gorgeous long blue dress and was beaming the whole time – often with a smoke in her hand. I had a couple of glasses of champagne and felt a bit tipsy, but I didn't go overboard as at Biddy's wedding. I stayed away from brother Will probably to avoid a repeat of the last wedding's debacle.

Overall, a good time was had by all. We got home late, so I used that as an excuse to not call Babs. I resolved, however, to ask her to the Prom tomorrow – the Maggot notwithstanding. He can go to Hades. Babs can only say no, I thought, and though that would devastate me, I'd get over it eventually. How does that old saying go – what doesn't kill you makes you stronger?

Cop-u-later.

APRIL 25,
1966 – Monday

Once again, I had my dream last night, but there was a twist. I was driving the car with Will as my passenger. Babs and the Maggot jumped in front of me. I slammed on my brakes. This time Will didn't go flying and wasn't impaled on glass. Indeed, I hit the Maggot, he went flying and he was impaled on a tree limb. The Prom tickets fell out of his pocket. Babs picked them up.

No one was laughing and she pleaded with me to take her to the Prom as she held the precious papers in the air. Will said he forgave me. Babs and I kissed. This time I was shaking my head, but up and down as if to say yes to Will and Babs. I woke up in the proverbial cold sweat, but the good kind. I knew what I had to do. My dream was an omen. Today would be the day.

When I got to school, I saw Katie crying on the steps. I liked Katie, but not in the way she wanted me to. I was flattered that she liked me and gave me attention though I'd never admit such. Concerned, I asked her what was wrong. Between tears, I got the story. She told me that Stan the Man – her alleged boyfriend – asked someone else to the Prom.

I could see she was devastated. I tried my best to console her, in fact I felt sorry for her. She's a good kid. I actually came within a whisker of asking her to the Prom, but the bell rang, and I had to get to class. This whole episode upset me so much I didn't get around to asking Babs.

Ironically, the Maggot wasn't at school (did I dream him away?) so it would have been easy. My dilemma: do I ask Babs who might say no because she's been asked, or do I do the honorable thing and ask Katie?

After school, I went to baseball practice expecting to be cut when the team was announced. Amazingly the team roster was posted, and my name was on it. I made the squad. I was as happy as a dog with a bone. Although I made the obligatory commiserations to Tim Adams who was cut, I was happy I made the team ahead of him. I felt on top of the world. I was now determined to ask someone to the Prom.

During dinner, I told my dad the baseball news. He gave me a big hug and had this large 'that's my boy' grin. This would give him something to tell my uncles and Grammy. Afterwards, I went upstairs and sat by the phone. I was shaking and even had a notion to back down. Finally, I mustered the strength to dial the number. I didn't beat around the bush. 'Would you go to the Prom with me?' I confidently asked. Immediately, she replied yes.

Wow, what a day. I made the baseball team, and I asked a girl to the Prom, and she accepted. We had a long chat afterwards. I definitely felt good about the decision. For now, I didn't care what anyone thought or said. I made the right choice. It would be a wonderful Prom. That's all that mattered. I couldn't wait to take Babs.

Cop-u-later.

APRIL 26,
1966 – Tuesday

What a day yesterday was! If I live to be one hundred, I don't think I'll ever forget it. I made the baseball team and Babs said she'd go with me to the Prom. When I saw her, she told me she didn't know what took me so long. I didn't mention the Maggot, but I'm nuts worrying as I do. I told Hep and he was feeling good too. And relieved.

He informed me that Voohaus had accepted his invitation to go to the Prom. So, it'll be like the Doublemint twins – double the pleasure, double the fun! I like Babs, but to double with the eminently kissable Janet Voohaus is more than I could imagine. Hep said we should order tuxes on Saturday. He knew a place. Of course, he did. It's good he knows what the hell he's doing.

I asked Hep about drugs being sold around school. I mentioned the distinctive smell when someone using the substance was near. He confessed he knew about it but kept his views to himself. He said those involved play rough and don't like a squealer. He didn't know who was selling the foul weed.

When I mentioned Pij's name, Hep got angry. He said I suspected Pij because he was black and that I had no proof he was involved. He didn't even go to school with us (I didn't tell Hep what the Chief had said about where he got the stuff). He said there was no finer person of any color than Pij.

I like to think race has nothing to do with it, but didn't Dad tell me to 'be careful?' Pij was loud and arrogant and not one I'd hang out with. Maybe we just don't click. Then again, it's difficult to escape our environment and the way we are raised.

The election for next year's officers is heating up. It takes place on Friday. Cavendish already has posters hanging throughout the school. 'What a Dish – Cavendish is his slogan. I have nothing up and the Munchkin has even fewer than that. It'll be tough competing with the socials.

Anyway, the Munch looked me up and asked what I was doing about my presidential candidacy. I don't know why, but I seem to be on a roll. I actually feel I could win this election. I originally told Munch that I was having second thoughts about the position. Now I told him I felt I'd be the better person to challenge that social asshole Cavendish.

The candidates are supposed to give a speech tomorrow to the student body about what each one will do if elected. Although I'm not crazy about speaking in front of my apathetic peers, I'm sure I could come up with any number of lies – just like our real politicians. I guess I'd have to write a speech, but I know I could pull it off.

I started daydreaming about me with a crown on my head dispensing truth, justice and the American way to my subjects. I told Munch I'd give him my answer as to whether I'm running tomorrow morning. For his part, the Munchkin said he wasn't going to back out and was sure he could beat Cavendish if I withdrew.

I had lunch with Babs. I told her about Hep and Voohaus. I'm hoping we're now on the same wavelength. Just like the Sadie, she talked about her dress, her hair, her accessories and all the things I could give a stuff about. I spied Katie sitting by herself and wondered if she would have been talking about these things if she was still going. I should do something nice for her.

In an afternoon Science class, we saw a movie about a woman delivering a baby. Wow! It showed everything from the time the mother was pregnant to – and including – the delivery. Hep whispered that it would be more realistic if they showed how the baby was conceived. It was sickening, yet fascinating viewing.

While watching I kept thinking how watching this film could cause girls to think twice about getting pregnant. How could a woman go through that torture? I'm glad I'm a guy, I thought. The worse we can do is go to Vietnam and get shot at.

After school, we had a baseball game at Roxborough Park. I got my uniform – no.55. It was way too big, but I'll live. We played our first game against the Richfield High School Bees (or wannabees as we called them). We lost 5-0 as we committed too many errors.

As a second stringer, it wasn't in the cards I'd get a game, but stranger things have happened. Just not this time. The first team catcher is a senior, so next year is my year. I sat on the bench bullshitting with the other subs – one of whom was Cavendish. If that isn't ironic!

After the game, I got dressed and called Dad to pick me up at school. While waiting for my ride, I saw Katie. I tried to avoid her as I really didn't know what to say. She saw me and called out, so I had to say hello. She looked terrible. I felt bad that she didn't have a date for the Prom. To think, I almost asked her.

She was waiting for a bus. My dad was going her way but hadn't arrived. I told her I was hitchhiking home and didn't offer her a ride. Just as well, the bus left before my dad got to school. So much for doing something nice for her. No use getting her hopes up about her and me with a cup of the milk of kindness.

Cop-u-later.

APRIL 27,
1966 – Wednesday

Got to school, and immediately had a pow-wow with the Munchkin about the election. He said he talked to 'some students' who thought it would be a good idea if one of us dropped out of the race so as to not to split the vote against Cavendish.

I told Munch that I thought I could win, but in order to beat the social Cavendish, I'd back out. This would have killed my father as his family has a long history in politics, but I had to look at the bigger picture. Besides, I really hadn't organised a speech for today's assembly and – although I'm confident I could have winged it – I'm sure it would have fallen flat.

Munch seemed very happy, made some inane comment about how I could take off my running shoes now, and shook my hand. I then went to the teacher in charge – the one we call Sister Mary 'What-What' - to tell her of my decision to pull out of the race. She said she was disappointed, but I got the feeling she couldn't have cared less. A minor hiccup in her day.

At lunch, I saw Babs and told her the news. She didn't say she was upset, but her manner turned frosty. Later, I saw her talking to Janet Voohaus. Once again, I felt jealous of Hep. If she isn't the toughest non-cheerleader in school, then I'm a monkey's uncle.

Indeed, my fantasies took hold of me at that moment, and I had to pinch myself to get back to reality. Voohaus is one of those chicks who gets me tongue-tied when I speak. Perhaps Babs noticed this about me and there was a bit of jealousy on her part. Then again, maybe she didn't want me to drop out of the race. Whether this or that, she hardly spoke to me at lunch. C'est la vie!

In the afternoon, we had a school assembly for the speeches for officers for next year. The speech for class president was last after a tedious round of boring efforts from the minor office candidates. I expected a stirring speech from the Munchkin and was ready to cheer my ass off for him. To my surprise – and most of the audience – Munch announced he was dropping out of the race in order to join Cavendish as his vice-president candidate.

I nearly shit myself when I heard this. Munch never had any interest in running for president I figured, but he was able to get rid of Cavendish's competition. From the first, he wanted to be vice-president. I should have been pissed off, but I guess I was mildly impressed with Munch's bastardry. That's the way the cookie crumbles. As a British politician once said, 'There is no justice in politics.' I had been outmaneuvered.

After the assembly, I saw Katie who said she was sorry I dropped out and that I would have made a good president. She's always so damned sweet! We talked for a little while. She seemed very sad about breaking up with Stan the Man. Especially as Stan sat by his new flame after giving a speech. Stan is running for the vice-president position as is drum-major Josh Shalich. With Munch on the Cavendish ticket, I expect he'll win. Stan is oatmeal.

After school, I went to the locker room to change for baseball practice. I was informed it had been cancelled due to rain. This was OK with me as it had been a long day and I was beat. I saw Cavendish and congratulated him – only to be told it was what he deserved.

Some people are bad losers, Cavendish is a bad winner. I was totally turned off by this conversation and tuned out for the rest of his arrogant rantings. As he was talking my mind wandered away from him. I pictured Janet Voohaus in a bikini.

Cop-u-later.

APRIL 28,
1966 – Thursday

I felt somewhat uncomfortable driving to school with Katie this morning. She barely said a word to me and didn't rub up against me as usual. She seemed quite vulnerable, but this made her oddly appealing. However, this thought didn't last long. I felt sorry for her, but I had no time to dwell on it.

When I got to school, I was confronted by a number of people wanting to know why I quit the race for president. I didn't want to seem stupid by telling them I was dudded by the Munch. I told them I wanted to concentrate on my schoolwork – as if they believed that. Whether stupidity or schoolwork, in reality it didn't really matter as I was out of the race. I already regretted it. The election was set for tomorrow. Cavendish and the Munchkin were shoe-ins.

I told Babs I would meet her after lunch, as I had some school stuff to do. The trouble is that we went on daylight time over the weekend, and I had forgotten to change my watch to the new time. So, I missed her.

After lunch there was a special screening of our 'Brigadoon' performance. If I do say so myself, I looked dashing – in a girly way – in my kilt. Hep, on the other hand, was told off by Sister Georgakopoulos because he had his socks pulled up too high. She said it didn't look like a skirt. From Hep's point of view, you would think that was a plus, but he brooded about it during the whole film. I looked for Babs, but she wasn't to be seen.

We had a baseball game scheduled to start after school, but it was rained out. Instead, we were sent to a study hall in the cafeteria the last two periods. It was like being in a prison. There was a space between each student, and we had to observe absolute silence. We were merged with a group already there. I made the mistake of talking briefly to Hep. Talk about your Russian Gulag!

Well, Sam Signoria, Sam-I-Am – our crack music teacher and

resident twit – was supervising this study hall. He came down on me like a ton of bricks. He started yelling at me and carrying on like a pork chop. What a screwball! Sure, I said a few words, but it wasn't like it was the Gettysburg Address or anything.

He told me I had a detention after school. Crap. Because of this I had to catch a later bus and didn't get home until after five p.m. SIA assigned me an essay on the life of a fly ('It's born, it annoys people, it procreates, it dies' – what else is there?) due tomorrow. I guess life wasn't meant to be easy.

I was so pissed off when I reached home that I didn't realise Biddy and Duane were back from their honeymoon (interrupted only by Pippa's fake nuptial announcement). They seemed in good spirits. Biddy told us how great Florida was; Duane was his usual nerdy self, but now that he's family I feigned interest. I wasn't really into it. I just wanted to get out of there so I wouldn't have to explain the election proceedings to Dad.

That night, I called Babs and apologised about missing her at lunchtime and at the screening. She didn't seem unhappy about it. In fact, she invited me to her place tomorrow evening. Fantastic – I don't feel we get much alone time. Now if only her Dad, Mom and siblings were gone, then we could make beautiful music together (did I really write that dribble?).

I told her it was a date and that I'd see her in school tomorrow. Funny enough, she said she had to miss school because she had some business to attend to. She would see me in the evening. For a brief moment, anyway, Sam-I-Am's essay was an irrelevant piece of garbage I'd like to have pissed on – metaphorically speaking.

Cop-u-later.

APRIL 29,
1966 – Friday

I had to tell my dad this morning that I wouldn't be class president. I'm sure he was disappointed. I told him I only lost by a few votes. I think that made him happy. In reality, the election is today and I'm not even on the ballot. So, I told Dad a fib. Is a fib worse than a white lie? I felt a bit disappointed myself that I didn't make a better fist of things. Then again, you've got to hand it to the Munch. No use crying over spilled milk! Or something like that.

As expected, Babs wasn't at school. At lunchtime I sat with Katie with the intention of cheering her up. What a downer that turned out to be. All she wanted to talk about was her rotten love life and how miserable she was. I tried to console her the best I could, but I couldn't help thinking that she was her worst enemy. Then again, maybe I was the cause of all her grief. I was never so happy to hear the bell as I was desperate to get away.

After lunch I voted – for Munch, but not Cavendish. (I left it blank as he was running unopposed). While I was walking to my next class, I ran into Janet 'va-va-va vroom' Voohaus. She actually stopped and talked about the Prom and doubling with Babs and me.

In reality, who knows what she said, as all I could do is stare at her, nod my head every so often and occasionally say something unintelligible? She smelled so nice! I've said it before, and I'll say it again – Voohaus is some babe. Hep is damn lucky! Too lucky! Then again, Babs is no shrinking violet.

No baseball practice, I decided to go home right away and stay in until seven-thirty before I went to Babs' place as arranged yesterday. However, at 6.30 Hep, JD, Frenchie and the Boob – a hanger oner – stopped in to play pool. JD and I teamed up to win four of five games of 8-ball against Hep and Frenchie. The Boob wasn't interested in playing.

Around seven-fifteen, I told the guys I was going to see Babs. Unfortunately, the whole group decided to come with me. I protested, but they insisted. They had a car and were going to go see Geist, as they put it, no matter what I said. Once again, I wouldn't get to spend any time with her alone. I was pretty pissed off.

I think Babs was a little surprised to see the gang when we arrived. Nonetheless, we went in, ate her grub and listened to the album 'Revolver' by the Beatles. The Turtle walked into the living room, sat beside me and rubbed against me. I wasn't flattered, but appalled. In front of her sister?

I was saved by the bell when Babs asked me into the kitchen to help with the food. I expected her to be angry about Turtle and me, but instead she kissed me quite passionately on the lips. She had spent the whole day with her mom looking for a Prom dress she said.

Well, I felt about two-inches tall as I thought she might have been with the Maggot. Her parents weren't home, so I kissed her again – this time with a bit of tongue. She seemed to like it. I regretted telling those assholes where I was going. What was I thinking?

We stayed for a while longer before leaving. The boys had kept busy by playing with Milly – the dog. Maybe it was my imagination, but I swear the Turtle winked at me as I was going out of the house. I pretended I didn't see it. After we left, Hep said we should have a double date before the Prom. A test run so to speak. The thought of being that close to Voohaus was inviting, but again I lamented that I never got to be alone with Babs.

Cop-u-later.

APRIL 30,
1966 – Saturday

Went with Hep to get measured for a tuxedo to rent – for the May 21st Prom – at 'Universal Tuxedo.' Considering how classy the clothes were, the shop itself was located in a dumpy part of town. The store itself was cluttered with jackets and shirts, store dummies and measuring tape, and not in any particular order. It had the smell of chalk and old men.

Both Hep and I got the traditional school formal white tuxes complete with black ties, cummerbunds, black pants and shoes. The renting of black shoes particularly galled me as they cost $15. Now I know what I'm going to do when I 'grow up.' Anyway, the guy took our measurements and told us to come back in a week or so to pick up the clothes. It cost us $50 each, but I guess it's worth it.

Afterwards, we went in Hep's car to Stuvers to celebrate our purchases. We bought five burgers each, large fries and a shake (me vanilla, Hep chocolate). I couldn't believe the outrageous cost of the burgers – 18c each (formerly 15c). We then moved to my place where we played pool for an hour before Hep had to go home. I told him I'd see him at the school dance this evening.

I hadn't been to confession for a long time. I figured before the Prom I might want to cleanse my soul in case I got lucky. Going to church would put me in the good graces with Dad when I ask him for the car for Prom night. He likes that religious stuff. I stopped off at the local Catholic Church – the Church of the Fear of the Lord - went into the Confessional and ticked off my check list of sins to the priest. I swore, didn't obey my parents, missed a few Masses, etc.

I ended my recitation by confessing the sin of 'impure thoughts and deeds.' I deliberately was vague as I figured this standard phrase covered the gamut of these passions. Normally, the priest would leave it at that. However, this time the priest asked for specifics. Did he get off on the details, I thought? I could hardly tell him my fantasies about doing it to Hep's Prom date – the lovely Voohaus.

Instead, I gave him a response half-true, half made-up and prayed it wouldn't send me to Hell. The priest was more than satisfied, and he's not allowed to reveal what was said in the Confessional. If he told anyone, I'd have to kill him!

Of course, there are Church guys who would do that first. For Penance he gave me five Our Fathers and five Hail Mary's. So, after my prayers, I was sin free – for the short time before I again would have impure thoughts about the fabulous Janet Voohaus.

In the evening, I drove to the school dance. Here I found that Cavendish and Munch had won the class election. I shook the Munchkin's hand and congratulated him, but I couldn't help thinking that – except for the grace of God and Munch's bastardry – it could have been me as President.

I looked for Babs, but she wasn't there. This was a pity as I had hoped to resume our lip sucking from last night. Babs' sister was there. I asked her to dance. It was OK when we fast danced, but then the music switched to a slow one. As we were on the dance floor, there was no escape.

She danced extremely close to me – so close I could smell her hairspray and sweat. It mixed in beautifully with the now obligatory stench of the shit making the rounds. I must be getting used to it because it didn't smell as foul as normal. Dancing with the Turtle was awkward, but not unpleasant by any means. A bit unnatural – if you know what I mean – under the circumstances.

After the dance, I went to talk to Hep, but the Turtle followed me. My ego told me she wanted to go outside and smooch, so I figured I'd better get the hell out of there. Having anything to do with Elaine would only complicate matters with her sister. The Turtle never did tell me why Babs wasn't at the dance in the first place.

Cop-u-later.

MAY 1,
1966 – Sunday

Called Babs and told her I'd be up to see her in the afternoon. I was about to take the car when Dad stopped me. He said I had to take Will to his girlfriend's place. I was pissed off, but then I thought I kind of owed Will after the wedding episode. What got me was that Dad only told me just before I was ready to go see Babs.

Anyway, before I took Will to see his squeeze, I was told I had to go with Dad to see Grammy. Well, I was livid and once Dad started the car and drove, I jumped out. I don't know what I was trying to prove. After the Steel City fiasco, Dad must really think I'm a nut case.

Maybe Mom was right about me needing to see a psychiatrist. The car wasn't moving fast, but I landed on my elbow. It hurt like hell. In fact, I thought I had broken it. Dad told me he'd better take me to the hospital to get it x-rayed.

Dad knows quite a few people in the hospital emergency area in his capacity as a dentist. At times, he uses the hospital facilities professionally. So, when he took me to get my elbow checked, he took me past all these people who had been waiting. Some possibly for hours. He went right to the head of the line. It's a bit embarrassing – although convenient – for me. I tried not to make eye contact with these patients.

Well, the x-rays proved negative. I was told to take two aspirin and call into the hospital tomorrow if the pain got worse, but my plans for the day were wrecked. I had to call Babs and tell her I couldn't make it. I had to stay in to rest my elbow.

After dinner, Hep and the gang – Frenchie, JD, Racovic - and the much maligned, for good reasons, Boob – came over to commiserate. I had called Hep earlier about my elbow. I didn't say anything about jumping from a moving car like in one of those gangster films. Instead, I told him I fell down the steps in my house. When I think about it, I don't know which reason for the elbow injury made me look the worst.

We went to the basement to play pool. During the game, Hep started talking about the Prom. We again gave him shit about how an ugly SOB like him got to go with a dish like Voohaus. JD said he was taking Arua Marhilles whose parents come from India. Arua is a nice girl, but Hep couldn't help himself and made a tasteless joke about she being a snake charmer. I'm surprised he didn't say she slept on a bed of nails.

Racovic naturally was going with Stephanie Bronkowski – the smartest girl in the class. Even Frenchie was going. He asked Adele Lagonski – a girl we often said looked like she had been mugged. Only the Boob was without a date. Understandable, as he had a double whammy on him. He was homely and an asshole.

The guys played pool for a while (not me as my elbow still hurt) when Kitty called down and said I had a phone call. It was the Chief who wanted to speak to me. I was reluctant to talk to him and for good reason. He said he wanted me to do something for him.

I lied and told him I was sick which was true, in a way, as my elbow still hurt like hell. Besides, Dad wouldn't have given me the car anyway after my daredevil routine. Then there was that thing about ripping me off to the tune of $10 the other day.

Well, the Chief wanted me to pick up some beer, and who knows what else? I suppose he would have owed me a favor had I done this chore, but the seniors had almost finished school so I figured I wouldn't need his protection. I would take my chances.

The Chief wasn't too happy when I told him my decision. He threw everything and the kitchen sink at me to get me to help him. He reminded me how he helped me with the Year 12s when I needed him. I held my ground. The Chief isn't one who takes no for an answer, but I prayed something wouldn't come of my refusal.

I asked the other guys, but they weren't too keen to take on the Chief's request either. The Boob told me to say he wasn't all there. Quite aptly for him in more ways than one, I thought. There was something rotten in the state of Denmark. That reminded me that I needed to brush up on my Shakespeare.

Cop-u-later.

MAY 2,
1966 – Monday

Back to school. The official result of the class election was announced at a short assembly this morning. As expected, Cavendish, who was unopposed, got elected President and Munchkin was his Vice-President. Because of my stupidity, I didn't run. Of course, that doesn't mean I would have beaten Cavendish. Munch beat Josh Shalich by forty-four votes for vice-president. Stan got two votes.

I thought Katie would be happy that Stan the Man lost because he dumped her. Yet she was crying when I saw her (kind of her normal look these days) as she said, 'she still liked him.' I wasn't about to touch that statement with a 10ft. pole or a 5ft. Hungarian (boom, boom) for that matter.

Katie had lost all sense of judgement. I quickly got the hell away from her and looked for Babs. I'd let her down twice this past weekend and, as Desi would say on 'I Love Lucy,' had some 'splaining' to do.

Due to my sore elbow, my arm was in a sling. This made for a good conversation piece but didn't get me much sympathy. As we had baseball practice later and I didn't want to look like a nong, I soon abandoned it. Hep is still pushing this double date thing before the Prom, but that doesn't solve my dilemma of never being alone with Babs. On a double, I suppose I'd get to see the eminently 'lickable' Voohaus.

I finally caught up with Babs and – although she was civil with me – something was missing. Maybe she found out I danced with her sister on Saturday. I joked about it, but she gave me a stare that conjured up scenes of a hypnotist attempting to put a person to sleep in order to make him or her act like a chicken.

I changed the subject. I had deliberately put my sling back on hoping to garner some sympathy from Babs. Even that didn't work, although she gave me a slight peck on the cheek before we split. Perhaps all was forgiven, and my paranoia wasn't real.

After school, I went to a brief meeting of the school newspaper. I signed up to be a reporter next school year and had already written an article recently. This meeting was followed by a baseball practice. Because of the newspaper meeting, I got there late and had to run some extra laps around the ground.

When I joined the team, I found the seniors weren't very sociable. They ignored me and big Jack Trident, aka 'Neptune', who was usually friendly, bumped me for no particular reason. Was it deliberate or accidental? As a junior, I wasn't about to push my luck and make a fuss. It was odd, nonetheless.

There's a big game against City High tomorrow – our Jakstown city rivals. I don't expect to play, but I got some great batting time today. In a practice game, I cracked a ground-rule double despite my sore elbow. Afterwards, we got changed. The bumping from the Year 12s continued. I was mystified by the treatment given to me by the older teammates.

As I was leaving school, I spotted the Chief. 'Thanks for the ride,' he sarcastically said. He didn't have to write a letter for me to know that my senior problem was all about my refusal to do his bidding last night. As a result, the Chief put the word out to the boys that I was fair game. I explained about my elbow, but he wasn't cool about my reason.

With only a month to go before the seniors finish school, I figured I could see things out without any of his help, but just to make sure, I asked the Chief if I could do anything for him to keep the hounds out of my hair (pun intended). He said he'd think about it. It was then that I knew I was in trouble.

Cop-u-later.

MAY 3,
1966 – Tuesday

Saw Babs talking to the Maggot at lunchtime. I told myself to stay calm externally if not internally. Babs already said she'd go to the Prom with me. Besides, the Maggot had a date – so I keep being told. I couldn't help thinking the Chief was inadvertently behind this reunion. Without his authority, I was fair game for the Seniors – as was my girlfriend it seems. Soon the Maggot left and, although I was seething inside, I didn't show my anger in front of Babs.

After lunch, I tried to avoid, read hide, but was found by the Chief. He'd be a natural at 'hide-and-go-seek.' He said he had something he wanted me to do this coming weekend. I reluctantly agreed. This reminded me of the Mafia where the godfather tells his minions what he wants done and you'd better not disagree. Otherwise, you get fitted for cement overshoes and thrown into the sea. For the time being, I was counting the days until the Seniors left.

In English class in the afternoon, I started chatting with Dave Penish (we might have nicknamed him 'Penis', but he was a big brute and not one to mess around with). Dave was a fellow baseballer and I asked him about the game after school. Well, Sister Mary All Buns – our English teacher – called me up on it. She wasn't happy when I gave her a ridiculous excuse – my pencil broke – and then blamed an innocent kid.

All Buns gave me a detention after school. When I told her I had a baseball game that afternoon, she gave me five demerit points. What a bitch! She told me I could have the detention tomorrow. I was in no position to argue. I did find out from Penish that our illustrious Principal – Georgie Porgie – had to go to the hospital for a rumored bowel obstruction. Appropriate, I thought, as the guy gives us the shits.

After school, I dressed for the big game against City (Public) High School. They were favored, but we won 2-0. Randy Shellhamer aka Shelly – our big lefty pitcher – was on fire and shut out the Trojans (we call them the 'Rubbers' after the brand of condoms called 'Trojans') on two hits.

Harrigan homered and I sat on the bench. We all celebrated after this great win. The seniors were noticeably nice to me. Did the Chief spread the word to lay off? Or maybe I didn't need him after all. Probably the former.

When I got home, I called Babs and had a long chat about many things. I didn't bring up the topic of the Maggot, but we did talk about our relationship. She said she really liked me. That was good enough for me. When she brought up the subject of Prom dress, I pretended to be interested. Would she want to hear all the details about my tuxedo?

In the evening, I watched the Steel City Buccaneers beat the Redlegs in twelve innings on TV. The Buccaneers are off to a great start and are in first place. Could this be a repeat of the World Series of a few years ago when Mas' home run beat the much-hated Knickerbockers?

Cop-u-later.

MAY 4,
1966 – Wednesday

Just an untypical day at school. Father McCracken took the boys aside to talk about sex. I assume a nun did the same with the girls. I'm not sure what a celibate man or woman could tell sixteen-year-olds, but it did spark my interest. In the course of his talk, I wondered if any of our Catholic girls would have had sex. I had my suspicions. I guess I'll never really know.

Hep says he can tell if a girl has 'done it' by the way she walks. I take his advice on girls with a grain of salt. Then again, he's going to the Prom with Voohaus. In my dreams, the girls would gladly be game for the home run if I asked. In reality, I'd get slapped first.

Not that there was anything new the priest could say to us – nothing any of the guys would admit to not knowing. I figure if you don't know about sex by the time you're in Year 11, there's no hope of ever getting any. I don't actually think of Babs in sexual terms, but I've thought about it with Voohaus, and Lisbeth, when she was around.

These things aside, the talk was interesting and humorous. Who would have thought a priest would know so much about sex? He even told us a few dirty jokes. Saw Babs at lunchtime. She seemed all perky. Perhaps the nun's sex talk wound her up. There was no sign of the Maggot. Maybe that horse had well and truly bolted.

Had a detention with Sister Mary All Buns after school. Man, she seems fatter up close than in class. And she stinks! A little bit of chat in English class yesterday and I'm stuck in detention writing an essay on 'Macbeth.' The other day, Hep asked me which Shakespeare play refers to a dog. 'I'll bite,' I sarcastically asked. 'Macbeth,' he answered. It's when Lady Macbeth cries, 'Out, damn spot.' I guess she was putting the dog outside for the night.

My favorite lines come from Macbeth's speech when he learns his wife has died.

'And all our yesterdays have lighted fools, the way to dusty death.

Out, out brief candle! Life's but a walking shadow, a poor player that struts and frets his hour upon the stage, and then is heard no more. It is a tale told by an idiot, full of sound and fury, signifying nothing.'

Makes me think of my own life and my place in this world.

All Buns let me go early as I told her I had baseball practice. She made me promise not to talk out of turn in class in the future. I said yes with my mouth, but my brain thought otherwise. Anyway, I hightailed it to the practice in record time. We have a big game tomorrow and I wanted to get there as fast as possible.

Things didn't go well once I put on my catcher's gear. I dropped a couple of pop ups and had to put up once again with the 'Radar 'moniker. The coach read the starting list. As expected, I wasn't in that group. Indeed, I was resigned to not getting a game this year. My best chance to play was if someone got hurt. Would it be right if I prayed that the starting catcher got injured?

Got home late only to see Dad passed out on the kitchen counter – drunk as a skunk. He had drunk far too many vodkas. If he thinks it can't be detected on his breath, then I'm the Pope!

Mom was asleep, so I helped Dad upstairs and into his bed. He's a good dad, but his drinking and smoking will catch up to him 'while he struts and frets his hour upon the stage.'

Cop-u-later.

MAY 5,
1966 – Thursday

Got my Thursday ride to school with Katie's dad, which is just as well as my dad was sleeping it off with a massive hangover. Katie has been chilly toward me recently, but on this ride, she embarrassingly cuddled up to me – if you get the picture. Considering I didn't ask her to the Prom, she seemed quite OK with me now. I was hoping she'd get a date, but then again – selfishly – I hoped she wouldn't as I've gotten used to her fawning all over me.

Anyway, had lunch with Babs. She, too, was quite frisky for lack of a better word. She even snuck in a lip kiss as we were leaving the lunchroom. Finally, we're a couple! If only she didn't constantly harp on about her damn Prom dress.

That topic would be on the bottom level of items of interest to me. Hep still wants to double date before the Prom. I finally gave in, and we agreed next Friday would be good. Whether I can control myself around Voohaus is another story.

I did my best to avoid the Chief as I knew he wanted me to do him a favor. His favors always seem to cause me grief. I can't wait until the end of the month when the seniors finish school, and I don't need his help. Well, I couldn't avoid him forever.

He caught up with me after lunch. He told me he needed me to pick up a package for him tomorrow night. I had an idea what the package would look like. I asked him what was in it, but he said it wasn't my concern.

The Chief told me to go to a place known by all as Dogshit Hill – so-called because the people living there are known to be out of it if you get my meaning. The area was 'down in the boondocks' as the song goes. It was filled with dilapidated homes usually with old cars parked on the front lawn. The people were rough, and the area noted for reports of crime and illegal activities. It wasn't an area I wanted to go to.

Dogshit Hill wasn't the area's real name, but for the life of me I didn't know it or how it got its nickname. The people habituating the area took great pride in the place and its bogus name. If one disparaged where they lived, he'd better watch his back. The rumor was that the white boys there were in-bred.

If you knew a guy named Touch Campdown (nicknamed 'Duda' after the song 'Camptown Races' sing this song, duda, duda), you'd readily agree with me. He'd been in jail multiple times for multiple offences. He'd sooner fight you than look at you. They say he once killed a man in cold blood.

The Chief gave me the address as to where to pick up the 'goods', followed by instructions to take it to the school dance tomorrow night. I was a bit squeamish about this task. Picking up beer I can understand, but what about a mysterious package? Would it be like the one I picked up when I performed my previous task for the Chief?

Like last time, I was a bit concerned about the goods I would receive and deliver. What if it was something illegal? And what if I was pulled over by the Fuzz – always a possibility? The whole thing was somewhat disturbing, but I had already agreed to do it so I could hardly back out. Where the hell's my backbone when I need it?

After school, had a baseball game against the Windlass Coalers – a high school from a coal mining region in the next county. I expected a tough game, but we won easily 6-0. Tom Scott – a sophomore – pitched wonderfully. I was hoping to get in as we were winning easily, but once again I was relegated to the bench. I kept amused by joking around with Sam Genovese – a senior – who was equipment manager and who also kept the stats.

So, the players were pretty upbeat afterwards. The team was doing well and had a good chance of winning our division this year. The All-Sports School Banquet and Awards Presentation was on Saturday, and the seniors were in a good mood as they anticipated receiving their letter sweaters. I wasn't getting one, but some juniors were so the coach expected all the Year 11 team members to attend as a sign of solidarity.

The Seniors treated me as one of the gang, which again made me wonder if I needed the Chief's protection anymore. Then I thought about that rabbit punch one of the seniors gave me earlier in the year and thought better of disconnecting myself.

The weather's been hot this spring, so the boys no longer have to wear ties or school sweaters. Ironically, the girls have to wear their whole uniform. What's good for the goose is definitely not good for the gander. It doesn't seem fair, but it reminded me of the golden rule. Whoever has the gold (in this case the male priests) makes the rules.

Called Babs when I got home. We talked for an hour and a half. Oddly enough, I can't remember much about what we said. I did ask her out on a date next Friday along with Hep and Voohaus. This double-date would either be double the fun or double the trouble. Six of one or a half-dozen of the other.

Cop-u-later.

MAY 6,
1966 – Friday

More of the same at school. Saw Babs and had lunch with her. She said she was busy and wouldn't be able to see me this weekend. I have a lot on my plate anyway, so I didn't really mind. I was already thinking of the job I was to do for the Chief.

Sister Mary Fuhrer was peeved at us at choir practice. We were gabbing throughout the rehearsal, so she lost it. She made us sit in silence for forty minutes without any talking at our chorus rehearsal. No singing, no nothing! Only staring straight ahead.

Was she pissed off at us? Do nuns get a period? No one could figure out what was with her, but the whole episode smacked of desperation. I figured it was just one of those crazy things as the song goes. It was very queer, nonetheless.

In the evening, I had the boys over – Hep, Frenchie, JD and Racovic - for pool. Luckily not the Boob. We were soon joined at the table by my new brothers-in-law Nerdy Duane and Horny Enny. We played some team doubles. The first match pitted JD and myself against the newly married guys. We wiped up the floor with those oldsters. Then we beat Frenchie and Racovic easily.

The match against Hep and Frenchie was a bit more difficult, but we beat them as well. Hep let out the f-word when he lost. Mom – in her robe – overheard him because she made a rare appearance downstairs to reprimand Hep. This kind of put a dampener on our game, and we left (without D & E). Besides, I had to go as I had that task to complete for the Chief.

Hep drove the others to the school dance. I told the boys I would meet them at the school as I had something to attend to. I was deliberately vague. So, I went to Dogshit Hill to pick up the mysterious package. Dogshit Hill is not a pleasant place to be – especially at night. I don't like doing things like this at the best of times, but I was super apprehensive in this case.

The address provided was to a seedy looking 'Munster-type' house on a dark street where half the streetlights weren't working. When I got to the said address, I flashed my car lights as the Chief had instructed just like in one of those spy movies.

With no response, I flashed my lights two more times. Finally, some dude came up to the car and handed me the package. I had never seen this dude before, but I had seen his picture in the paper. It was Duda – the barbarian. If I wasn't scared before, I certainly was now. He gave me different instructions than the Chief. He told me not to deliver the item where I had been told, but to a bar in the City to a guy named Jones.

I protested and told him that wasn't what I was supposed to do. Anyhow, I wasn't old enough to go to a bar, but he insisted I follow what he said. He looked like he could step on me like a bug and his only regret would be the gunk on his shoe.

There was a bulge in his pants, and I don't think he was glad to see me. The package he gave me was short and square, covered in brown paper and tied with string. Just like the previous one I picked up. At the time, the Chief told me they were cigarettes. Who was I to disagree?

The package was similar to one I had received last time I did something for the Chief. I saw the same type of package in a room upstairs at Mrs. Pride's house the day I was sprung by her and Columbus. The guy gave me the address of the bar and he was gone. I thought about taking it to the dance anyway but nixed that idea for obvious reasons. I think I mentioned the bulge.

I was shaking and praying I wouldn't be stopped as I drove to the destination. The designated address was in a poor part of the City. After a short search I found the place – a dimly lit bar with a big 'Pabst Blue Ribbon' sign on the front. Also, in the window was a tattered notice from 1963 about a march to Washington to hear Dr. Martin Luther King.

I opened the door. It was dark inside and very quiet except for the juke box blaring a 'James Brown' song in the corner. All eyes were on me as I went to the bar and asked to see a Mr. Jones. The bartender called upstairs and three big Negroes came bounding down the stairs and then toward me. One of them demanded I give him the package, but when I asked if any of them was Mr. Jones, I got no response.

I tried to leave, but a couple of the guys blocked the door. One of them said he was Jones, but I didn't believe him. I asked for some identification, but he ignored my request. He asked again for the package, but again I refused. They started walking toward me like they meant business. Viciousness was carved on their faces.

I thought I was a goner. I put a hand up in front of my face, but I knew what I was doing was futile. I prepared myself for a whole bunch of pain. It was then that I heard a familiar voice. 'Gussie, is that you?' Everyone stopped. I turned toward the voice. I couldn't believe my eyes. It was Columbus – Mrs. Pride's chauffer. 'What chu doing here, boy?'

I was never so relieved in all my life. I explained the situation to him. Columbus, in a firm voice, told the others to back away and they did without hesitation. He asked for the package. As I trusted Columbus, I gave it to him.

He passed it on to a guy I spotted sitting in a corner booth. Jones, I presumed. It was dark so I was only able to get a quick glance of him. Somehow, he looked terribly familiar. Columbus then he told me I'd best leave. I didn't need an invitation. I thanked him and hightailed it to the dance.

When I got there, the first person I ran into was the Chief. He asked me for the package. I told him what had happened. When I mentioned Jones, he genuinely seemed scared – unusual for him – and dropped the subject. I didn't tell anyone else what I had been up to as who would believe me anyway?

I was in no mood to dance – particularly as the Turtle was eyeing me. I was still shaking, so I told the boys I was leaving. We went to Stuvers where I had three of those ridiculously priced 18c burgers. Then the boys followed me home where we shot pool for another hour before they left. I went outside to see them off as Hep drove them home.

The interesting thing was while I was outside, I saw a light on in Mrs. Pride's house. I could make out Columbus. He had what looked amazingly like a short and square brown paper package tied up with string. Five will get you ten it was one of his favorite things.

Cop-u-later.

MAY 7,
1966 – Saturday

I'm still sweating after last night's close encounter with death. Columbus saved my ass that's for sure. Perhaps I'm exaggerating it, but it sure seemed my life was on the line. What does he have to do with the Chief? Columbus took the package that was earmarked for the Chief. The Chief said there were only cigarettes in the package. So why the fuss? I have my life to live so for the time being I decided to put all this on hold.

Anyway, I'm through with the Chief. I've paid my dues to him with interest. Besides, the seniors are leaving in a few weeks, and till then I have senior friends on the baseball team to look after me. His services were no longer required.

Went to the Public Library this afternoon to finish a magazine article on the Cold War. Things are still going well in Vietnam with our troops. I'm sure we'll be out of there in a few months. Doc Ranan – our history teacher – thinks otherwise. He told the boys in his class that we are the ones who will be fighting there when we get out of school. As we're sure the whole thing will be over by then, we all laughed.

I had written to the sailor from USS Kitty Hawk who wrote me earlier in the year. He replied. His ship was stationed off the coast of Vietnam. He couldn't tell me exactly where, as that knowledge was classified. He indicated the ship had been under fire to some extent and they had responded. As I hadn't read about any of this in the newspaper, I wondered if Ross Rawlings – the sailor – had reported something he shouldn't have. Loose lips sink ships, I thought.

He told me the ship would be going to Japan soon and then back to the States for repairs. Being in a war zone seems so exciting. It would be great if the war wasn't over soon so we could experience some of that action. I wished him well.

Before I went to the library, I had baseball practice with my summer team. I had gotten a letter recently which stated that training for the season would be starting today. Games begin in a few weeks. My team is sponsored by Lichtenfels' Used Car Motors ('If it's not a Lichtenfels, it's not a used car').

I'm on the team with my brother which I suppose could be somewhat awkward – especially as he's better than me, but I wouldn't tell him that. Then there's that unspoken incident. I anticipate this will be my last year on the team as it's pretty obvious I don't have a career in professional baseball.

On the other hand, Will is good enough to move up to the high-end amateurs or even the professionals if he takes things seriously. My baseball career is kaput especially since I've discovered girls in general and Babs in particular.

At the library, I ran into Hep. I guess he was doing some similar work to me for school, but it seemed out of character for him. He suggested we go back to my place to shoot some pool. I said I'd drive him to my place, but that he'd have to find a way home as I was going to the All-Sports School Banquet this evening.

Although the coaches expected me to turn up, I'm not sure why as I haven't gotten into a game this year. The whole affair is a bit like the Oscars – a mutual jock admiration society. I'm far from being a jock, but que sera, sera. Whatever will be, will be!

Hep and I played a few games of 8-ball before I had to go get ready for the evening. I was able to drop him off at the Inclined Plane. Before he left, Hep reminded me of our double date next week. He suggested we take the girls bowling. I said OK, but his idea to go bowling struck me as very 1950s. I sarcastically asked him if Hazel – the maid from the TV show – would be there.

So, I went to the awards night banquet in the evening. The food was crap – leathery beef with lumpy gravy, broccoli with runny cheese sauce, mashed potatoes that tasted like starch and chocolate ice cream. The latter was the best part of the meal.

Afterwards, the seniors – and some good Juniors like Rudy Mingo – got awards and letter sweaters for being involved in sports. The champion basketball team was given a special trophy. There were other awards for cheerleaders and for the coaches.

Later there was a dance. Babs wasn't there, so I hooked up with Mary Lou LaPorchetto – a good looking girl who lived a few blocks from

286

me. She was part of the home economic catering group. I wondered why I had never asked her out as she had looks, personality, smarts and – oddly enough – no obvious boyfriend.

It was rumored that her dad was a gangster so maybe that turned off not only me, but apparently other suitors. We talked and danced but left it at that as anything beyond talking would surely get back to Babs.

I couldn't believe my eyes when I spotted the Chief. As far as I know, he has nothing to do with sport, yet there he was. He has a way of turning up at where he's least expected. He told me we were in big trouble over last night's package fiasco.

I thought of the joke where the Lone Ranger and Tonto are surrounded by Indians and the Lone Ranger says, 'We're in big trouble, Tonto.' At which point Tonto looks at him and says, 'What do you mean we, white man?'

I didn't want a bar of this tomfoolery. Life was good and last night's package to me was ancient history. He asked me who took it, but I didn't mention Columbus. Instead, I again mentioned Jones. He said he'd be seeing me, but I replied, 'Not if I see you first.' Barring this interruption, I had a good time. I took Mary Lou home but didn't try to steal a kiss. I knew how to swim but didn't fancy swimming with the fishes!

Cop-u-later.

MAY 8,
1966 – Sunday

Really had to get to the library to finish my research assignment on the Cold War. I didn't get much done yesterday with Hep there. The family had a big Sunday roast dinner – beef of course. Dad is a meat and potatoes man from way back and wouldn't eat anything else on a Sunday.

Mom, who hasn't cooked all that much recently as she still says she feels weak from her gall bladder operation, actually cooked. Duane and Ennis were there along with the rest of the family. Ennis had to leave early – probably had some snatch lined up! Duane was just Duane – bland and beige.

Gran-King was also there. GK had a couple of pre-dinner drinks. Her constant tirades against Negroes and Jews gets a bit tiresome. After the events of Friday, I have nothing but good things to say about Columbus. Mind you, the only other colored person I know is Hep's friend Pij. The jury's still out on him.

I'd rather Gran-King talks about the good old days than this racist shit. I reminded her that Dr. Martin Luther King, a Negro, won the Nobel Peace Prize. I doubt this changed her perceptions. GK is very lonely. Her husband died two years ago and – according to Dad – she's taken up drinking.

To say our 'formal' family meals in the dining room are bizarre would be an understatement. Dad no sooner cuts the roast and piles it on everyone's plate (you have no choice how much meat he serves) than he gobbles his food down in a couple of bites.

He then feels he has to get our approval for the meat because he looks at each person in order starting to the left of him and goes around the table asking the person his or her opinion of the roast. Woe behold anyone who disparages the cow. He takes it as a personal affront if we don't want seconds.

Anyway, I ate my meal (there were other things with the roast that I won't get into), gulped some apple pie down and then announced I had to go to the library to finish some work. Unfortunately, I was told I had to take Gran-King home.

I couldn't get out of it, or I wouldn't have the car, so I didn't have much of a choice. GK didn't say much despite her tipsiness. I don't think I could have taken any more of her comments or her morbidity. I took her home and was soon on my way to the library.

Before I arrived, I realised I'd forgotten my notes and the assignment guidelines. I went back home but couldn't find either. I was going nuts, but Mom came to the rescue and discovered both under some of Dad's old 'Playboys'. I guess I left my notes with them when I was having a peek. He only buys the magazines for the articles he once told me. Funny that because I only look at them for the girly pictures.

Take two. When I got to the City Public Library, I saw Peter Pells – a History classmate. I wanted to finish my report at home, but I could only borrow five books with my card. I needed more. Pells said he would borrow four more for me as he only needed one book. Go figure? Perhaps I've overdone the sources.

Oddly enough, sitting at a far table was Voohaus. She always struck me as a dumb blonde so this is the last place, I would have expected to see her. As usual, I was mesmerized by the sheer gorgeousness of the girl. She saw me and waved thus I felt obliged to say hello.

I said a few words but managed to sound inept and stupid all at once. Looking at her, I actually thought she was better looking than the cheerleaders. Well, line ball! I reminded her of our double date next Friday. She said she was looking forward to it. What the hell does she see in Hep, I thought?

Stayed up until one a.m. finishing the report. I alternated working on the assignment and reading Theodore White's book 'The Making of the President 1960.' My Dad, a Republican, says that Kennedy really stole that election from the schmuck Nixon. I doubt 'Tricky' Dick will ever be President.

Cop-u-later.

MAY 9,
1966 – Monday

A bit tired this morning after staying up late finishing my Cold War report, but I was pleased with my effort and expect a good grade. When I got to school, Hep asked if he could 'borrow' my report to look over. I reluctantly said OK but told him I wanted it back in time for my afternoon class.

'No problem,' he said.

'What are friends for?' I replied, almost sure he would be copying large parts of the report.

Saw Babs at lunch. Reminded her about our double date with Hep and Voohaus on Friday. She said she was happy about it, and even gave me a peck on the cheek to seal the deal. It was only a peck, but in front of everyone it had more status than a private kiss.

Going to class, I ran into Katie who was smiling like the cat who ate the canary. She said she was back with Stan the Man so her Prom campaign (the girls always look on Prom preparations as a military engagement) was on again. Understandably, nothing was said about STM's so-called girlfriend. I thought he had asked her to the Prom. Anyway, the big event is less than two weeks away. Things need to be done. For me, probably at the last minute!

Before my next class, I went to get my report from Hep. He told me he lent it to one of the jocks – Pat Fitzgerald. I was pissed off to no end and told Hep I'd retrieve it myself. I didn't know him all that well, but Fitzgerald always seemed like one of the less conceited jocks. He gave it to me right away. But when I looked at it, I discovered a page was missing. I had some kind of brain fade lending it to Hep in the first place.

When I got to class, I told my POD (Problems of Democracy) teacher about the missing page. I told her I left it at home, but I would re-do it after school and hand it in by the end of the day. I'm not totally sure she believed me. My excuse probably ranked up there with 'my dog ate my homework,' but she said it was OK to submit it after school.

Accordingly, I went to the school library to complete the report – again. Without my notes, it was a struggle, but I got it done. Probably it wasn't as good as the original, but it was completed. It was after four when I finished, so I thought I would be handing the report in late and be given a lower mark. Sister Mary Donuts – the teacher – was surprisingly pleasant about the whole thing. She took my paper, then asked me to sit down for a chat.

She caught me off guard by asking me what I was planning after I left school. I was supposed to make an appointment to talk to the counsellor, but never got around to it. Now I was asked by this nun to confront my future. Ten years ago, I would have said I wanted to be a fireman or cowboy. I told her I'd like to go to college where I'd decide my future path.

She said I should be able to enroll in college but put me on the spot by asking me to be more specific about my intentions. Under pressure, all I could think of was that I'd like a good-paying job. When pushed to name something, I went blank. I told her I wanted a job that paid $20,000 a year. Man, I'd be in clover if I got that much, I thought.

She laughed and wished me well, but our short discussion made me wonder what I would do after I finished school. It entered my mind for a few seconds anyway. Soon I was thinking about the Prom, the double date and how relieved I was getting my work handed in. I should have stayed pissed off at Hep, but how can you stay mad at your best friend? Besides, all's well that ends well (is that another Shakespeare reference?).

Later I thought some more about my future. I'm sure my dad would like me to be a doctor or lawyer, but I'd love to be a radio DJ. That would be so cool! I'm not sure it pays all that much, but so what. I could be another Long John! For now, I had other things on my mind. With my future plans on hold, I settled down at home to study for a Chemistry test tomorrow. Occasionally my mind wondered about what job I'd do when I 'grow up.'

Butcher, baker, candlestick maker? I kind of like the idea of making candles!

Cop-u-later.

MAY 10,
1966 – Tuesday

Last night I called Hep. We talked for an hour about school and our big double date on Friday. I probably sound like a broken record, but I still wonder how he got Voohaus to go to the Prom with him. The rumor is that her boyfriend is in the Army, and she wanted to go to the Prom so badly she'd have gone with anyone.

I wanted to believe that – I really did – if only because it would explain a lot. Hep isn't ugly by any means, but he's no Cary Grant. More like Boris Karloff, and he's not the sharpest whip in the stable.

I confess I'm a bit jealous of Hep. I really like Babs – I'd even use the l-word if it didn't make me feel trapped – and she's cute as a button. But Voohaus is Raquel Welch and Jayne Mansfield wrapped up into one. How am I supposed to control myself on a double date, much less a Prom? I've been trying to keep away from her if only to avoid temptation.

Well, I'm being punished for a past life as, to make matters worse, I ran into JV at school for the second time in three days. How come when you're trying to avoid someone you run into them all the time? I was anxious as I approached her, but I quickly composed myself and said hello.

I was somewhat tongue-tied, but not as much as usual. I managed to say all the right things and avoid embarrassing myself. The bell rang, and it was time to go to my Chemistry class. Despite limited study and the obvious distraction, I think I did OK on the test.

Anyway, sat with Babs at lunchtime. She was friendly enough. We held hands and she gave me a little peck when we were leaving the cafeteria. We've really become an item in the minds of our fellow students. The best thing about her affection for me is that it was in front of the Maggot.

Who cares, as he's history in a few weeks. I have some friends on the baseball team, so I'm not worried about retaliation by the seniors. I'm more worried about the Chief asking me to do another favor for him. I almost wish he hadn't saved my life from the Year 12s.

Had a baseball game after school. It was damn cold – unseasonably cold – for once. Even though it was close to freezing, the game went ahead. We were playing Richfield High – one of the suburban public schools. This game was for first place in our division. As usual, I was on the bench helping Sam Genovese keep score.

Going into the seventh inning (our games go for seven innings), the score was tied 0-0. The first batter for them walked. The next batter hit the ball into the left-center field gap. The outfielder got the ball and relayed it to the shortstop who made a fantastic throw to the plate that appeared to get their man out at home, but the umpire claimed the catcher interfered and called the runner safe.

Well, our team gave that umpire bloody hell. One guy used a swear word and was chucked out of the game. The coach went right up to the ump's face, no holds barred, and told the blind man (my words) what he thought of him. The rest of us were shouting and screaming. While we were arguing, the other Richfield guy came home as our coach had neglected to call time out when arguing with the ump. He was ejected from the game. We ended up losing 2–0.

The result gave everyone on our team the shits. Afterwards – in the locker room – the coach apologised for his actions. He told us we should accept the umpire's ruling even if we don't think he's right. Fine words for sure, but we wouldn't have a bar of them. We were robbed and wanted the coach to appeal to a higher authority.

Fat chance. One good thing came out of the game from my perspective. We got our school baseball caps. This made us officially cool or dorky – depending on your point of view. This was little consolation for today's 'blind' justice.

The rest of the evening, it was all I could do to put the game out of my mind. Only thoughts of Voohaus – I mean Babs – would be able to do that.

Cop-u-later.

MAY 11,
1966 – Wednesday

Was playing a scrub game with the team split into two. In the third inning, I got a hit and made it to first base. Our assistant coach – Dean Shiffauer – was pitching. He's a big hard-throwing lefty with a wicked fastball. Anyway, I took a lead off first base when he made a pickoff move to the base to try to get me out. The ball hit me flush on the head and 'dehorned' me.

I was momentarily knocked out. While under, I swear I saw Voohaus. I dreamed I went up to her and kissed her passionately on the lips. Not only didn't she resist but contributed some of her own moves. I'm pretty sure there was some tongue involved.

I don't think I was out for long, but the whole Voohaus thing seemed so real. Finally, I heard someone asking me to count to one hundred – backwards. I was alive. The coach was around me as were the rest of the team. I made a weak joke when I inquired about the condition of the ball, then jumped up like nothing had happened. What a lump I had. I was examined by the trainer, then told to go home and get it checked by a doctor.

I wasn't feeling the best, but what disturbed me more than the substantial lump on my head was that I thought of Voohaus in my otherworldly state. Why not Babs? I really like Babs I kept telling myself. How often did I have to say it? Didn't I trust my emotions? Did I have feelings for Voohaus instead of Babs?

When I got home, I asked Mom to check out my lump. She said it was a nasty 'goose egg,' but that I'd get over it. When Dad got home and checked my noggin, he said the same thing. He didn't think a doctor was necessary. After dinner, I was still feeling the effects of me using my head as a fielder's glove.

I decided to call Babs. The excuse was to make plans for Friday's date, but I kind of wanted to test my feelings. Babs was my true love, I kept thinking. She was my Prom date in ten days. She was the one I loved. I was temporarily captivated by Voohaus' looks. Babs and I had a great chat and said a lot of personal things. Babs was the one for me.

After I hung up, I asked Dad for the car on Friday, as I had a date. He was overwhelmed. Me with a girl! He seemed in a good mood, so I figured it was a good time to hit him up about driving the Wildcat to the Prom. Before I got up the nerve, he had some news for me. Ennis was enlisting in the Army for Officer Training. He would be inducted next week. Dad, a former army officer, ate that shit up.

Dad loved everything about Ennis. He wasn't the brightest crayon in the pack, but he was athletic, a high school sporting hero and was now going in the service as an officer. He was also a known philanderer that everyone sort of knew about except Pippa. I doubt if I could ever have lived up to Ennis according to Dad's standards. He was a 'man's man.'

Biddy's husband, Duane, was nerdy, but reliable and a loving husband. Dad respected Duane, but never really warmed to him he once told me. Dad said there was going to be a farewell party for Ennis on Saturday afternoon that he expected me to attend. That was all right with me. I had been blasted with a baseball and had wrestled with my mental demons over two girls. I could handle a boring armed forces party.

Cop-u-later.

MAY 12,
1966 – Thursday

Once again, Thursday. Rode to school with Katie and her dad. As is her habit, Katie sat next to me in a most inappropriate – yet oddly comforting – position. Her leg was right next to mine. Every so often she would rub it against me. I wonder if her father ever noticed. Not that I didn't like it. If only she would do something about her braces and nose. I guess I'm being cruel going there. Besides, I thought she now had a thing with Stan the Man.

As far as Voohaus was concerned, I told myself – not for the first time – I would no longer think of her. My sole concentration would be Babs. The problem with that is that we have our big double date tomorrow. I feel a bit like 'Dobie Gillis' contemplating his love life in front of the sculpture of 'The Thinker.' There's two women to consider – Babs and Voohaus, and Katie is my Zelda.

Hep had said we were going bowling Friday evening with our dates. I mentioned this to Babs who told me she liked bowling. Whether she obligatorily said that didn't matter. In my mind, I'd rather be alone with Babs, but Hep wanted a Prom night preview date. So be it. The big Prom night is a little over a week away.

Babs was, again, very frisky – for lack of a better word – at lunchtime. She snuggled up to me, held my hand and gave me little pecks on the cheek. These actions led to some ribbing – some good-natured, some jealous – from my friends. Eat your heart out, losers, I thought.

Actions speak louder than words, so I didn't bite at their cretinous soundings. I saw Voohaus, but I ignored her. You wouldn't give alcohol to an alcoholic, would you? However, that dream of kissing her when I was out like a light, was so vivid. I needed to stay focused on Babs.

Today was my lucky day. First, I won a Baby Ruth candy bar in Rock's math class for answering a problem correctly. The Rock weighs 70lb. soaking wet, so the nickname is somewhat ironic. My second bit of good luck occurred when rain postponed our scheduled baseball game. I wouldn't have played anyway, and I had a book report on Shakespeare's 'A Midsummer Night's Dream' to complete.

As far as I'm concerned, Puck can get fucked. I really didn't understand the play – something about fairies I gather. So, I used a 'Cliff Notes' summary of the play, which I had bought at the local five and dime to help me. Where would we be without 'Cliff Notes?'

I was working on my report in my room when the phone rang. It was answered by my sister Kitty who yelled for all the family to hear, 'It's for you – a girl.' She particularly emphasised the girl part of her message to let everyone know in the household that someone of the opposite sex actually wanted to talk to me. I quickly rushed to the phone expecting it to be Babs, but instead it was Voohaus.

She said she wanted to know about tomorrow's double date. I'm sure we filled her in at school, but also, why didn't she call Hep to get that information? I know I swore off Voohaus this morning, but that was then, this is now. Secretly, I was glad she phoned me despite my silent protestations. We talked about the usual crap that goes on around school. We also talked about the Prom. I was eternally grateful she didn't talk about her dress.

Then, she told me in that Marilyn Monroe voice of hers that she was happy we were double dating tomorrow. She didn't mention Hep at all. I said I, too, was looking forward to it. We ended our call after about an hour's chat. I never did get around to giving her details about the date.

Was God tempting me like the devil tempted Jesus in the desert? Do I tell my best friend that I talked to his date (it's not as if she's his girlfriend) on the phone? I dare not mention it to Babs. All my good intentions to avoid Voohaus were for naught. Remember, she called me and not vice versa.

Meanwhile, strange things were happening to me physically such as severe pain in my lower extremities. This date would be something to behold – as would the Prom.

Cop-u-later.

MAY 13,
1966 – Friday

Big double date or, as Hep put it, a making out warm-up for next week's Prom. Hep certainly has a way with words. As I'm driving on the night of the Prom, Hep said he'd drive tonight. He picked me up first. Then we went to Janet Voohaus' place to get her. Voohaus was gorgeous as always but was dressed as if she was going to a cocktail party rather than bowling.

She wore a semi-short black dress with a low-cut back and sparkles all over. She wore stockings and boots as well. How does that Nancy Sinatra's song go, 'These Boots Are Made for Walkin'.' I sure hope one of these days her boots are 'gonna walk all over me' (boom, boom, boom, boom, etc.). I admit I've been hot for Voohaus recently. Her attire did nothing to dampen those feelings.

Finally, we picked up Babs. Babs looked great – obviously dressed for bowling so not as spectacular as Voohaus. When I went to her door to collect Babs, I was greeted by her sister – the Turtle. I blatantly flirted with her which I'm sure didn't impress Babs. Anyway, when Voohaus saw Babs' attire, she insisted we take her back to her place to change. Hep and I – as red-blooded American boys – tried to talk her out of it, but she was insistent. So, we backtracked.

Around eight, we got to the Westside Bowling Lanes near my home. I'm shit-house at bowling, but not as bad as Babs who maybe was playing the helpless female and letting me beat her. On the other hand, Hep and Voohaus were really good at the game which made me look somewhat inadequate in front of my girlfriend.

While I was bowling, I was confronted by my public-school friends Cooey Procco and Beetle Bailey. They started making fun of my clothes and my bowling action. They laughed and mockingly asked how someone as ugly as me could get such a tough girlfriend. 'Eat your heart out, losers,' I said. 'At least I have a date.'

I playfully told them I hope they like kissing each other. That didn't totally stop their rantings, but it did silence them temporarily. I didn't mean to, well maybe I did, but in the course of the match, I started flirting with Voohaus. This put both Hep and Babs off. Neither were happy!

After the match (I think Hep won, Voohaus was second; my score was embarrassingly low, though just above Babs), we stopped off at the local Dairy Queen for ice cream. We parked in the Dairy Queen lot where Hep and Voohaus started smooching hot and heavy like. I got a couple of kisses from Babs, but nothing as passionate as the other couple. Babs just wasn't all that receptive in this environment.

Between flirting with Voohaus and the Turtle, I didn't make a very good impression with Babs. I suggested we go to my place for a bit of pool. This was one game where I could shine. When we got there, Will and his friends were drinking, swearing and looking the worse for wear. Babs was annoyed. Voohaus, however, reveled in it. Will's gang managed to be civil with us, but nonetheless, rowdy. They offered us a drink, but we refrained from imbibing. I'm sure Voohaus was tempted.

Babs remembered Will from her party and briefly spoke to him. Will, meanwhile, cornered Voohaus and asked her out. I'd had enough of this circus. I decided to get the hell out of there. I went with Hep as he drove the girls home. On the way, he parked the car on a side street.

I got a few kisses from Babs while Hep furiously made out with Voohaus. We then dropped them off. I thanked the girls for coming on this date and told them I was looking forward to the Prom. As she was leaving the car, Voohaus blew me a kiss.

The double was successful to a point, though I did think that Babs could loosen up a bit. The big day was coming up soon. After we dropped Babs off, Hep and I talked about the Prom and how great it would be. That night, I went to bed pretty happy with the way things had gone. Just as at Christmas, I had visions, but this time of Voohaus dancing in my head.

Cop-u-later.

MAY 14,
1966 – Saturday

Only a week before the Prom, and all I can think of is Janet Voohaus – Hep's date. I do everything I can to think of other things like Babs, but 'The Big V' keeps popping into my head. Am I in love? I like Babs a lot, but Voohaus really turns me on. I've got to get my shit together before next Saturday.

I got the car in the morning and drove by Voohaus' house – more than once I might add. I wanted to see her. I knew the address as Hep had picked her up for our date yesterday. I guess I'm kind of getting into a weird area here. I just hope I wasn't noticed.

And what about my best friend, Hep? Maybe I'm jealous of all the smooching he did with her last night. They say all is fair in love and war. This is both. Babs is a great girl. I should concentrate on wanting to be with her.

In the afternoon, the family attended Ennis' farewell party at the Country Club as he's to be inducted into the service at the end of the month. Though boring, as expected, at least it helped me forget my love woes by giving me some distractions. Drinks were plentiful – though I was a bit restrained as I wanted the car in the evening – and there were some tough-looking chicks (very expensive if you wished to take them out) as eye candy.

Ennis was at his blowhard best and had his sleaze-ball pretentious buddies with him as an audience. Good riddance, I thought. Soon after we got home – thankfully, we left early – I reminded myself I still haven't told Dad about the car and the Prom. Shades of the Sadie.

I'll need some money as well so I'd better clear this up soon. Speaking of the old man, Dad was prancing around the house in his underwear, socks and slippers. He even went outside and said hello to Mrs. Pride in that garb. I wish I could be so uninhibited.

Hep got a job at a restaurant/ice cream place called the 'Dairy Dall.' In the evening I picked up the other boys – Frenchie, JD, Racovic and, the much-derided hanger-on, the Boob. We played a bit of pool at my basement (Will and his imbecile friends, thank the heavens, weren't there).

I easily beat the lot, though JD is improving daily and becoming a real threat.

Anyway, JD had a little flask of gin with him and shared it with us. We were a might tipsy because we (except for the mammoth Frenchie) played hockey using a cue ball, and brooms on top of the pool table (I think it was just a little flask). I shouldn't have been driving, but I got the car and suggested we visit Hep at his place of work. He gave us free ice cream even as we gave him shit for his white outfit, and a stupid-looking white and red-striped hat.

We didn't know what to do afterwards. As we were feeling our oats, I thought some hot dogs would do us fine. I drove down to Coney Island and ordered five dogs with everything on. It was fascinating seeing Pickles do his thing. It's got to be one of the wonders of the world.

While there, I noticed Pij sitting by himself in a corner booth. Against my better judgement and feeling the gin, I sat beside him and started mouthing off about him supplying those funny cigarettes to students. Well, he got quite irate, and accused me of being a racist. The argument got us quite a bit agitated.

I told him it had nothing to do with race, but I noticed he wasn't interested in finding out who was the culprit. I continued. People acted funny when he was at a dance like they were on something, and I knew of a black guy who may be involved. In reality, I wasn't actually sure Columbus was involved.

At this, Pij nearly blew his stack. He wanted to fight me right then and there. My friends had heard the commotion and came over to back me up, but I was aware of Pij's fighting ability and I told them to back off. Pij had fire in his veins and was ready to come at me.

Then he stopped and said it wasn't any of my business whether he was involved in any of that shit. He said he'd let this incident pass for now because I was Danny's (read Hep's) friend, but he wouldn't forget it. Frenchie then dragged me out of the place most likely to save me from myself.

I wasn't sure what had come over me. Was Gran-King and Dad's influence that strong? Where was the proof that Pij was involved in selling that shit? We made it to the car safely and got the hell out of there. It was quiet as I dropped off the guys. Some things are better left unsaid.

Cop-u-later.

MAY 15,
1966 – Sunday

Thought I'd stay home to get on Dad's good side. I'll need the car next Saturday and will probably be out all night. Plus, I need some dough. Besides, the less I see Hep, the less I'll think of Voohaus and what a rat I am. Thinking about her all the time, wishing she was with me, being jealous of Hep. Driving by her house and hoping to catch a glimpse of her. What kind of friend am I?

This morning I was called in to serve Mass. The new service is being used where the priest faces the congregation. There's no Latin either. The service went much faster than previously. Thank the Lord! After Mass, I went right home and helped Dad put screens up and cut back some of the backyard plants. He continues to walk around in his boxer shorts – even out back – thus I'm reluctant to bring the girls home before the Prom. I'll decide later.

I doubt that Mom – still recovering from her operation – will want to make an appearance on Prom night. Dad may want to see the gals dressed to the nines, but I'm not quite sure I want them to see him if in his 'Fruit of the Looms.'

Called Babs to ask her how she was doing. She said she had a good time on Friday and was excited about the Prom. She couldn't wait to go.

Anyway, I was about to ring Hep when I picked up the phone and overheard Ennis talking to a woman on the other phone. I shouldn't have been eavesdropping, but I guess I just couldn't help myself. Ennis was setting up a date – I use that term loosely – for the evening. Well, Mom warned us that he was a bastard, but this was too much. I heard the word motel mentioned as well as some things an innocent like me barely understood.

I didn't know what to think. Do I tell Pip? Do I confront Ennis? His wife's pregnant. Shouldn't they be together? I might have forgotten the whole sordid affair, except that he told Pippa he was going to play poker with his old high school chums and would be gone all night. I decided to confront him about these lies and ask him what he was planning. After all, Pippa is my sis!

I caught up with him privately that afternoon and spilled the beans. Ennis was momentarily taken aback but recovered nicely like the Army Officer he was about to become. He said he had to set his girl cousin up in a motel apartment (I hadn't mention motel to him) before he went to a poker game tonight. The whole thing smelled to high heaven. Naturally, I didn't believe a word he said, and I wondered whether I should sing to Pippa.

On reflection, I figured it would be too much stress to mention this to my sister or anyone else for that matter as it could get back to her. The news would hurt her, which could possibly harm the baby-to-be. Besides, she most likely wouldn't believe me anyhow.

Dad would probably applaud Ennis' actions and tell me to keep my big mouth shut. Mom would condemn the action and give me that 'I told you so' look. Then she'd tell me to let it be as she took a drag from her cigarette.

I needed to get out of there. I asked Dad for the car and made up an excuse that I was putting some gas in. I'm still hung up on Voohaus so instead I drove it to where she lived. Maybe it was to upset Hep, but really it was because I just wanted to catch a glimpse of her. I parked it so I could see the house but not be seen.

While parked, I spotted Voohaus in her nightie in her upstairs bedroom. Man, that was all I needed. The image would keep me going for weeks. Then I thought I saw a guy half-dressed in her room. Some bad vibes there. Someone may have seen me as the front light was turned on. I got the hell out of there as I didn't want to get caught, accused of being a stalker and possibly arrested. I prayed I hadn't been seen.

I'd seen enough. I got the gas for the car and went home for dinner. The whole weekend had been an eye opener for me.

Cop-u-later.

MAY 16,
1966 – Monday

'Monday, Monday, can't trust that day' sang the 'Mamas and Papas.' That's how I feel. I'm sick of thinking of Voohaus all the time when I have an amazing girl like Babs who wants to be with me. My opinion of Voohaus went south when I saw the guy in her room half-undressed. How can I trust her – despite her looks? I'm going to concentrate on being the best boyfriend I can with Babs and not worry about things over which I have no control.

Hep is my best friend for crying out loud. I shouldn't be farting in his face. He's with Voohaus and not me! As for that mystery gentleman I saw in her bedroom last night, he wasn't a mirage. My eyes did not play tricks on me. I'd swear on a stack of Bibles he existed.

I decided not to tell Hep. Would he believe me anyway? He'd probably say I was just jealous of his relationship with Voohaus. Then there was that whole Pij thing the other night. Would Hep and I still be friends if he knew about that?

My sense of right and wrong was definitely on the blink. I had accused Hep's friend Pij of selling drugs to students. I had perved on my best friend's Prom date. And I had done a 'Casper Milquetoast' by not telling Pippa about my brother-in-law's nocturnal activities.

I sat with Babs at lunch while Hep sat with Voohaus in her area of the cafeteria. Babs and I held hands openly. This is unusual, as both of us aren't fond of overt public displays of affection. With some exceptions! Anyway, I had to leave the lunchroom early for a baseball game. As I walked out, I turned away from Voohaus and did what I could to avoid any eye contact.

We had a game after school. As usual, I sat on the bench. We beat Adams High School (named after one or the other of the Presidents Adams) in an exciting game 1-0. We scored in the bottom of the seventh on an error, but we'll take it any way we can get it. We still have a chance to win our division – although it's hard to get excited when you don't play.

After school, I met Hep to discuss arrangements for the Prom. I expected him to mention my encounter with Pij, but he said nothing. Either he wasn't told anything or he's waiting until after the Prom to confront me. Either way, it's a recipe for anxiety. My fingernails will be bitten to the bone in anticipation. Anyway, I told Hep I made reservations at the Xanadu restaurant – a classy joint in the City. We'll go there after the Prom dance.

Then there's a post-Prom party at the Pig's Whistle Nightclub nearby. This is being organised by the Seniors. We should be out until five a.m. at the earliest. Naturally, I'm driving my dad's big red Buick Wildcat. If that doesn't impress the ladies, nothing will. So, we're all set for Saturday after I talk to Dad. Decided to call Babs to tell her the details.

I'm a bit behind in some of my work so I called Charles Frick aka Frickn' Chuck. Frickn' Chuck is in my English class so I asked him if I could borrow his notes for a 'Pride and Prejudice' book report due this week. He offered me the whole report and said I could copy as much as I want for All Buns' class.

I knew she would catch me if I copied the information word for word, but it would be good to read Chuck's ideas and get the gist of the book (as boring as it is). My moral compass is all over the place lately.

When I got home, I saw Pippa and Ennis. Ennis is to be inducted into the Army shortly. Pip will be joining him after he's settled. After she left the room, Ennis took me aside and asked me not to mention the phone call to his 'cousin'. He said it would only upset Pippa which would not be good for the baby. He then put the boot in and said he knew about me stabbing my brother and it would be a shame if the news got out.

I hadn't planned to say anything to my sister about her husband's dalliance with his 'cousin,' but the fact that he mentioned the unfortunate wedding stabbing confirmed to me he was guilty as hell for cheating on Pip. Not that I needed much convincing. As for bringing up the incident, I thought he was a real pig for blackmailing me.

He said he would never do anything like that again (did he mean the blackmailing or the nocturnal exercise?). I agreed to stay silent as I figured it was better not to open this can of worms. I knew in my heart that this wouldn't be the last incident of this nature in their marriage. In my head I could hear my mom's prediction she once made that their union wouldn't last.

Cop-u-later.

MAY 17,
1966 – Tuesday

The Prom is only four days away. At school, I ran into Katie who's going to the Prom with Stan the Man. This on-again, off-again romance can only end up in hurt for her. Stan the Man is a no-good-nik. But if going to the Prom with him makes her happy, then I'm happy. She was smiling broadly and willing to bear her soul – not that I was all that interested in her feelings for Stan or her Prom arrangements. But I felt good for her.

Caught up with Babs at lunch. She looked great. My plan to avoid the temptress Voohaus was working. Babs and I held hands and after lunch she even gave me a kiss – a long one though far away from the crowd. Like Babs, I'm really hyped up about the Prom and can't wait for the day to come.

Had to leave school early as the team had a baseball game against Fernmount High School. We lost 6-3 so look out of the running for the division championship. Not that I'm too hung up on it in my role as a bench jockey. Actually, I almost got to play. Our regular catcher – Ralph Chiodo – was late arriving for the game.

Apparently, Ralph – one of the Year 12 officers – was arguing with Georgie Porgie over the after-Prom party at the Pig's Whistle. Porgie was back after being mysteriously treated in the hospital. From what I heard later, he had concerns about a social function with our school kids at that nightclub. He needed convincing by Ralph, who organized the function, that it would be above board.

As the substitute catcher, I was warming up the starting pitcher for the match. The game was within minutes of beginning when Ralph came roaring in like the Cavalry in a John Wayne western movie. He took over and that was that. I'm not sure if I was happy or relieved about it. I wanted to play, but I hadn't had time to get my head around starting the game. I guess I'm used to being on the bench.

After the game, I had to rush home immediately after I got changed and showered as I had baseball practice with my summer team –

Lichtenfels Motors. Our coach – Bobby Jenkins – is a great guy. He's in his twenties and relates well with the players.

Unlike the school team, I get to play. I usually play second base, though sometimes catcher. Our first game is in a couple of weeks. Will is on the team. He also plays for his school team – Westwood Suburban Public High School. After last month's tragedy with him, I've tried to keep my distance for fear of another incident occurring.

Will and I got a ride home with one of our teammate's parents. When we got there, Mom was still in bed. This wasn't the first incident of this type. It's always leads to a bad scene when it occurs, and so it did.

Dad wasn't too happy when he got home as Mom had been in bed all day. There ensued a major argument with shouting and words that could have come from a sailor. It wasn't a pretty sight by any means. Will, Kitty and I stayed downstairs and out of it. From what I heard, Mom blamed her gall bladder operation for her inactivity, but Dad wasn't sympathetic.

Dad called her a lazy so-and-so and told her to make dinner, but she held her ground and refused. It didn't help that she was puffing on a cigarette throughout the conflict. Dad looked on the verge of fisticuffs but managed to restrain himself.

As always, Mom won, Dad surrendered and went out for Clarke's Submarine Sandwiches, which I don't mind as they're great. They say it's the jalapenos old man Clarke liberally throws into the sandwich that makes them legends of food. Arguments of this nature hardly bode well for me bringing Babs, Hep and Voohaus home to speak to the folks before the Prom.

Cop-u-later.

MAY 18,
1966 – Wednesday

It rained like hell last night and today. One might say it was raining cats and dogs - if you were some old fart. The streets were really bad as there were gushes of water running down the side of the road, and there were deposits of mud and debris dropped by the torrent of water.

Someone said it reminded them of the great floods of 1888 and 1937 that more or less destroyed the town. Since then, the Government has made sure our town was flood free and this would never happen again.

I didn't want to get caught up in the flood comparisons. I was happy to skip school. I thought I was going to until Dad said I had no choice. He said he'd drive me. I couldn't see the point. It seemed even more pointless when I got to school, and half the students hadn't shown up.

Even Babs didn't make the trip, and I certainly didn't see Voohaus (not that I was looking for her). As much as I thought it was crazy braving the water to get to school, I had no choice but to listen to Dad and not rock the boat (boom, boom) if I wanted the car this weekend.

Hep was there. We talked about the Prom on Saturday. I was worried that if this rain continued, I wouldn't be able to drive the car. Can you imagine your father picking up your date with you, dropping you off at the Prom, picking you up to go to a restaurant in the city, afterwards dropping you off at the Pig's Whistle and then taking you home at five a.m.?

Hep was more worried about what the wetness would do to the girls' gowns. I'd heard enough about the gowns. Tell someone who cares! I just hoped that the downpour was a one off. I wouldn't want it to ruin our Prom date.

Anyway, Hep said we'd pick up our tuxes on Saturday morning. It was all arranged. Just bring money. On the night, I told him I'd get the car and pick him up first, then Voohaus followed by Babs. Like the Sadie, we'd return to his place for pictures. As I hadn't told Dad, this was wishful thinking. I still need to secure the car for the night. Maybe there's a chance I can get my parents to see the couples. I'm forever the optimist.

Once again, if Hep knew about my weekend encounter with Pij, he didn't say anything. Should I tell him and get the whole ugly incident out into the open? I thought I'd wait to see how things unfolded.

We were supposed to play a baseball game against City High, but it was rained out. We have to win this game to have any chance of making the finals, so the game will have to be rescheduled – not that I was unhappy about that.

Because of the rain, we were dismissed from school early, so I hitchhiked home rather than wait for the public bus. To get to the highway, you have to climb this steep and now wet hill, but considering the alternatives, it was worth it. I got a ride faster than had I waited for the 'slow boat to China' City bus.

When I got home, lo and behold the place was clean. Mom was out of bed, the beds were made, and she was cooking dinner. All of last night's drama had done some good. Dad would be pleased. Maybe I would be able to bring my friends home on Saturday.

After dinner, I went upstairs and caught my brother Will in my room stealing money from my drawer. Naturally, I went ape shit. I didn't want to lose my temper. I politely asked him what the hell he was doing. He said he needed money for something or another. I plum forget his irrelevant reason.

I was irate and was about to give him shit when he said, 'Go ahead, stab me again.' Well that just about floored me. I decided to control myself. When I had calmed down, I told him I would gladly lend him some money, but he should ask me next time.

I asked how much he had taken and told him I expected him to pay it back. It's amazing how a guilty conscience changes one's attitude.

After he left, I hid the rest of my money.

Cop-u-later.

MAY 19,
1966 – Thursday

Thursday, and a ride to school with Katie and her dad. The worst of the deluge was over, but mud and ripped-up shrubs told the tale of a Noah's Ark-type storm. I expected Katie to be on top of the world with the Prom in two days, but her eyes were all red as if she had been crying. I didn't say anything in the car indeed we barely said a word to each other. When we got to school, I asked her if everything was OK.

She didn't say anything at first, then reluctantly told me that Stan the Man was sick and wouldn't be able to take her to the Prom. This was after she had bought a dress and was to go to the hairdresser on Friday. I gave her a little hug as it was hard not to feel sorry for her. She seemed so vulnerable.

There were tears in her eyes. In this mode, she was not unattractive. I consoled her and told her all would be good. She still had me as a friend if she needed someone to talk to. In reality, I had no idea what else I could do. I really had deeper shit on my mind.

Because the rain had washed out the cafeteria, students had lunch throughout the school. Our Home Room was assigned to dine in the Science Lab. Because of the different environment, Babs was a bit standoffish. She wasn't as affectionate as she had been the last few days. Babs said all she could think of was the Prom. She was picking up that infernal dress from the store tomorrow. She then proceeded to describe the frock in great detail for the umpteenth time.

I should be more supportive, I guess, but she lost me at dress! My mind tuned to other things such as Katie's plight, but not Voohaus. I've had enough of that old chestnut. I still can't help thinking about that guy I saw in her bedroom the other day. I'm of two minds whether or not to tell Hep. As for the Pij incident, I decided to not worry about it anymore. What's done is done. I'll have to live with it.

When Babs finished babbling on, I gave her some details of the Prom evening. As I had mentioned some of these things before, I suppose it was her turn to tune out. Keep in mind, I still have to tell Dad.

During lunch, Ralph Chiodo rushed into the lab and announced that those attending the after-Prom function would have to get a parent signature to go to the Pig's Whistle. Permission forms were passed out. Everyone was pissed off at Georgie Porgie.

Who wants to tell their parents they'll be out until five a.m.? Particularly the good Catholic girls. We were told it had to be done if we wanted to attend. The form had to be handed in tomorrow – signed! I figure I'll have to tell Dad tonight.

Meanwhile, the baseball game – scheduled for after school – was cancelled, so I got to go home early. I wasn't unhappy at this development. Winning the division is a long shot anyway. As I was waiting for the City bus, I noticed Stan the Man, who hadn't been at school today, talking to a girl. This really bugged me as he obviously wasn't sick.

I was ready to give him hell when my bus arrived. I made a note to confront the bastard at some future time. How strange that I was the defender of Katie – a girl who liked me a lot, but with whom I couldn't care less about developing a relationship.

When I got home, I was ready to tell Dad about the Prom, the car and the note that needed signing. However, he was busy cutting out coupons for the weekend's grocery shopping. I chickened out just like before the Sadie. Now I have to talk to him in the morning. What's the old saying – always put off today that which you can do tomorrow?

Cop-u-later.

MAY 20,
1966 – Friday

How does that poem start – the bastardized version. 'Twas the night before Prom when all through the house, not a creature was stirring not even a mouse?' I've been reluctant to tell Dad about the Prom for one reason or another that I really can't articulate. This morning I had no alternative as I had to get him to sign the permission form to be handed in today at school. Also, I had to reserve the car for Saturday night.

Anyway, I broke it to him at breakfast. He was overwhelmed by the news. Unlike Will, I don't bring girls home to meet my family. He particularly liked that I was taking Barbara Geist whose father was on the City Council. A fact I didn't know. Thus, I achieved both of my goals. He signed the permission form and let me have the car tomorrow. I felt on top of the world as I made my way to school.

We're getting back to normal after the 'big wet' of Wednesday. The water that had soaked into the buildings had subsided. We were again able to use the cafeteria for lunch – although it was muddy in places. Saw Babs, and she continued to talk up the Prom tomorrow night.

For once she didn't go on about her dress. Ironically, I brought up the subject when I asked her if the mud would cause any problems with her long gown. She dismissed this concern by quoting what she said was a Buddhist text: 'it is what it is.' I was suitably impressed with the reference.

Hep, too, was in good spirits. We agreed to meet tomorrow morning in the City to finalise our tux arrangements. As for Voohaus, I think I'm getting over her, but avoided her nonetheless just to make sure. I may not have that luxury come tomorrow evening. I decided not to tell Hep about Voohaus' mystery man until after the Prom. Why ruin the evening?

I looked around for Stan the Man during the day as I wanted to have a word with him about the way he treated Katie. I needed to get it off my chest. It wasn't that I liked Katie, not in that way she wanted, I just figured she needed some justice after a number of bad breaks. But Stan was away.

Got home early to talk to Dad. He gave me some bad news that I half expected to hear anyway. He said Mom didn't want to meet the group before the Prom as she wasn't up to it. I went up to see her in her bedroom as I hoped she'd change her mind, but it wasn't to be. We're being greeted by the three other parents and I'm the one driving.

I admit to feeling a bit hurt that my parents didn't want to see my date and I on this special occasion. When I asked her why, she could only say, 'I can't, I just can't.' She's been increasingly withdrawn since her gall bladder operation. She's been smoking and drinking more than ever.

Called Babs and told her how lucky I was to have her as my Prom date. She said she was picking up her dress after school. Her mom, a hairdresser, was doing her hair. Amidst all the preparations she was undertaking, she told me she really cared for me.

I was ecstatic. Her words were stronger than like, but weaker than love. I'll take it! Voohaus be damned!

After I hung up, I was on pins and needles. I couldn't sit still. I called Cooey and Beetle – my public-school friends – and asked them to come over to play pool. When they got here, I told them about the Prom and Babs and all that stuff.

They both gave me shit, but I didn't give a damn. What Prom were they going to? We played pool for a while before going to Stuvers where I only had 3-18c burgers, fries and a choc milk shake. I wasn't all that hungry.

After I dropped the boys off at their houses, I returned home. Funnily enough, when I pulled into the driveway, I noticed the dirt over the hole I had dug up in Mrs. Pride's place last month had been disturbed. As the bones I had discovered at one time had been removed, there should have been nothing there of note, I thought. I had questions, but that was then, this is now. It would have to wait as I had a Prom to go to.

That night I had visions of sugarplums dancing through my head!

Cop-u-later.

MAY 21,
1966
Saturday – The Prom

Prom day – finally! I've been waiting for this day since 'Moby Dick was a minnow', if I may steal an expression commonly used by my history teacher Mr. Ranan. I hope I don't blow it (boom, boom.) You might say I was chomping at the bit to get things started when I got up for the big day.

After breakfast, Dad asked me to take Will to the sporting goods store to pick up some golf clubs, and then to drop him off at the golf course. I guess I have to do things like this to get the car all day – and all night. After this brief interlude, I picked up Hep to get our tuxes (white with black trim, bow tie and a pink carnation) and corsages for our dates. We also picked up some black shoes and had time to grab a couple burgers and a shake at Stuvers.

I took Hep home. The calm before the storm. The rest of the afternoon was filled with anxiety mixed with anticipation saddled around a couple of activities. I watched Muhammed Ali beat Henry Cooper in a fight. I picked up Will after his golf game.

After getting ready, I had to pass Mom's inspection. She proclaimed I'd be the handsomest one at the ball, but then moms are supposed to say those things. Dad, Kitty and even Will wished me well. Will said something about not forgetting my rubber.

Kitty gave me a little kiss. Pictures were taken. I was a bit sad I couldn't show off my date to Dad and Mom and share my happiness with them, but such is life! I wasn't going to let Mom's idiosyncrasies ruin my night. I was now ready to paint the town red!

Picked Hep up at seven-thirty. Talked to his parents for a bit. His Mom thought we looked like twins in our matching outfits. Did she think she was flattering me? Our next stop was to pick up Voohaus. She was gorgeous as ever in her long blue gown. She was wearing stockings and white shoes with short heels. She had long white gloves on. Her hair was pulled up. Hep pinned her corsage and the inevitable photos were taken. We had a chat with the parents, and we were off.

Now to Babs. Babs was exquisite in a green gown with flowers on it and a sash across his midriff. She also had the heels, stockings and gloves. Her hair was worn down with little sparkles throughout. Babs looked beautiful. I don't know why I was so hung up on Voohaus as Babs looked even better than her.

She looked like a little angel to me. I fell more in love than ever when I saw her. Once again, the corsage was pinned, and the photos were taken. We talked to the parents as well as her Gran and the Turtle before moving on.

There was one last stop, and that was at Hep's place as his parents wanted to see his date and take pictures. I felt like a male model with all these photos taken. This made me even more disappointed at my mom's decision not to see us. Anyway, when we got to the Prom venue, we couldn't find a place to park. Mr. Voohaus saved the day by beating us there and reserving a parking spot.

Inside the Hall, we found our way to our table. Racovic, Frenchie and JD were already sitting with their dates. We then settled down to three hours of dancing, listening to the music by a crappy band made up of teachers that only knew Cole Porter songs, and staring into our dates' eyes.

The dancing was great, but I particularly liked the slow ones where I could cuddle right up to Babs and smell her beautiful hair. I did manage one dance with Voohaus, but it did nothing for me as I'm hung up on Babs.

Babs wanted to get a formal Prom picture. 'Try and stop me,' I joked. The theme of the Prom was Blue Hawaii. The picture was taken in front of a backdrop of a fake beach with palm trees, Hula girls and lays for decoration. A cliche, sure, but magical, nonetheless. Another cliche, I hoped this night would never end.

Only one thing ruined the mood. In the course of the evening, I noticed Stan the Man with a date. He was supposed to be sick so he couldn't go to the Prom with Katie. Yet here he was with his girlfriend.

I couldn't let this betrayal of Katie pass. I would give him a piece of my mind later. It was approaching midnight when it was time to go. They say time flies when you're having a good time. All good things come to an end I suppose. Next stop – the Xanadu restaurant.

Cop-u-later.

MAY 22,
1966
Sunday – After-Prom

After the Prom, we had a short drive to the Xanadu Restaurant in the City. They specialize in Chinese food, but since no one knew what the hell to order, we all passed. To a person we said we didn't like Chinese food anyway, but I doubt if any of us had ever eaten it.

I guess I had some at Amy Sing's place, though I couldn't tell you what I ate. At home I once had frozen, heat-up and ready to serve chop suey (which isn't really Chinese food I've been told). Here we all had turkey, mashed potatoes, peas and apple crisp for dessert.

It was after one a.m. when we were on our way to the 'Pig's Whistle' Nightclub for the After-Prom party. Before we got there, Hep suggested we go parking. So, I drove up this dark, secluded road amidst screams from the girls. I don't know whether they were fake screams or not – though it hardly mattered.

I pulled over to the side of the road. Hep and Voohaus immediately started to go at it hot and heavy like there was no tomorrow. Up front, Babs and I kissed at a less frantic pace and at a more subdued level than in the back seat.

After a few minutes, I got more aggressive. I went for second base and tried to touch Babs' boobs. Unfortunately, she backed away at a certain moment and I tore her corsage. I felt terrible and stopped.

This didn't deter Voohaus and Hep as they continued on, oblivious to the drama up front. Babs maybe felt a bit sorry for me and cuddled closer. We resumed our more sedate making out which included some tongue. Now on to the 'Pig's Whistle' around two.

The 'Pig's Whistle' is a beautiful venue nestled in the hills outside the City. It was decorated to the hilt by the organizers. Streamers, balloons, painted signs, you name it. Once there, we had a great time dancing to 'juke box' music we could rock to, and not that crap dished out at the Prom. The atmosphere was informal, and many girls even discarded their shoes for the occasion. Babs got quite affectionate. We kissed and held hands throughout.

We had been there for a while when I excused myself to go to the bathroom. That's where I spotted Stan the Man. Already pissed off that he had left Katie in the lurch, I called him a 'dirty prick' and showered him with unmentionable names and nasty insults.

None of this bothered Stan. He laughed at me and told me Katie was a dog. For this, I pushed him as hard as I could. He went backwards and fell down. His head hit the floor and started bleeding. I thought I'd better get out of there before the chaperones found out. They surely would pass on this news to the principal. As it was four-thirty a.m., I figured it was time to go anyway.

As soon as we got in the car, Hep started to go at it again with Voohaus. We parked at the same desolate place as before. This time Babs was the aggressive one. We kissed like we had never kissed before. I made second base with a bit of boob action but stopped there for a double.

I looked on Babs and me as a long-term thing and decided to pace myself. No use getting greedy. It was now five a.m., and time to get the girls home. I didn't want a 'Wake up little Suzie' on my hands. I dropped off Babs first. I told her what a wonderful time I had, and she said likewise. She gave me a super passionate kiss. What a night!

I then took Voohaus home and stayed in the car for Hep's 'leaving is such sweet sorrow' on her porch. Unlike Babs' place, the light was on, and the parents were up, so I didn't fancy Hep's chances for much more than a peck. I was taking Hep home when he suggested we go to Coney Island for a hot dog.

Here we caught up with Pij who referred to Hep as fuck'n James Bond in his tux. I greeted him, but – as expected – things were tense. Pij acted as if nothing was wrong, but a blind person could have sensed otherwise. I think Hep realised something was up, but the two of them weren't giving anything away, like they were under Maxwell Smart's 'Cone of Silence.'

Surprisingly, Pij asked me for money. I couldn't believe his boldness. I guess I wanted to try to bury the hatchet. I still had my suspicions about his selling and supplying students with that shit, but he was Hep's friend, and I didn't want Pij to come between us. I reluctantly obliged him.

Then Hep and I went across the street for a six a.m. Mass of which I barely remember a thing. Afterwards, I took Hep home. I got home at seven-thirty a.m. – about twelve hours after leaving for the Prom. I was on top of the world the whole evening, and so revved up that it took a while before I came down from the clouds enough to sleep.

The next day, I woke up around noon and immediately called Babs to tell her how I felt about the night. I almost used the l-word. I then went downstairs and talked to Mom and Dad about the night (except for the boob touching and the shove of Stan the Man). They asked a lot of questions, but I could tell they were proud of me.

In the afternoon, I went to the Mount to play a game of pick-up baseball. I told a few whoppers about last night along the way as boys will be boys. I think I got everyone sufficiently jealous. Yes, I was in love. I even wondered if a sixteen-year-old could get married.

The greatest time of my life was over. I barely gave Stan the Man and the consequences a thought. I went to bed early on Sunday evening with Babs floating through my brain.

Cop-u-later.

MAY 23,
1966 – Monday

I was in the zone after Saturday (and early Sunday), but I came down to Earth quickly when I got to school. During period one, I was called to the principal's office. I knew exactly the reason – my push of Stan the Man at the 'Pig's Whistle.'

I expected a suspension, but I only got a dressing down from Porgie plus three detentions this week. No demerits. I tried to make like the fracas was an accident, but there were witnesses and also the chaperone's report. I had to throw myself on the mercy of the court.

As we are only two weeks from the end of the school year, perhaps I was given some leniency. Then again, this wasn't the first time I'd gone in front of the 'Pudding and Pie Man,' so I should count myself lucky. This leniency will probably lead to some students thinking I have my head up the Prin's ass. I'll take my chances.

Between classes, I ran into Katie. I didn't really want her to know what I did on the Prom night, but the rumors were rife. She thanked me for sticking up for her. The downside is that she'll be wanting to hang around me even more, but not everything was roses. Stan the Man's cousin was a senior. Although they only have a week to go (seniors leave school at the end of this week), I was concerned he and his gorillas might want to make a going away present of my head.

Naturally, this led me to the Chief. I doubt his services will be required next year. But for the next week the Chief agreed to have my back and keep the dreaded Year 12s from making my face look like it had been put through a meatgrinder.

Of course, this required a quid pro quo. He said he'd need me to do something for him this weekend. He'd give me the details later. I almost thought I'd rather face the seniors than do the Chief's bidding but, 'discretion was the better part of valor' (is that from Shakespeare?).

I happened to run into Stan the Man in the course of the day. As we passed in the corridor, I told him what a rat he was. He had a bandage on

319

his head like some karate guy. What a fake, I thought. In a threatening tone, he told me that I'd be sorry for what I did to him. 'OO, I'm scared,' I replied with a bit of bravado. I probably made things worse with my sarcasm. Now I was glad I had the Chief on my side.

Oddly enough, with all that was happening, I only briefly caught up with Babs at Home room and lunchtime. As I mentioned before (not to her yet), I'm in love – at least as much as a sixteen-year-old can be. I told her I had a great time on Saturday. She looked beautiful. I love being her boyfriend. She said she really enjoyed the Prom. She had some errands to run, and we'd talk later. Talk later? I'm not paranoid, but what's the old saying, 'you're not paranoid if they really are after you.'

Anyway, we got our yearbooks this afternoon. They're bound in a sickly pale green cover with some avant-garde scribblings on it with the year in big letters. I was in a few of the pictures which was OK with me, though I look like a dork in most of them.

The custom at OLPS is to have classmates write some inane words and then sign the book. Stuff like 'I had fun in English class'; 'keep your sense of humor'; remember the great French classes.' These are stupid, but safe. There are always other comments I'd rather not have in my yearbook that would knock your sock off.

Hep wrote something about me ripping Babs' flower on Saturday. I thought he was occupied with Voohaus and didn't see that. Even the Turtle added her two cents worth. She wrote something screwy – and somewhat suggestive. For some reason, I didn't see Babs to get her to sign.

Had a baseball game against City H.S. after school. If we won, we had an outside chance of making the finals. We lost so the season's over. I, of course, missed the game as I had my days of detention to fulfill (it was not like I missed anything). I had to write an essay on 'What goes up, must come down.'

To add to my woes, while serving my penance, a teacher came in and gave me a bill for $2.50 for my lock rental. It's amazing how a day that began with such euphoria, ended up so crappily. I don't know if that's a word, but it described my mood perfectly.

Cop-u-later.

MAY 24,
1966 – Tuesday

Only two more days of classes this week. Then there's final exams which count for a third of the semester mark. So, I suppose I should get cracking! I'm not sure what happens next week, but school ends the Friday after next. Then, summer vacation. I should be happy the school year is finishing, but I'll miss the daily contact with Babs.

I think I'm in love, but does Babs feel as I do? She seemed preoccupied. Was she humiliated that I touched her boobs after the Prom? I spoke with her briefly at lunch, but she made an excuse and left early. And without signing my Yearbook. One person I tried to avoid, without success, was the Chief. He reminded me of the task he said I had to do this weekend. As the seniors finish up on Friday, I figured I could possibly wait him out and not do the deed.

I figured wrong. At one point, I was confronted by Stan the Man and his Year 12 cronies. Baseball is over and I'm no longer flavor of the month with the older team members. Perhaps the seniors felt they had some scores to settle. The Maggot was among them salivating for one last bullying session. With the Prom over, maybe he thought he could reclaim Babs.

Stan wanted to fight then and there – even with his head bandaged. I was happy to just fight him one on one and GIOW (get it over with). But tackling the cretins with him was another story. It could be one for all, all for one. Anyway, I wanted to get it done and agreed to Stan's challenge. All of a sudden, who should walk past but the Chief. Stan and his mob quickly broke up and walked away with their tails between their legs.

It might have been better if I had fought Stan. The Chief having my back didn't make me look all that courageous, and I still owed the favor. A bashed head might have been worth it. Eventually the day of reckoning with Stan would come. Hopefully, this year, maybe next year. When he least expected it.

After school, we had solos for the choir. I guess the Fuhrer wanted to test us out our voice range before next year. I was a bit late because of my detention. One by one, she made everyone – boys and girls – sing the overdone sugary song 'Secret Love' from the movie 'Calamity Jane'. Babs was mysteriously missing from this exercise.

We sat in the audience while each person performed. After about two-dozen renditions of this madness – none of them Doris Day-like – it was my turn. I was sick of this song and asked if I could sing another.

Well, Sister Georgakopoulos picked the song 'There's No Business Like Show Business' from the musical 'Annie Get Your Gun.' I didn't mind singing it, but when you sing that song there's a tendency to sing it loud and nasally like Ethel Merman who made it famous.

After I sang a few bars in that style, Sister Fuhrer made me stop. I was directed to sing 'Secret Love' like the others. 'Now I shout it from the highest hill, even told the golden daffodil,' I sang. (Gag, gag) I did think of my love for Babs while singing.

After my rendition, I re-joined the others in the audience – including Hep – for the rest of this monotonous exercise. When the singing finished, our group sang, 'At last my ear's an open sore, for we don't have to hear this anymore.' Don't call us, we'll call you!

Cop-u-later.

MAY 25,
1966 – Wednesday

The last day of regular classes before final exams. I dreaded going to school for two reasons: the humiliation of not facing up to Stan yesterday; and learning about the diabolical task the Chief had in mind for me. First things first. As soon as I got to school, I walked up to Babs and had her sign my yearbook and I signed hers.

I wasn't crazy about what she wrote. 'Thanks for all the good times – particularly how nice you were after the Prom.' I certainly hope no one sees this message as my reputation, what little I have, would be shot if someone reads that I was 'nice' to her. Aggressive, manly, animalistic – yes. Nice – no. I figured no one would see what she wrote other than Hep, so I should be OK. Before I went to class, Babs gave me a peck on the cheek.

Had a few classes – mainly revision of boring old stuff. Later, there was a big school assembly to farewell the seniors or the 'Class of '66' as they were now called. They've had their finals and finish on Friday. I think they have a graduation ceremony on Sunday. Anyway, the whole shebang was a farce, as we were told how wonderful they were and how we juniors had a lot to live up to. I thought, good riddance. I only ever got hassles from the Year 12s.

Next year's president and vice-president were then introduced. Cavendish and the Munch. I'm still a bit bitter about how I was maneuvered out of running for president – although masterfully. My payback list gets bigger all the time. I noticed some of our girls were crying about the year ending. We still have another week, and don't they realise we have another year of this torture. Man, I'm getting twisted as I get older.

When the assembly ended, I had my last detention to go to. I tried to leave quickly to avoid the Chief. I was almost to the detention room when he materialized from nowhere. Who is he – Houdini? I was trapped like a rat in a maze and had no place to hide as he filled me in on his latest plan. I was to pick up a package on Friday evening at the canteen from someone who would find me. I was to deliver said package to a house on Prospectors Hill.

I would get the address at the canteen from the guy who handed me the package. I asked if any part of this was illegal. The Chief assured me it was all above board. What else would he say? He also said to follow the instructions carefully as he didn't want another screw up like last time.

Well, I wasn't crazy about this idea as Prospectors Hill is where mostly Negroes live. I've been told those on the Hill don't take kindly to white boys. What if the rumors are true? The only Negro I know reasonably well is Columbus – Mrs. Pride's chauffer. I can trust him as he saved me a few weeks ago. Then there's Pij, but I don't know Jack Shit of any others.

This task was not going to be easy or pleasant. Perhaps, I thought, I can get Hep to go with me. The seniors will be history after Friday, so what's the point doing this anyhow? I was going to tell the Chief to forget the whole thing. Then again, he saved my bacon numerous times from serious hurt. I guess I owed him. That didn't stop me from thinking what a fat SOB he was. What was that about a tangled web?

Cop-u-later.

MAY 26,
1966 – Thursday

Got my final Thursday ride for this school year with Katie and her dad. Katie seemed unusually chatty and quite frisky. She snuggled embarrassingly close to me. Normally I don't mind these displays of affection, but as I'm 'going steady' (what is this 'The Adventures of Ozzie and Harriet'?) with Babs, I didn't think her actions were prudent under the circumstances.

When we got out of the car, she took me aside and again thanked me for sticking up for her the other night. By now, word of my confrontation with Stan the Man was all over the school. When we got to school, she then gave me a little peck on the cheek. I guess she's not all that bad, but – ugh! – that kiss. What if someone saw it?

Had a French final and a History test amongst my exams. Caught up afterwards with Babs who had a Spanish exam at the same time as my French. She asked if I wanted to come to her place on Friday.

She had something important to say to me. I wanted to see her more than anything as I'm head over heels in love with her. Could it be that she wants to tell me she loves me? But how could I go see her when I have that project to do for the Chief? She seemed disappointed when I told her no. I sure was.

We got our Prom pictures today. I guess I'm prejudiced, but Babs and I made a great couple. I usually take a horse-shit photo, but I was pleased with the way we looked. I suggested we see each other on Saturday (if I'm still alive). She said she'd get back to me.

To add to my dilemma, I ran into the Chief who gave me the finger across the neck motion. In other words, do my chore or else. I wasn't sure what the 'or else' entailed and frankly I didn't want to know. As the seniors are history after tomorrow, I considered backing out of our arrangement. I do that at my own peril. I asked Hep if he'd go with me tomorrow to Prospectors Hill. He grudgingly agreed but didn't seem all that keen. What a pal! What a nut!

Anyway, exams finished for the day, and we were allowed to go home early. Hep suggested a nine-hole golf game at the Berkshire Community Golf Course. So, I went home, changed, grabbed my clubs and got picked up by him. When I got there, I was greeted by my worst nightmare.

Unfortunately, Hep had neglected to tell me that Stan the Man and one of his friends would be part of a foursome. I couldn't help thinking that STM set up this whole thing. Whatever I thought of Stan, and that's not much, he was a damn good golfer. As a golfer, I made a good ten-pin bowler. With every hole we played, he rubbed my ineptness in my face. Revenge would be sweet, I thought, but on my own terms.

On the last hole, Stan was still on the fairway. I was on the green putting out when a golf ball came out of nowhere and almost hit me. The word 'fore' was shouted well after the fact. As Stan was playing with his friend, I couldn't tell who made that errant shot.

I gave both Stan and his partner a piece of my mind when I saw them, though I doubt they really cared. I got some revenge on the asshole when I sank a twenty-foot putt on the last green. That gave me a fifty-nine for nine holes. This was ten strokes more than Stan, but still the source of some satisfaction when he three-putted the ninth.

In the evening, I stayed at home to study for my final exams tomorrow. I had a number of them, but I concentrated on studying for my English final. Who can think of Macbeth when I have my own problems? "To thine own self be true,' I thought. Not Macbeth, but Hamlet I believe. Still handy advice, nonetheless.

Cop-u-later.

MAY 27,
1966 – Friday

One more week and Year 11 is a memory. I didn't have much time to dwell on this, as I had an English final. I think I did OK. I got my Chaucer and Shakespeare right anyway. I had a POD exam later which I aced. Babs finished her exam, so I told her I'd give her a lift home.

Before that, I saw Hep and reminded him that he said he'd come with me to Prospectors Hill tonight as I was to complete the Chief's errand. I could tell by looking at him that he wanted to 'punk out,' but I begged enough that I finally shamed him into coming. I had to use the friendship card to get him to tag along. A bit below the belt, granted, but I'll take it.

I drove Babs home and told her I'd see her tomorrow evening. She hesitated to answer, but then seemed happy to go along with me. We had a pleasant drive to her home, and she even gave me a quick kiss – on the lips - when we reached her destination.

I was going to tell her I loved her as I expected she would reply likewise. How's that song go, 'Love is a many splendid thing?' I think that's how it goes. It could wait until tomorrow, as my mind was on tonight's task. Then it was home for a quick bite. I asked Dad for the car – hoping he'd say no, but no dice. The die was cast. I guess I've learned a few phrases from English class.

Around eight-thirty, I drove to the canteen parking lot. I spotted Hep right away. He asked me to wait ten minutes before we got the instructions and went to the Hill. He didn't give me the impression he wanted to go with me, but he didn't refuse either. His request to delay our task was odd, but I humored him.

While we were waiting for who knows what – it could have been for Godot for all I knew – he told me he knew about the confrontation I had with Pij. He said I was wrong about him and even considered ending our friendship. He decided that we'd been through a lot this year and wanted to give me the benefit of the doubt. From my side, I said I could have phrased what I said to Pij a bit better, but it would be difficult for us to be friends.

Just then Pij appeared. We didn't say boo to each other and there was enough tension you could cut it with a knife. I was pissed off at first as I felt Hep was setting me up, but then realised there's safety in numbers. Whether his motive was security or my reconciliation, I had to hand it to Hep. Bringing Pij to a Negro neighborhood was a no-brainer.

Anyway, Hep and Pij stayed in the car while I went into the canteen to find the friend of the Chief who was to hand me the item to be delivered and supply the address. I expected some kind of signal from the said person and looked around the dance floor.

I didn't expect the Chief himself to be there, but there he was – in the flesh! He gave me a package covered in brown-paper wrapping and tied up with string. 'Who do I give it to, Julie Andrews?' I joked. I doubt the Chief got the reference.

He then gave me an address on Gravel St., Prospectors Hill. He told me to go to that address, ask for a girl named Sydney, deliver the package, and then get the hell out of there 'as fast as you can.' He repeated that last instruction slowly and urgently. I understood the instructions, but that last piece of information was somewhat disturbing. I wondered why the Chief didn't deliver the package himself. Now I think I knew and wasn't thrilled about it.

Off the three of us went. It was a steep climb going up the Hill. Pij seemed right at home and was singing a 'Supreme' song as I drove. All of a sudden, before we reached the appointed street, he told me to stop the car and he got out.

I was bewildered as I felt Pij was abandoning us. I had no alternative and obliged. Now I really was scared as instead of three of us, there were only two. I suppose he only wanted a ride to the Hill. I thought of what my dad said about the Negroes. When I asked Hep about Pij bailing, he shrugged his shoulders and said, 'that's Pij.' He said Pij was his own person, and he couldn't force him to stay with us. So Hep and I continued our journey up the Hill until we spied the street and drove to the appointed address.

Gravel St. was gloomy and dark as a number of streetlights were out.

It was hard finding the place, but we finally reached our destination – an old beat-up house with a couple of broken windows and in badly need of a paint job. Ironically, there was a Cadillac parked in front of it. Talk about clichés! I asked Hep to come to the door with me, but he said he'd stay in the car. Indeed, he locked the doors as soon as I left.

I walked up to the front door with the package and used the quaint woodpecker knocker to get the occupant's attention. After three knocks, the device fell off. Then I tried the doorbell. I rang, then waited. The wait seemed like hours as I kept looking over my shoulder, though I'm not sure what I was expecting if anything.

Within thirty seconds, a girl answered. A Negro girl – maybe fifteen or sixteen I guessed. She had a beautiful face, I thought when I saw her. I also saw she was noticeably pregnant, but I wasn't here to dwell on her condition.

I asked her what her name was. When she answered correctly, I gave her the package. In front of me, she opened the box and counted out $5000. She then gave me a package – similar to the one I had brought and told me to give it to the Chief. I questioned her instruction and insisted this wasn't the plan. But my protests were in vain.

I reluctantly took the package. She thanked me, and offered me some money, but I respectfully turned her down. She asked if I wanted a drink of something, but I politely declined this as well. I was anxious to get the hell out of there – as the Chief had warned.

I ran to the car, hopped in, as Hep had unlocked the door when he saw me coming, and took off. When I told Hep that the package, I gave the girl had $5000 in it, he nearly shit his pants. I started down the hill toward the City when I noticed someone was following me. I told Hep and he said to floor it. I'm sure our blood pressures went considerably north.

Behind us was this blue Cadillac (naturally) trying to pass me. I turned into a side road and waved the driver on. At that point, he turned, overtook me, pulled his Caddy in front of me and blocked my car. The three of them – two Negroes and a white man – got out of their vehicle, and they weren't happy.

'What are you two doing up here with my girl Laurel?' one of the Blacks said. I wasn't about to tell him the girl's name was Sydney. Maybe the Chief used a fake name. Maybe the guys were shaking the Chief down.

I played it cool and stayed in the car. He aggressively told me and Hep to get out. I was as scared as I had ever been. I thought of the Chief's warning. This wasn't about a pregnant girl, but the package I had.

We were in no position to turn down his request. Hep swore he saw a weapon of some sort. So, we got out. The guys slowly came toward us. Once again, he asked me why I had gone to that house. I told him everything.

The leader of the group, a muscular Negro with a mean expression demanded the package I had received. Something stunk to high heaven as how did he know about the package? Hep told me to give it to him, but I told the man it was for my friend. The guys looked ready to tear us apart. I closed my eyes and thought of England, as all my mind conjured up as I faced this danger was that old sexual reference. Hep later told me his life flashed in front of him – all sixteen years.

Finally, I gave in and gave the guys what they wanted. Even then, they still were itching for a fight. They came after Hep and me, and they weren't about to reward us. There was fire in the leader's eyes. The three of them were going to have their idea of fun at our expense.

All of a sudden, I heard the screech of tires. Their pals joining them to cause us damage. But no, it was Pij. I wasn't about to ask Pij where he got a car as I was just glad to see him. Pij got out of the car, went up to the guys and said we were his friends. He told them to let us go. Their reply was to 'get the f… out of there.'

Pij didn't back away. He told them that I hadn't knocked the girl up and we were just delivering something to her. That didn't seem to mean anything to them. It looked as if we were in for a brawl. I only prayed there weren't any knives or guns involved. Now it was three against three. Despite the numbers, it still was not even by any stretch of the imagination. All I could think of was Babs and wondered what she would say as my eulogy.

Just then, we heard sirens blaring. Two cop cars piled into the street and blocked the others. The three ran, but quickly were caught. The cops found the package which, when opened, turned out to be those smelly cigarettes. Drugs, I overheard one of the coppers say.

Although the goons said the package was ours, we denied it. Pij must have called the cops, though it wouldn't have been cool for him to admit that. He explained everything to them. After asking us a few questions the head cop took our names and addresses and let us go.

Pij had saved us. I for one had a new appreciation of him. I felt ashamed that I had doubted him and thoughtlessly disparaged him and, by association, his race. Dad and Gran-King's old-fashioned prejudices were very wrong. I would never convince them otherwise, but I could try very hard to overcome my own misgivings.

$5000, a pregnant girl, a Negro area, drugs, police, Hep, and guys trying to kill me. Count me out! Of all people to save my life – Pij. He turned out to be an OK guy and I was grateful. I was sorry for believing he was selling drugs to the students. I apologised to him.

Pij told me not to worry. He suspected I didn't care for him probably because of his race. As much as I hated to admit it, maybe he was right. I didn't realise that was the case, but if I was honest with myself, I'd guess there was some truth in what he was saying.

I told him from this day forward I would try to judge a person as an individual. He told me it was good I had learned a lesson, but that I should respect people regardless of whether they help you. There's good and bad in all races. I asked him why he didn't bash me up when I confronted him about selling the drugs. He said I was Danny's (Hep's) friend and besides, he thought I was an OK guy – just ignorant.

Pij then surprised me by giving me a hug and paying me $50 for all the money he had borrowed this year. Well at that I was totally ashamed of the way I had acted. I certainly was humbled by Pij's actions.

I asked him to give the money to the pregnant girl who gave me the package. She looked like she needed it more than me. I told him I hoped to run into him this summer. He called me bro. This time I gave Pij a hug. Perhaps now we were OK with each other.

Hep and I were so relieved that we weren't dead that we couldn't go home. I felt invincible and drove extra fast on the bypass road to relieve some of the stress I had encountered. I was OK with it, but I'm not sure if Hep was. Now to Stuvers. I discussed the evening with Hep amidst three burgers, a large fry and a vanilla shake. Hep had the same, but also an apple pie.

It was obvious now that the Chief was the one who had been selling the drugs to the students. The story about someone from the public school supplying the drugs was a way of distracting me from the truth. I felt stupid as I should have figured this out long ago.

What about the three guys who tried to harm Hep and me? Were these guys working for the Chief? Perhaps that was why he warned us to get out of there quickly. He had an inkling of what they were going to do. They were bad dudes. Why would the Chief have them hold us up if he was going to get the goods anyway?

I'd say they were playing the dirty on him and planning to take the goods themselves. The Chief sensed their aggression, or he personally would have collected the goods, but even more intriguing, who was behind all this illegal activity?

Was the Chief the father of the pregnant girl (I told Hep about the girl being pregnant)? Was the $5000 for the drugs or to pay off the girl? None of our business, Hep told me. After all this, I was only interested in eating. I didn't care if the burgers were now 18c. I gladly paid the extra money.

Cop-u-later.

MAY 28,
1966 – Saturday

Got home late last night so slept in this morning until ten. I had to pinch myself to remind myself I was still alive. To think it was Pij who saved the day. I would never do anything for the Chief again. I was so naïve. Rudy warned me about where to find the person selling the drugs to students.

I never considered the Chief as someone part of my group. I guess he had often crossed my path this semester and was seen in effect to be part of 'my own house'. The answers were there. It took me all this time to realise what Rudy meant. Someone I had done favors for in return for protection.

The whole Chief protection thing was now irrelevant, as the seniors were done and dusted. My need for the Chief was no longer required. Hopefully, the drug trade at the schools would stop with the actions of the police.

I had my own ideas about this drug bust. There's been something fishy about the doings next door for quite a while. I saw a similar package in Mrs. Pride's house to the one intercepted by the cops yesterday. I was determined to find out about it. Last week I noticed that the mound of dirt in Mrs. Pride's backyard just wasn't quite right. Had it been tampered with recently? It was time to dig out the truth. I prayed Columbus wasn't involved in something illegal.

Regardless of my anxieties, I had a baseball game this afternoon for Lichtenfels Motors and a date with Babs in the evening. Hep rang and said we were lucky to be alive. He was told by someone (as always, with Hep there was always a someone) that the gang members had knives and maybe even guns. Lucky, Pij was there.

He then mentioned that the pop group 'The Shondells' were coming to the 'Pig's Whistle' Nightclub next Friday and wanted to know if I wanted to see them. 'Of course,' I said. Naturally, he expected me to drive. 'The Shondell's with lead singer Tommy James? With their hit song 'Hanky Panky'? 'Wild horses couldn't keep me away,' I said.

So, I was pretty upbeat when I got to the game for my summer team against Acme Supermarket. When I thought of them, I had visions of Wile E. Coyote chasing the Roadrunner. He always used Acme equipment in his unusual, but unsuccessful, ways of attempting to catch the bird.

The game was going well in the third inning. I was the catcher. In my first at-bat, I hit a single and scored. Now they were batting. We were ahead in the game when Dirk (aka Dork) Shneider – our pitcher – threw a fastball to the batter.

The ball caught the edge of the bat and hit my exposed right hand – my throwing hand. Well, I heard a crack. After that, I couldn't move my hand. I was sure it was a break. It was all purple, thus I figured it was a bad break. I had to leave the game. Our team eventually lost.

Dad was at the game and told me to shake it off as it was only a sprain. He might as well have said to put leeches on the hand cause his advice smacked of quackery. It was a break – I was sure! When we got home, Dad's advice was to put some butter on it. This to me was from the bogus 'old housewife school of medicine'. Was I to cure it or eat it? The mound of dirt I wanted to dig would have to wait.

Naturally, I couldn't drive which ruined my date with destiny. Tonight, I was going to tell Babs I loved her. I guess it wasn't to be. I called her and told her about last night. She seemed interested in my story. She was OK about not seeing me. Maybe a bit too OK, I thought. My expression of love would have to wait.

So, I reluctantly settled in for a quiet Saturday night at home. Around ten p.m., I got this strange phone call. 'I saw you last night,' the voice said in a high squeaky voice. The line was repeated over and over. I didn't want anything to do with it and hung up. I figured it was Hep playing a joke on me. Ten minutes later, the phone rang again. I got the same message as before. I asked who was calling, but whoever was on the other end hung up.

Later, the same song. It was now near eleven and I was tired of this game, so I called Babs. I was told by her mom that she wasn't home. What the …? Why wasn't Babs home?

I got the same crazy phone message three more times. I'd had enough. I told those at home not to call me again to answer if the phone call was for me. I didn't want to deal with this anymore. I instructed them to say I was asleep. I still thought Hep or someone was playing a trick on me.

'To be or not to be, that is the question' wrote Shakespeare. If only I knew the answer.

Cop-u-later.

MAY 29,
1966 – Sunday

My finger, damaged at yesterday's baseball game, swelled up so much overnight that Dad thought it necessary to take me to the hospital this morning. Obviously, butter was not the solution and leeches weren't available.

As usual, Dad took no notice of a big group of people waiting in the Emergency Room and walked straight into the consulting room in the back for me to be treated – much to my embarrassment. We got a lot of dirty looks from those who had been waiting for hours. I guess privilege has its advantages.

I had x-rays taken and – after a short wait – it was found that, as expected, I had a break in my right index finger. I wasn't the least bit happy about this, but I wasn't about to cry me a river as the song goes. I just had to grin and bear – even if I couldn't bear to grin (boom, boom).

The doctor gave me some pain pills. He said to stay away from any strenuous activity. This means I'll have to sit out three weeks before I can go back to playing baseball. Boo hoo! It was sore, but not too sore to do some digging tonight.

Perhaps this break isn't such a bad thing, I thought, as I'm getting tired of the baseball grind after five years on this team. I'm obviously not going to be a major leaguer. Anyway, the doctor put a splint on my finger. He scheduled me to get a cast put on this Tuesday, so I won't be able to drive until then.

Thus, I had to call Babs and cancel a planned trip to see her this afternoon. Once again, my plan to tell her I love her was foiled. With summer vacation starting on Friday, I wasn't sure I would see her as often after then, so I was anxious to tell her how I felt.

I thought I was stuck at home for the day, when I got a call from my friend Beetle Bailey. Beetle, who lives nearby, and I went to the Catholic primary school together, but we go to different high schools. He asked if

I wanted to go out. Beetle can be a bit strange, but I agreed to go as long as he drove. Half an hour later, he picked me up in his parent's cool VW van.

Beetle drove me to see this girl he knew from Year 11 at his school. Before we got to her house, he said he was confident he could get some 'snatch'- as we crudely refer to any girl we could possibly hook up with. He told me that when, not if, he 'scored' I'd have to walk home as he would be 'using' the back of his van.' He didn't have to hit me on the head with a hammer. Beetle is nothing if not optimistic although somewhat delusional. I wasn't worried about having to walk.

On the way there, he stopped for gas. When he reached into his wallet to pay, a rubber fell out – deliberately, I gathered, as he wanted me to know he was prepared for the inevitable. This made me wonder if all the young guys carried these 'Trojans' with them. Maybe I'm the odd one out. I didn't know the girl, but I knew Beetle. I was 99-44/100% sure that his plans would be thwarted. I was right.

Once there, he introduced me to the girl without mentioning her name. The girl might have been sixteen, but she was made-up like a twenty-year-old. Mascara, lipstick, rouge, the whole shebang. Beetle talked to her for a few minutes, then she brushed him off with a hair-washing story.

She's all made up like she's going out on the town and she's washing her hair? Please! We soon left her. The whole scene was hilarious, though I refrained from laughing in order to spare Beetle's now fragile ego.

Next, we went to Stuvers where I had a few over-priced burgers, some fries and a shake. Beetle suggested we drive around and pick up girls out for a walk. I immediately sensed the futility of this exercise and asked him to take me home. With summer vacation beginning soon, I figured I'd see more of him. Maybe more than I wanted. For now, when it got dark, I had a hole to dig.

When I got home, Dad asked me about my finger. I told him it hurt like hell, but I no doubt exaggerated the severity of the pain to get a bit of sympathy (and maybe some dough). He said the pain would lessen when I got my cast on in two days. As tomorrow is a public holiday, the doctor wasn't available on Monday.

There was something just that little bit off about the events of Friday night. The Chief was supplying those foul-smelling cigarettes to students this year. I'm sure he'll get torched by the police as the three perpetrators who attacked us will have to blame someone. It was classic double-cross if I remembered my crime shows on TV. Did he know that would happen? Is that why he didn't want to deliver the package himself. But who supplied him?

The leader of the men who took the package from me the other night was the big muscly guy I saw at Mrs. Pride's house who had moved furniture with the truck. I'm sure he was the same guy as the person named Jones at the bar when Columbus saved me. Columbus took the package from me to give it to Jones. I thought. Later, I saw Columbus with a similar package at Mrs. Pride's place. And what about the bones?

The first time I looked here I found some bones which I thought were Mrs. Pride's. Columbus said he didn't know of any bones unless they belonged to a dog Mrs. Pride once owned, but I don't remember Mrs. Pride ever having a dog, and they were gone by my second dig. So, was there more to that hole than met the eye? There was only one way to find out.

Anyway, I waited until it was dark before I snuck out of the house, grabbed a shovel from the garage and slowly made my way to the area that had been dug up previously. After making sure the coast was clear, I started. Digging was somewhat difficult because of the recent rain, but I persevered. As expected, just under the surface there were no bones to be found. I decided to dig deeper.

I had to be careful as from my experience the other night, these guys play for keeps and – as Hep said – could have knives or guns. I like Columbus, but he could be involved. The ground was like glue. Another month and it would be rock hard from the sun. As I dug, I kept an eye and ear open for any strange sounds or movements in case someone interrupted me.

Finally, after more digging, I came to a large box buried deep underground. I retrieved the box from the hole and took it under a nearby streetlight to see what was in it. Inside were similar packages like the ones I had received on my errands for the Chief.

I didn't have to open a package to look at the contents because I knew what was in it. It wasn't 'Camels.' The packages were full of the cigarette drugs, the type of which I was sure had been circulating at school and around town. I had seen the type on a couple of occasions and quickly identified them.

It was then that I saw Columbus coming toward me with an object in his hand. Was that a weapon he was carrying? I couldn't believe Columbus would do anything to harm me, but desperate times sometimes call for desperate measures. He didn't look happy, that's for sure. I prepared myself for the worst.

As he approached me, I saw that the object was a flashlight and not something sinister my mind had imagined. That was some relief. Columbus looked at me and shook his head. 'Gussie, where did you get that stuff?' I expected him to be furious at me which could have meant anything.

When I told him, he flashed a huge grin and said he had been looking for this. Some men had come to the house and must have hidden these packages. He said he would take them and hand them over to the police.

Was Columbus telling the truth? Did the same guys who had removed Mrs. Pride's furniture also bury what looked to be drugs? What was Columbus' role in all of this? Should I believe him? In the past two months, wasn't he the least bit curious as to what was obviously buried there?

I was ready to confront him when a local cop pulled up in his squad car. When the cop saw the goods, he didn't appear all that surprised. He certainly didn't have his gun drawn. Columbus wasn't all that anxious either and told the policeman the packages weren't his and he would gladly hand them over and cooperate with the authorities.

The cop took a statement from Columbus and then me. He confiscated the packages and told us to be available in case more information was required. No one was under arrest which was strange to begin with. The packages were found on Mrs. Pride's property. Columbus, her employee, was the only Negro in a white neighborhood. There were illegal drugs found.

The way suburban white policemen operate, they shoot first and ask questions later in instances such as this. Right or wrong, I would have expected Columbus to be arrested or been taken to the station and questioned. His innocence had to be presumed. Yet the evidence pointed his way. Was Columbus guilty or not? Was he the head guy or an innocent bystander? Was I missing something?

It was late and I just wanted to get to bed. It had been quite a night. Much had happened and I was tired. My hand hurt like hell. However, before I even got to my room, the phone rang, and I answered. It was another phone call from the same mystery caller as last night. He had the same squeaky voice. Again, I was told he – I was convinced by the way the person spoke that it was a male – saw me on Friday.

I asked if the phoner was Hep – playing a joke, but I only got static. Two nights in a row. Should I be concerned or scared? I decided not to think about it. Instead, I nursed my sore thumb and thought of Babs. 'How do I love thee, let me count the ways,' I thought. I just wondered when I would get the opportunity to say those romantic three little words to her.

Cop-u-later.

MAY 30,
1966 – Monday

Today was the Memorial Day holiday honoring the soldiers of all wars. No school. Dad was up early to put up the flag outside our upstairs window. He often boasted about his war exploits in Korea. He couldn't get in the Service in World War II because of his bad hearing. He was embarrassed because his brothers were serving so he joined the Reserves.

During the Korean Conflict of the early `50s, his Reserve unit was called up. Even though he was near forty at the time and semi-deaf, he was pleased as punch – though he was stuck in the dental corps in Washington D.C. throughout the duration. That's what his brother – Uncle Andy – told us. We would humor Dad when he talked about his time in Korea fighting the reds.

Anyhoo, in the morning, Kitty, Will, Dad and I went to the street corner to watch the servicemen and scouts walk past in formation. It was a stirring sight. It wasn't that long ago that I was one of those scouts marching. The parents and Grammy would be watching and cheering.

After it was over, I went back home and fell asleep. I didn't get up until after noon. A good way to waste the day. My finger was still throbbing after last night's strenuous activity. The bandage/splint came off when I showered. I called Hep after a quick breakfast to tell him about the phone calls and the activities of last night. He denied being the caller (would he admit otherwise, I thought?).

I still had Hep as my number one suspect crank caller. As for the drugs and the police, he told me to talk to the Chief tomorrow at school. Somehow, I didn't expect the Chief would be there after the events of the past few days.

I didn't want anything to do with the Chief anyway after Hep and I were almost killed on Friday. Not to mention his association with the drug trade and his selling and supplying drugs to kids. I was through doing his favors.

What made the day even more surreal was that Columbus was acting as if nothing had happened last night. When I went outside, I saw he had washed Mrs. Pride's car and now he was giving it a polish. The story about the 'hidden' drugs was all over the media.

The newspaper, radio stations and the one TV station in Jakstown were in a frenzy breaking the story of a drug bust in Jakstown. There were pictures of the confiscated booty, with armed policemen standing guard over the drugs and taking credit for the bust.

And I thought I had discovered the buried drugs. Perhaps not dragging me into this was for the best, as there were notorious people who might have been inclined to retaliate against the one who found the shit. The funny thing was that on the news there seemed to be fewer numbers of packages than what I had found.

The story went on to say that three men had been arrested for their part in the drug bust. A Mr. Jones was mentioned as well as two others – one other Negro and one white man. An unnamed minor had also been questioned under suspicion of distributing drugs to school children. I pretty much knew the identity of that person.

I went over to talk to Columbus to find out what had happened. I was confused to say the least. 'Well, Gussie, it appears that everything worked out for the best,' he said as he continued his task. He didn't initially mention anything about the events of last night. It didn't appear anything had or would happen to him, but I wanted to know.

The car was shining so brightly from the polish that one could see his face reflected on it. He continued, 'I was picking up Mrs. Pride in Florida when whatever was in that hole was buried. It's a real tragedy. Yessir, crime does not pay.'

'Did you know the fellas who were arrested?' I asked.

'Not really. They aren't the kind of people I like to hang around with.'

'Cool,' I replied sarcastically. I saw the Jones character at the time Columbus rescued me at the bar and I'm sure the others weren't far away. They seemed to know him. Did they take the rap for Columbus? What would he have promised them?

'But what happened to the box and why was it buried in Mrs. Pride's backyard'? I continued.

'They were bad people, real bad men. They took advantage of me not being home to hide their ill-gotten gains. They were just waiting for a day when I was gone to dig up the stuff, but none you mind, son, it's all been worked out,' he confidently replied.

'One thing. How did the cops know to come to the house after I found the box?'

'Well, Gussie, I thought I heard a burglar and called them. It was quite the bonus when they discovered the drugs.'

I really didn't understand what the hell he was on about. Whose bones did I dig up if it wasn't a dog? Columbus had already denied their existence. There was something sinister about these bones. I'm not talking dog either.

What was Mrs. Pride doing while all this was happening? She probably didn't know anything about this as she was more interested in listening to her beloved Buccaneers. Only Columbus really knew.

Columbus then inquired about 'that little gal of yours.' I said I loved her and was going to tell her. He laughed. 'That's mighty fine stuff,' he replied, 'but at your age, things aren't always what they seem.'

Was he talking about Babs or was he talking about the drug bust? The latter still didn't add up. I had seen Columbus four days before he supposedly picked up Mrs. Pride in Florida, and then caught me in her house. It was during this time that the drugs were allegedly buried. Why was the dirt over the hole recently disturbed?

Columbus must have had one f'n fast car to drive to Florida, pick up Mrs. Pride and return in the space of a few days. I assume the drugs were buried recently maybe because the police were getting close to discovering the bounty. The perpetrators were waiting for the right moment to retrieve the shit until I ruined things.

Well should he say crime doesn't pay. I had my ideas centering around Columbus, but it was time to move on. I'm only sixteen. Who would believe anything I said? Especially as the cops seemed to have his back just as Columbus had my back on occasions. Besides, where was the proof? So, it was goodbye to him and goodbye to me.

Later that afternoon, Beetle came over. For lack of anything better to do and to clear my mind, I went riding in his car with him. We had a brief stopover to see the girl who crapped on him yesterday. He told me he likes her. Lo and behold, today she really was washing her hair.

Beetle didn't mince any words. He told me he had a rubber – as if the whole world didn't know. He was conspicuous enough making sure I noticed it yesterday. And – knowing him – it was plausible others were given that dubious privilege.

He said he was ready to get some use out of it. I thought right – at the girl's home in her bedroom with her father in the house. Not to mention the fact she was washing her hair for the second day in a row just as you showed up. The message she sent was loud and clear. Anyway, what was I to do while this activity was being performed? Best he employs 'Harry Palm'!

I then asked Beetle to take me to Babs' place. When we got there, I found out she wasn't at home. I talked to her sister the Turtle. I chatted and flirted with her – careful not to overstep the mark – before Beetle and I left. Interesting – Babs was out Saturday night and now this afternoon.

When am I going to see her to express my love for her? And despite the fact she's making herself scarce these days, I'm confident she'll express her love for me. We had a thing going as our love had blossomed on our Prom date. I was distressed (hot and bothered, said Beetle) and the splint on my hand was falling off, so I asked him to take me home. That evening, I tried to call Babs. She still wasn't home. As I had a Chem and Math finals tomorrow, I spent a few hours studying.

Once again, before I turned in, I got my 'I saw you on Friday' phone call. I told the caller to piss off and not phone again. I warned the asshole that the call would be traced, and he would go to jail. Of course, I was bluffing. I was hoping I could put the fear of God in him and get him to lay off. As for the calls, who was behind them? What was the point? If this was a serial like 'Captain Midnight,' I thought, I'd add, 'make sure you don't miss the next exciting episode.'

Cop-u-later.

MAY 31,
1966 – Tuesday

Went to the hospital before school to get a cast put on my finger. I guess I'll only be wearing it for a few weeks, but not to worry. I won't have to play baseball. I'm kind of bored with the sport, but Dad likes me playing and he controls the car. Enough said. After the traumatic events of the weekend, now I can turn my attention to Babs. Getting the cast put on was painless though a broken finger could cramp my style.

Sat for my Math exam, then took a Chemistry final. Both went reasonably well for me. As a southpaw, I was easily able to complete the tests. When finished with the latter, I was asked by Chubs to 'volunteer' to correct some of the exams. Multiple-choice, tick the box. Supplied with the answers. No problem. I'm not sure why I was picked for this task except perhaps that I was there. I certainly didn't have any special qualifications for this job. Though a long shot, I was hoping I might be able to mark my own paper.

I looked around the school for the Chief but couldn't find him. I didn't expect him, but I thought I'd check – just to make sure. As he was the supplier of the drugs to the students, I thought he might be in jail.

If I do see him, I'd like to hear if he knows anything about these phone calls. If so, what do they have to do with last Friday as the caller implied? Should he be informed? Do I really want anything to do with him? A dilemma for sure!

Babs was still at school after my corrections were completed so I asked her if she needed a ride home. After the hospital, I had dropped off my dad in the City and took the car to school. With my cast on, there's no problem driving. Anyway, Babs thanked me and said she could use the ride.

I thought this was the perfect time to tell Babs I love her. I just needed to get her alone. Unfortunately, Stan the Man poked his head in before we left and asked for a ride as well. Normally I'd have told him to f--- off, but as Babs was there, I thought I'd better control myself.

Well, on the way to Babs' house, S the M dominated the conversation. I couldn't get a word in edgewise. He mentioned he was going to Friday's concert to see the Shondells – his favorite group. Bummer. He sat awfully close to Babs. I was glad to drop him off first. By the time I got to Babs' home, I guess the romantic moment had passed.

Babs asked me about the cast, and we sat in the car parked in front of her house and talked about this and that. Then I gave her a peck on the cheek, and she was gone. Now I'm down to three days to tell her how I feel and – if I'm right – she feels the same. I did ask if she'd like to go out tomorrow, but she said she had 'cleaning up to do' – whatever that means.

I had to get home as it was my parents' twenty-fifth wedding anniversary, and there was a celebration to be had. All the family (Biddy, Pippa, Will, Kitty and I) and the hubbies were invited to meet with Mom and Dad at the 'Shangra-la in the Pines' restaurant – the best steaks in the business they advertise. Pippa was pregnant with her 'illegitimate' kid – wink, wink.

Ennis – as expected – was nowhere to be seen. Pippa said he was preparing to go into the Army tomorrow. Really? Duane – Biddy's hubby – was there. Before Biddy and Duane arrived, Dad once again mentioned the butter knife story (to recap, Duane had once buttered his bread with the butterknife). We'll be hearing that story from now until the cows come home – although I'm sure Duane's not the only person to have ever committed this so-called faux pas.

Dad got very sentimental after the dinner when he read some mushy anniversary cards we had brought for the occasion. For a present we got Dad an acoustic guitar. Always 'gracious,' he asked what the hell he was going to do with a freak'n guitar. Mom was given a new bathrobe and some perfume.

Dad said he was the luckiest guy in the world (shades of Lou Gehrig) and shed a tear. Mom was too busy smoking and drinking her highball to get misty-eyed. We all requested they kiss to which they obliged. Photos were taken. As good offspring, we all clapped.

We then retired to our place to drink and play Bridge. By the time we had finished the game, it was as usual – people yelling at each other and casting blame as we rotated partners. Pippa was particularly annoyed at my bidding. Drinking and smoking. And Duane was exasperated and losing.

Dad – the heaviest drinker and craziest player who hardly knows the rules and breaks the few he does – came out the winner. A fun day – one to remember in years to come when we look back at things. The best part of the evening was no one answered the phone, so I didn't have to talk to that douche bag anonymous caller.

At the end of the day, Dad locked his bedroom door – a sure sign his twenty-fifth anniversary would have a happy ending.

Cop-u-later.

JUNE 1,
1966 – Wednesday

Stayed up late playing cards last night so I wasn't in the mood for school. I was a might tipsy too, as Dad let me drink one or four beers. Luckily, my last final was yesterday, and classes were finished. I felt loose as a goose. It was a glorious sunny early spring day hardly conducive to school. We're now counting down the minutes much less the hours until we're free.

Again, I drove the car. Once at school, I helped a bit more with Chem corrections but didn't come across my paper. I guess I won't get a perfect score! After, I cleaned out my locker. I was wondering where that sandwich went last January. The end is nigh! The school picnic is tomorrow. I told Hep and the boys I'd take them. Babs unfortunately declined my offer, but she agreed to let me take her home again. Was this the time to express my innermost feelings to her?

Before we left, she asked me if I would take her mother home as well. Apparently, Irena Geist had a meeting with a teacher about Babs and took a bus to school. So, I saved her money by giving her a ride. Mrs. Geist was in her mid-late thirties, but very well preserved.

She wore a short blue miniskirt, with dark stockings and a white top. She had on just the right amount of make-up. Her blond – not her true color – hair was hanging down. She wore small heels that accentuated her walk. She smelled a million dollars. I always thought she looked good, and not just for her age.

Admittedly, I had a young man/older woman fantasy about her, but she was definitely off limits and beyond my pay grade. I was tongue-tied talking to her. To say my speech to her was disjointed and silly would be an understatement. I knew I didn't make any sense.

Although she was sitting in the back seat, I found myself looking at her often through my rear-view mirror. I'm surprised I didn't have an accident. Anyway, the twenty-minute trip went well. Irena thanked me when I got to her house. I don't remember saying goodbye to Babs as my eyes followed her mom all the way to the door. I did tell Babs I'd see her on Friday. My last chance to tell her how I feel and vice versa.

After dropping the two off, I went to Hep's place to tell him about my encounter with Mrs. Geist. He agreed she was beautiful and added that 'he wouldn't kick her out of bed of for eating crackers.' I didn't want to ruin my experience today with sordid words. Though I thought as he did.

Hep mentioned that Voohaus told him she didn't want to see him anymore. After I saw that guy in her room the other week, I figured this breakup was inevitable. I felt bad for Hep and didn't tell him about seeing the half-naked dude in her room as it would only rub salt into his wound.

Now I believe the rumor that Voohaus only dates college boys. It still won't stop me from ogling her from afar. She's too tasty! With Hep out of the way, perhaps my chance would eventually come. That is, if she'd be willing to go out with a mere high school 'boy.'

We picked up Frenchie, JD and Racovic and went to my place to play pool. I told everyone about the phone calls. Again, I asked Hep to admit it was him. He denied it a second time (if he did a third time like St. Peter, then he's either a good liar or not guilty). He's my best friend, so I have to believe him.

Around three, I dropped off Racovic and Hep asked me to pick up Mike Kang aka Mondo after a movie about weird stuff happening around the world. Mondo, a member of our intermural team, is a thin weasly-looking guy with a Beatle haircut. Hep asked me to take Mondo to this indoor raceway so he could race his model car.

Mondo is OK, but he travels to the beat of a different drum. He can be a bit strange at times. We watched him race for a short while (he wasn't all that good) before going to Stuvers. Mondo preferred to wait at the indoor track. At the burger joint, I had three of the overpriced hamburgers. What's the alternative if you want a burger? Then I dropped the lads where they wanted to go and went home.

That evening, I got the same call I had been getting all week. 'I saw you on Friday,' the voice repeated over and over. This time I didn't say a word and just hung up. How long was this going to go on? This was worse than a Chinese water torture.

Cop-u-later.

JUNE 2,
1966 – Thursday

No school, as the annual picnic was held at the Lakefront Amusement Park in Altona – about thirty-five miles away. There were rides, swimming, food, but no Babs. Except for a brief thought about the mystery caller, my dreams last night were mainly about Mrs. Geist – or Irena as I called her in my subconscious state. I think I married her, even though there is a Mr. Geist. Back to reality, I wondered why Babs didn't want to go to the picnic.

As I had the car, the boys skipped taking the bus from school. I picked up JD, Hep and his friend Pii (even though Tony was playing hooky from City Public High), and we were off. Luckily, Frenchie didn't want to go, as his size would have been quite the hindrance going over the mountains to Altona.

We were barely out of Jakstown when I noticed the brakes weren't quite right. When I was going downhill, I had limited braking. I told the others, and they nearly shit themselves, but I used the emergency brake, and it was all good.

This temporary solution would not do for the longish trip over steep grades. The others encouraged me to go on using the hand brake, but I wasn't dumb enough to do that – especially with a hand in a cast. I pulled the plug on the trip. We limped back, disappointed, but carefully, into town before I took the car to Shark's Service Station near home.

One of the attendants, Crazy Henry, was there. He briefly looked at the car and then told me I had run out of gas. I guess that's how he got his name. I went straight to Sharky – the owner – and explained what the problem was. He told me to leave it with him and collect it later after repairs.

I told the guys we could go to my place and play some pool. There was a lot of whining when I told them we had to walk about two miles to get there. However, on the way we stopped off at the local elementary school and took some of the kids' bikes for the rest of the trip.

When we got to my place, we played a bit of pool and then som basketball (there was a hoop on my garage). When Dad got home, I told him the story and he let me use the VW to drive the guys home.

After I got back, I called Babs, but she wasn't at home. I was starting to feel like Beetle Bailey and his hair-wash girl. Was Babs seeing the Maggot again? I knew what I had to do tomorrow. I would finally express my feelings to the girl I loved. Babs. Or was it, Irena? Babs naturally.

That evening, I again got my phone call about last Friday. This time I asked the asshole what he thought I had done. For once, he actually talked. In a squeaky voice, he told me I knew what he meant – before laughing and hanging up. The way he answered and spoke and laughed indicated to me who he was. I should have suspected him all along. It wasn't Hep.

I would take care of things tomorrow – the final day of the school year. It would be my last day as a Junior. I was determined to tie up any loose ends. That night I dreamed of Irena again and how her experience could teach me a thing or two. And now I could appeal to her as a mature senior student.

Cop-u-later.

June 3,
1966
Friday – Last Day as a Junior

My last day of Year 11. Had a brief assembly where awards (I didn't get one) were given and report cards passed out. I did very well in English, Math, Chem, POD and History, but less so in French. I don't have any plans to go to Paris anyway. Georgie Porgie, the principal, gave a short speech (for him) thanking everyone from the janitors to the teachers and finally the students. Some of the girls were crying, but I thought good riddance – just get me out of here.

Then Cavendish, as next year's class president, said a few words. I can't remember anything he said, as all I thought as he was crapping on was that it could have been me up there crapping on while I was being ignored. Finally, we sang our forgettable school song – once again bastardizing it as the guys I hang around with barely know the words. We're good at pretending to sing.

'By the banks of the mighty Stringybank River,
We dedicate our lives to you,
Dear Old Lady of Succour
We love you through and through.
Today may be passing, tomorrow we'll be through,
But we will never forget you (we always say lick instead of forget).
Our Lady, we love you.'

Then, after this dribble, it was ten a.m., and it was all over but the shouting. A loud cheer filled the auditorium as the students were leaving. I said au revoir (I guess I learned something in French class) to a few people I probably wouldn't see until September. JD, Racovic, Frenchie and Hep I'd see at tonight's concert.

Saw the Chief for the first time this week. As expected, he was fingered by the guys who had tried to kill us on Friday. The Chief was questioned by the police. As he's only sixteen, he went before a Juvenile

Court. The Chief pleaded guilty and was sentenced to three months Juvenile Hall (read a kind of prison for minors) this summer.

He would be free to resume his schooling here in the fall (and, hopefully, not his life of crime). He said he was only at school to talk to Porgie before the assembly and to clean out his locker before beginning his sentence. I would have expected him to be expelled, but us Catholics are a forgiving lot. There's justice for you!

As for the pregnant girl at the Hill, the Chief denied everything. 'She sleeps with everyone,' he cried in anguish. The Chief outweighed me by many pounds, but I felt like giving it to him. He wasn't showing much compassion for her. He deserved to be locked up and the key thrown away.

Funny, he didn't mention anything about my role in his demise. He wasn't pissed off at me for all of this – or was he? It could wait till September.

I left school quickly. I didn't care to say goodbye to the teachers or anyone else. I figured I'd see enough of them next school year. As I was leaving, I eyed Voohaus one more time. I stopped and stared. *That's one fine looking lady*, I thought. But fickle.

Finally, I spotted Katie and said I'd see her next year. I told her to thank her dad for me for the rides. She gave me a big hug and told me to come by her house anytime. I said sure – not all that sincerely – and was out of there.

I had seen Babs at the assembly earlier, and she agreed to accept a lift home. I met her in the parking lot. This time it was only Babs and me. I wasn't about to blow my chance to tell her how much I cared for her. About a block before her house, I pulled over to the side of the road. With a feeling of apprehension, I looked into her eyes and said it: 'Babs, I love you.'

There was silence for what seemed like an eternity. I expected Babs to kiss me and pledge her everlasting love right back. Instead, she mentioned what a great time she had this past year, especially at the Sadie and the Prom. She had memories she would never forget.

Then came the 'but'! Why must there always be a 'but'? 'But since we might not see each other this summer, we should give each other some space,' she said. She didn't have to say anything further because I realised what the important statement was that she wanted to tell me. She wasn't going to say she loved me. She was breaking up with me. Now she spoke that dreaded line guys have hated to hear from time immemorial: 'Let's be friends.' It was as if someone had ripped my heart out.

'But why?' I stuttered.

'It's not your fault, it's mine.' Another classic break-up line. The silence was deafening.

'Is there someone else,' I asked – thinking of the Maggot.

Babs didn't answer, but finally all the time she was away these past weeks hit me. She didn't have to say anything else. I didn't say anything either but drove her the rest of the way to her house. Before she left the car, she gave me a peck on the cheek and wished me a good summer. Then she reached into her bag, pulled out my school ring and gave it back to me, and that was that. As Abe Lincoln once said after a defeat, 'I'm too old to cry, but it hurts too much to laugh.' Life as I knew it was shot.

school and took some of the kids' bikes for the rest of the trip.

When we got to my place, we played a bit of pool and then some basketball (there was a hoop on my garage). When Dad got home, I told him the story and he let me use the VW to drive the guys home.

After I got back, I called Babs, but she wasn't at home. I was starting to feel like Beetle Bailey and his hair-wash girl. Was Babs seeing the Maggot again? I knew what I had to do tomorrow. I would finally express my feelings to the girl I loved. Babs. Or was it, Irena? Babs naturally.

That evening, I again got my phone call about last Friday. This time I asked the asshole what he thought I had done. For once, he actually talked. In a squeaky voice, he told me I knew what he meant – before laughing and hanging up. The way he answered and spoke and laughed indicated to me who he was. I should have suspected him all along. It wasn't Hep.

I would take care of things tomorrow – the final day of the school year. It would be my last day as a Junior. I was determined to tie up any loose ends. That night I dreamed of Irena again and how her experience could teach me a thing or two. And now I could appeal to her as a mature senior student.

Cop-u-later.

June 3,
1966
Friday – Last Day as a Junior

My last day of Year 11. Had a brief assembly where awards (I didn't get one) were given and report cards passed out. I did very well in English, Math, Chem, POD and History, but less so in French. I don't have any plans to go to Paris anyway. Georgie Porgie, the principal, gave a short speech (for him) thanking everyone from the janitors to the teachers and finally the students. Some of the girls were crying, but I thought good riddance – just get me out of here.

Then Cavendish, as next year's class president, said a few words. I can't remember anything he said, as all I thought as he was crapping on was that it could have been me up there crapping on while I was being ignored. Finally, we sang our forgettable school song – once again bastardizing it as the guys I hang around with barely know the words. We're good at pretending to sing.

'By the banks of the mighty Stringybank River,
We dedicate our lives to you,
Dear Old Lady of Succour
We love you through and through.
Today may be passing, tomorrow we'll be through,
But we will never forget you (we always say lick instead of forget).
Our Lady, we love you.'

Then, after this dribble, it was ten a.m., and it was all over but the shouting. A loud cheer filled the auditorium as the students were leaving. I said au revoir (I guess I learned something in French class) to a few people I probably wouldn't see until September. JD, Racovic, Frenchie and Hep I'd see at tonight's concert.

Saw the Chief for the first time this week. As expected, he was fingered by the guys who had tried to kill us on Friday. The Chief was questioned by the police. As he's only sixteen, he went before a Juvenile

June 3,
1966
Friday – The Nightclub

I immediately went to Hep's house to tell him the news. He suggested we play a bit of mini-golf and talk it over. I don't remember much about the game, but I'm sure my score was shocking. 'There's plenty of hairpie (aka available girls) to go around,' he said.

He then reminded me of the dance/concert tonight at the 'Pig's Whistle' teenage nightclub. He said there would be lots of good-looking chicks there to feast on. If I've said it once, I've said it a thousand times, Hep has a way with words.

I was devastated and really not in the mood to go, but then I remembered I had some unfinished business to attend to. I had to see someone and knew that person would be there. I told Hep I'd pick him and the others up around eight. Got home around four. Gave Dad and Mom my report card. (The end-of-year report wasn't passed out at the church.) They liked it. After a small congratulatory dinner for making it to Year 12, I asked for and got the car.

Picked up Hep, JD, Frenchie and Racovic at the appointed time. Frenchie had a six-pack which we split, so I was feeling my oats when we got to the venue. Hoping to save the $5 entry fee, Hep knew a guy (of course) named Bud whose father owned the nightclub. Bud got Hep and I in for nothing though the unfortunates JD, Frenchie and Racovic had to pay. They were all upset – particularly Frenchie who had gotten us the beer. 'That's life in the fast lane,' I quipped.

'The Shondells' (with lead singer Tommy James) – a nationally recognised band who had been on the TV show 'American Bandstand' with Dick Clark – were playing. They immediately got stuck into their hit song 'Hanky Panky' – much to the delight of the audience. Unfortunately, they only knew about half-a-dozen songs, so they played 'Hanky Panky' loud and often.

You'd have thought the crowd would have gotten sick of hearing this song sung over and over, but people didn't mind one bit. We all had a wild time dancing and singing along ('My baby does the hanky panky, my baby does the hanky panky…'). At least Hep made an effort to pick up some girls though, if he was successful, it was not obvious. My heart wasn't in this girl chase. I was still heartbroken about Babs dumping me this afternoon. I was just grateful she wasn't here.

Then, I spotted the person I had been looking for. I saw him go into the lavatory and followed him. I confronted him. 'You've been calling me the past week,' I said, 'What's the big idea?'

'No, not me,' he replied. He looked shocked by the accusation.

'I recognised your voice, your laugh, and how you spit your words out. Don't shit me. It was you – Stan Lopata.' Well, Stan the Man was as weak as rainwater – especially as his cousin wasn't there. He didn't try to hide it.

'Yes, it was me,' he admitted, 'I had to get even with you for what you did to me at the Prom.' Then came the coup de gras. 'Not only that, I've also been going out with Barbara Geist the past weeks. Perhaps you did me a favour.'

Then it hit me. Babs hadn't been at home recently because she was with Stan the Asshole. It wasn't the Maggot. Stan had gotten his information about the events at the Hill from her. Stan stood there and laughed.

'You're such a sap, Gaughan. The day after you shoved me, Babs said she found out what you had done to me from one of her friends. She phoned me to apologise. I suggested we get together, and we hit it off right away. Of course, you helped things by not being around her the past two weeks. You truly are a goose by name and a goose by nature.' He continued his maniacal chortling and gloating.

Well, I wasn't about to take that insult lying down. I went up to him and punched him in the mouth with my good hand. He fell like a ton of bricks and was bleeding. He was sprawled on the floor almost passed out. I felt like finishing him off with a kick to the ribs. Instead, I left the bathroom, saw the others, and told them I was leaving. They protested, especially Hep who swore he had a girl lined up, but I had the car.

I said goodbye, and dropped the other three at their houses, then spilled my guts to Hep. We talked, I cried, we split a bottle of beer left by Frenchie, then went to Coney Island for a hot dog. We talked about going to Rachael's House of Ill-repute, but – as always – it was only talk. I dropped Hep off and got home at one a.m.

I wasn't feeling all that crash-hot when I made it to bed. The room was spinning, and I was in free fall. I was now a Year 12 Senior. My time as a Year 11 Junior at Our Lady of Perpetual Succour Catholic High School was history.

'Things don't just happen, they happen just.'

Cop-u-later.